COLONIAL LAND POLICIES
IN PALESTINE, 1917–1936

OXFORD HISTORICAL MONOGRAPHS

Editors

R. J. W. EVANS   J. HARRIS
J. MADDICOTT   J. ROBERTSON
R. SERVICE   P. A. SLACK
B. WARD-PERKINS

Colonial Land Policies in Palestine, 1917–1936

MARTIN BUNTON

OXFORD
UNIVERSITY PRESS

OXFORD

UNIVERSITY PRESS

Great Clarendon Street, Oxford OX2 6DP

Oxford University Press is a department of the University of Oxford.
It furthers the University's objective of excellence in research, scholarship,
and education by publishing worldwide in

Oxford New York

Auckland Cape Town Dar es Salaam Hong Kong Karachi
Kuala Lumpur Madrid Melbourne Mexico City Nairobi
New Delhi Shanghai Taipei Toronto

With offices in

Argentina Austria Brazil Chile Czech Republic France Greece
Guatemala Hungary Italy Japan Poland Portugal Singapore
South Korea Switzerland Thailand Turkey Ukraine Vietnam

Oxford is a registered trade mark of Oxford University Press
in the UK and in certain other countries

Published in the United States
by Oxford University Press Inc., New York

British Library Cataloguing in Publication Data
Data available

Library of Congress Cataloging in Publication Data
Data available

Typeset by Graphicraft Ltd., Hong Kong
Printed in Great Britain
on acid-free paper by
Biddles Ltd., King's Lynn, Norfolk

ISBN 978-0-19-921108-1

To Saija

Acknowledgements

This book began as a doctoral project in the early 1990s at St Antony's College, Oxford. It was written with the support and encouragement provided since 1997 by the University of Victoria, British Columbia. I have incurred a number of debts over the years and I am very pleased now to acknowledge the assistance I have received.

Research was conducted at the Public Records Office in London, the Israel State Archives in Jerusalem, and the Harvard, Oxford, Cambridge, and Victoria university law libraries, and I would like to thank the staffs of all these institutions for their help with the material. I would also like to acknowledge that chapters included in this book have appeared previously, in slightly different form, in *Colonialism and the Modern World: Selected Studies* (Armonk, NY: M. E. Sharpe, 2002), and *New Perspectives on Property and Land in the Middle East* (Cambridge, Mass.: Distributed for the Center for Middle Eastern Studies of Harvard University by Harvard University Press, 2000); they have been used here with permission of the publishers.

At the University of Victoria, I have learned a great deal from long conversations about property rights and policy making with Rod Dobell and about colonialism with Greg Blue, and I thank them for always having the time to share their knowledge. For invaluable comments on particular chapters I would especially like to thank Gus Thaiss and Michael Thornhill. Many others have also helped me in various ways over the years with the writing and rewriting of this book and I would especially like to thank William Cleveland, Ralph Croizier, Edward Ingram, John Lutz, John MacLaren, Eric Sager, and Ted Wooley. For their participation in workshops and panels at which portions of this book have been presented, I thank Michael Fischbach, Ellen Fleischmann, Geremy Forman, Rob Home, Niall O'Murchu, and Jane Power. I thank my parents who have supported this project since the beginning. My deepest gratitude goes to Saija Maarit Tissari, and I owe a special debt of gratitude to Roger Owen and Eugene Rogan for their long-standing support, and Eugene Rogan also deserves my particular thanks for guiding this book through to publication. I have benefited from the helpful assistance of Sarah Mann, and I thank all at Oxford Historical Monographs for their assistance, and patience.

Saija Maarit Tissari has lived with this project since the beginning. She has been the greatest source of support, and it is to her that the book is dedicated.

Contents

List of Maps

List of Table

Introduction

Though effectively run as a crown colony in the inter-war period, Palestine was in 1923 recognized by the newly formed League of Nations as an 'A' mandate. Technically it was to be administered like a trust by Britain until ready for self-government, but it was also subject to special stipulations recognizing Britain's earlier promise in 1917 to facilitate the establishment of a Jewish national home. Several important implications for land rights directly followed. The British mandatory government, 'while ensuring that the rights and position of other sections of the population are not prejudiced', was expected to encourage 'close settlement of Jews on the land, including State lands and waste lands not required for public purposes'.[1] The mandate also specifically enjoined the British to establish a Jewish agency for the purpose of advising on economic issues. Indirectly, owing to the pace and volume of Jewish immigration and to continual failures in advancing constitutional issues—the debates over which usually hinged on the powers to control immigration—the inter-war period witnessed a general politicization of the Arab and Jewish communities which affected other issues, such as property ownership, in significant ways.

Much of the literature on the conflict has focused on the question of transfers of land from Arab owners to Jewish purchasers. For example, attempts to assess the dynamics of establishing a Jewish national home have emphasized the role of British colonial policies in providing the protective umbrella necessary to assume legal possession of a national territory. Seen from another perspective, the focus on political troubles between Arabs and Jews has narrowed the history of land policies to a narrative of loss, with an emphasis on how colonial policies were inimical to, and disruptive of, the indigenous Arab society. The focus in these accounts tends to be on Zionism as a determinant force in the development in Palestine of a new land regime, which itself thus comes to represent a fundamental disjunction from what was there before. To be sure, histories of the events of 1948—the creation of the state of Israel

[1] The 'Mandate for Palestine' is reproduced in *A Survey of Palestine: Prepared in December 1945 and January 1946 for the Information of the Anglo-American Committee of Inquiry* (Washington: Institute for Palestine Studies, 1991), 2–11.

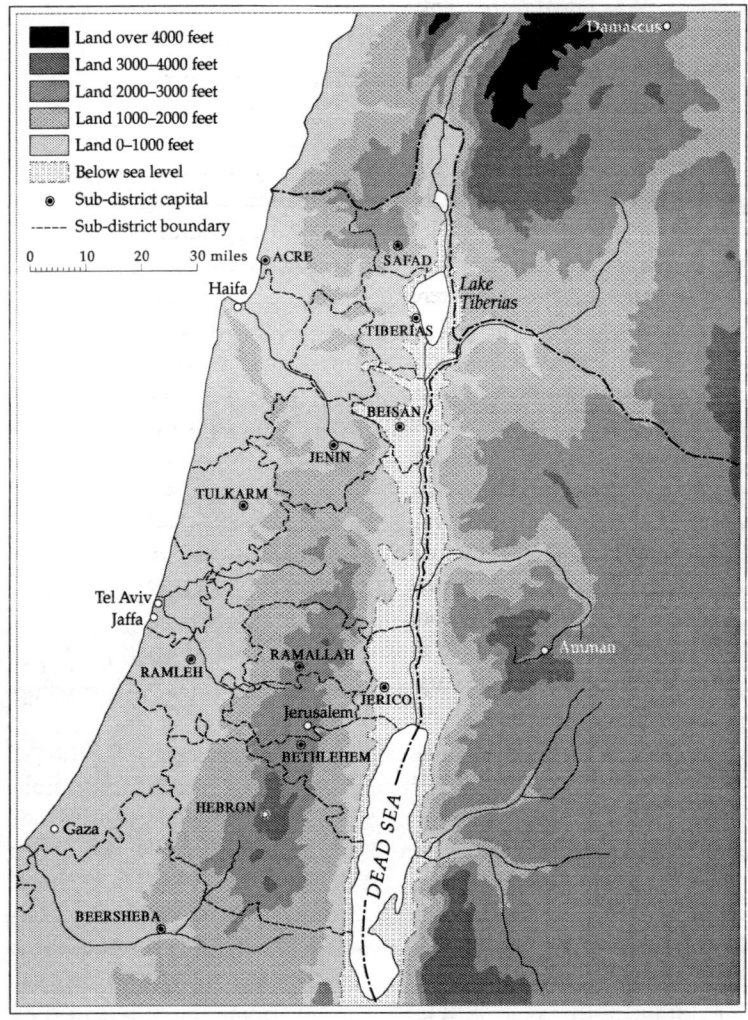

Land over 4000 feet
Land 3000–4000 feet
Land 2000–3000 feet
Land 1000–2000 feet
Land 0–1000 feet
Below sea level
● Sub-district capital
----- Sub-district boundary

0   10   20   30 miles

Damascus●

●ACRE   SAFAD

Haifa

TIBERIAS

Lake Tiberias

BEISAN

JENIN

TULKARM

Tel Aviv
Jaffa

RAMALLAH

RAMLEH

JERICO

Jerusalem

●Amman

BETHLEHEM

HEBRON

○ Gaza

DEAD SEA

BEERSHEBA

Map 1. Relief map of Palestine showing administrative divisions and centres

and of the failure of a Palestinian Arab state to emerge—must necessarily analyse and weigh appropriately significant trends of the preceding
decades. But in doing so one must be wary of reading history backwards.
The location of areas purchased by Jewish agencies in the nineteenth and
twentieth centuries was clearly of great political significance, shaping as it

did the 1947 United Nations plan of partition.[2] However, concentrating too heavily on the politics of the Jewish national home, and on the struggles between Arab and Jew, risks denying the overall subject of rural property during the mandate of its own history, with its many winding paths and lack of final destinations.

A review of the published law reports during the mandate reveals the significance of land disputes that took place not as formative political struggles between Arab and Jew, but between government and land-owners, or among Arab landowners themselves.[3] It is estimated that 70 per cent of land transactions registered during the mandate consisted of intra-communal transfers (only 30 per cent consisting of land sold by Arabs to Jews).[4] By 1948, a relatively small proportion of the land of Palestine, approximately 10 per cent, was acquired by Jewish land purchasers, a sub-stantial proportion of which was purchased prior to the mandate coming into effect.[5] The bulk of these transactions, Rashid Khalidi notes, 'were no more than straight-forward commercial transactions', a conclusion that draws heavily from the observation that a dominant role was played by absentee Arab landlords, many of whom found themselves on the other side of new international borders drawn by European powers during the post-war partition of the Ottoman Empire.[6] A further consideration in weighing the role of Zionism in the formation and implementation of colonial land policies is the emphases of colonial reports themselves, not

[2] See Beshara Doumani, *Rediscovering Palestine: Merchants and Peasants in Jabal Nablus, 1700–1900* (Berkeley and Los Angeles: University of California Press, 1995), Haim Gerber, *The Social Origins of the Modern Middle East* (London: Mansell, 1987), Gershon Shafir, *Land, Labor, and the Origins of the Israeli–Palestinian Conflict, 1882–1914* (Cambridge: Cambridge University Press, 1989), Kenneth W. Stein, *The Land Question in Palestine, 1917–1939* (Chapel Hill: University of North Carolina Press, 1984).

[3] Michael McDonnell and Henry E. Baker (eds.), *The Law Reports of Palestine . . . : [1920–1946]*, 14 vols. (London: Waterlow & Sons, 1933–47), Naomi Shepherd, *Ploughing Sand: British Rule in Palestine 1917–1948* (New Brunswick, NJ: Rutgers University Press, 2000), 120.

[4] Jacob Metzer, *The Divided Economy of Mandatory Palestine* (Cambridge: Cambridge University Press, 1998), 86. Note that this doesn't take into account the probable under-registration of intra-Arab land exchanges. See also Lewis French, 'First Report on Agricultural Development and Land Settlement in Palestine, Draft', 23 Dec. 1931, CO 733/214/5, 92.

[5] Stein, *The Land Question in Palestine, 1917–1939*, appendix 2, *A Survey of Palestine: Prepared in December 1945 and January 1946 for the Information of the Anglo-American Committee of Inquiry*, 244. Including registered transactions prior to the mandate period, total land purchase to 15 May 1948 is estimated by Stein at approximately 2 million dunams, representing less than 8% of the total area, and 20% of the cultivable area.

[6] Rashid Khalidi, *Palestinian Identity: The Construction of Modern National Consciousness* (New York: Columbia University Press, 1997), 113–14.

least the hugely influential, though circumlocutory, reports on the land system in Palestine by Sir Ernest Dowson. A pre-eminent adviser during the 1920s to the Palestine government in Jerusalem, as well as to the Colonial Office in London thereafter, Dowson authored three papers on Palestine's land regime in 1925 alone which are noteworthy for the limited attention directed at the subject of Jewish land acquisition.[7] In 1938, reflecting on two decades worth of colonial administration of Palestine's land regime, Dowson concluded that

The establishment in Palestine of a national home for the Jewish people accentuated the urgency of the reform and imposed a higher standard of performance than might otherwise have been necessary; but basically the measures that were adopted were evoked by the economic needs of the land and the inhabitants, irrespective of creed or race, and would have been intrinsically just as necessary if the Balfour declaration had never been conceived.[8]

That the political struggle between Arabs and Jews is due significant attention in analyses of colonial land policies during the mandate cannot be denied. Nor can it be disputed that the integrated impact of the forces of colonial rule and those of Jewish colonization were at times together more significant than either alone.[9] Care must be taken nonetheless to not reduce the study of how policies were framed, evolved, and applied throughout all of Palestine from 1917 to 1936 to a discussion confined to Jewish land acquisition. Disproportionate emphasis on Zionism wrongly underestimates the significance of other factors essential to an overall frame of reference.[10] The need for a broader, comparative approach has not generally been recognized in the literature on land in Palestine which instead has shown a tendency to accentuate the uniqueness of the period.

---

[7] See, for example: 'Preliminary Study of Land Tenure in Palestine', 'Covering Memorandum to the Report on the Land System in Palestine, 5th December 1925', and 'The Land System in Palestine', CO 733/109, 143–277.

[8] 'Memorandum II. Reviewing the History of Cadastral Survey Settlement of Title and Associated Measures in Palestine between 1913 and 1936', CO 733/361/12, 17.

[9] See discussion in Geremy Forman and Alexandre Kedar, 'Colonialism, Colonization and Land Law in Mandate Palestine: The Zor Al-Zarqa and Barrat Qisarya Land Disputes in Historical Perspective', *Theoretical Inquiries in Law*, 4/2 (2003). Also Raya Adler, 'The Tenants of Wadi Hawarith: Another View of the Land Question in Palestine', *International Journal of Middle East Studies*, 20/2 (1988).

[10] Historiographical discussions can be found in Roger Owen, 'Introduction', in Roger Owen (ed.), *Studies in the Economic and Social History of Palestine in the Nineteenth and Twentieth Centuries* (Carbondale: Southern Illinois University Press, 1982), Ibrahim Abu-Lughod, 'The Pitfalls of Palestiniology', *Arab Studies Quarterly*, 3/4 (1981), Zachary Lockman, 'Railway Workers and Relational History: Arabs and Jews in British-Ruled Palestine', *Journal of Comparative Society and History*, 35/3 (1993).

This book focuses attention on the contexts in which imported ideas and presumptions about land were continually being adapted to changing circumstances. Abstract theories of property informed official policies, but analysis of colonial land policies is best anchored in specific historical developments. Adapting at times a case study approach allows for a clearer recognition of the complexity and historical contingency of property rights, of the conditions defined by time and place under which various claims were enforced and legitimized. As one prominent theorist of property explains, 'the actual institution, and the way people see it, and hence the meaning they give to it, all change over time'.[11] It is the necessarily highly contextualized nature of land policy that this book hopes to capture for the case of Palestine in the inter-war years.

This examination of the ways in which land policies were defined and redefined, frequently changing direction in the process, is organized around two main themes. The first is the uneven impact on the policy formation process of the ideals that informed land policies elsewhere in the British empire. Ideals presented coherently and logically in the abstract nonetheless broke down in political practice and thus failed to achieve in Palestine the place of actual policy. The primacy of the negotiated and contested nature of property rights leads to the second important theme: the legacy of Ottoman administrative practices regarding land and the ways in which the implementation of colonial policies was bound up with broader historical processes in the region itself. Simplifications of British colonial land policy which reduce it to a coherent force that is basically metropolitan, monolithic, and fundamentally a disjunction (good or bad) from the land regime which preceded it have been proven elsewhere to yield limited insights.[12] The argument presented in this book is that British land policies in Palestine were constantly in flux, and are best understood in terms of wider frames of reference which recognize property as a fluid social construction, informed as much or more by structures and patterns inherited from the Ottoman past and by assumptions about changing realities on the ground, than by those idealized and imported

[11] C. B. Macpherson, 'The Meaning of Property', in C. B. Macpherson (ed.), *Property: Mainstream and Critical Positions* (Oxford: Blackwell, 1978).

[12] See, for comparison, Peter Robb, 'Landed Property, Agrarian Categories, and the Agricultural Frontier: Some Reflections on Colonial India', in Gregory Blue, Martin Bunton, and Ralph Croizier (eds.), *Colonialism and the Modern World: Selected Studies* (Armonk, NY: M. E. Sharpe, 2002), David Washbrook, 'Sovereignty, Property, Land and Labour in Colonial South India', in Huri Islamoglu (ed.), *Constituting Modernity: Private Property in the East and West* (London: I. B. Tauris, 2004).

from London. This may be little more than the established historical practice of balancing continuity and change, but it has not always been brought to bear in the study of land in mandate Palestine.

For these reasons, the official entry by General Allenby in Jerusalem in December 1917 obviously presents problems as a starting point for a study of colonial land policies. As military and civilian government officials came to realize, colonial policies risked confrontation or irrelevance if they strayed unwarrantedly from processes rooted administratively in the Ottoman past, or held in continuous social traditions. Colonial policies were constrained in important ways by the need to align with notions of property that prevailed in Palestine. Whatever the understandings or aims that contributed to the design of official land policies, it became clear that for land policies to work in practice it needed to be feasible at some level for the landholders or claimants to adopt or fit them into their interests. The need therefore to explore Ottoman definitions of land rights demands that this study reach back to the transformative reforms of the mid-nineteenth century, a stage commonly known as the *Tanzimat*, while recognizing of course the tremendous scope for reinterpretation in the inter-war period. Conversely, 1936 presents itself as a relatively useful finishing point in this examination of the governmental processes of defining and settling rights to agricultural land. The political turmoil following the outbreak in 1936 of sporadic violence and then full-on revolt caused widespread breakdown of the structures set up by the British administration particularly in rural areas: 'The roads became unsafe for use,' explained one official report, 'and the economic and social life of the country was seriously disrupted', causing the suspension of normal government activities.[13] Some officials claimed to be content with the progress made during the first months of the Arab revolt, catching up on paperwork that had fallen into arrears. But procedures in the field came to a standstill as officers either feared for their safety or were seconded for security duty. 'I have no intention of taking up settlement work', the commissioner for lands and surveys, for example, insisted in 1938, 'until public security markedly improves.'[14] Further, the circumstances after 1939 in the Middle East of military operations and international diplomacy inserted a new dynamic into colonial administrative practices in Palestine which deserves a study of its own.

[13] *A Survey of Palestine: Prepared in December 1945 and January 1946 for the Information of the Anglo-American Committee of Inquiry*, 44.
[14] Commissioner for lands and surveys to Haifa settlement officer, 4 Mar. 1938, ISA LS 8/16, box 3568. See also department of lands and surveys' *Annual Reports*, 1936–9.

In addition to its periodization, this examination of official land policies is also constrained by its focus on agricultural land. Though reference is made indirectly to issues concerning urban land and religious endowments, their study is outside the purview of this book. Under Ottoman law, the legal categorization of these lands as *mülk* and *vakif*, respectively, separated them from the main land codes that dealt with rural, agricultural land (placing them instead under the *mecelle*, the Ottoman civil code, and *sharia*, Muslim religious law). Land held as *vakif* tended to be regarded as 'a genus of land distinguishable in kind from other categories. It was not of any practical importance to determine who was the owner.'[15] The British tried to avoid interfering with religious institutions and in 1921 the administration approved the creation of the Supreme Muslim Council. For the next sixteen years the council managed for itself the creation and maintenance of *vakif*, using it both as a way to stimulate economic development in urban areas and as a political tool in the struggle against Zionism.

1. LAND AND COLONIAL IDEOLOGY

In addition to a consideration of official conceptualizations of property, as absorbed during an official's rural or semi-rural background at home or as learned elsewhere in the empire, this work focuses on processes unfolding at the local level, and rooted in the Ottoman administrative legacy with which British officials had to negotiate. These two themes, and how they frame this study of property rights in mandate Palestine, require some elaboration.

Formulations of colonial land policies flowed in part from imagining what an unknown territory ought to look like, in part from theorizing about what systems provided the most reliable guidance for its improvement.[16] In this sense, policies derived both from Britain's intellectual heritage and from the growing reservoir of administrative experience in the colonies. Of course, it can be difficult to disentangle the two sources.

---

[15] 'Acquisition of Property by Religious Bodies', ISA Chief Secretary's Office, RG 2 L/122/32, 1178. On *vakif* generally see Yitzhak Reiter, *Islamic Endowments in Jerusalem under British Mandate* (London: Frank Cass, 1996). Michael Dumper, *Islam and Israel: Muslim Religious Endowments and the Jewish State* (Washington: Institute for Palestine Studies, 1994).

[16] John McLaren, A. R. Buck, and Nancy E. Wright, 'Property Rights in the Colonial Imagination and Experience', in John McLaren, A. R. Buck, and Nancy E. Wright (eds.), *Despotic Dominion: Property Rights in British Settler Societies* (Vancouver: UBC Press, 2004), 4.

The emergence over centuries of liberal ideas of property in England overlapped with the development of colonial power structures (and with elaborations of their justification). Yet, the linkages and interrelations between theories of property rights entitlements in Britain and what took place in the colonies are often neglected.[17] Colonies were both a testing ground for European ideas, as well as a source for new ideas that flowed west (and east). Britain's intellectual heritage as well as its colonial experience played important roles in the formulation of land policies in Palestine. Both would be worth considering in some detail.

European conceptualizations of 'improvement' and 'progress' played an important role in the formulation of land policies. As a reflection of historical trends in Britain dating back to the story of enclosure, and as a way to justify ruling over foreign territories, the relationship between notions of improvement and ideas of private property can usefully be seen to have developed with Enlightenment-era social theories from the seventeenth century onwards.[18] In 1940, *The Times* argued that the personal acquisition of property was based 'on fundamental principles of the British political philosophy'.[19] The representation of land as external to individual rights holders, as abstract space 'to do with what one wants', resonated strongly in the larger enlightenment project—a conception of reality that reduced landed resources to a multitude of individual and separate commodities whose interactions could be understood by rational schemes that promised wealth-generating improvement.[20] Laws were passed enforcing transferable rights to precisely defined individual plots of land in order to support economic systems that relied on efficient trade between entrepreneurial strangers. As Carol Rose has observed, attempting to secure fixed rights to property required 'an ability to bound off

---

[17] 'The problem with Europe', Salman Rushdie has written 'is that it has forgotten its history, most of which takes place outside its borders.' Quoted in Edmund Burke III, 'Orientalism and World History: Representing Middle Eastern Nationalism and Islamism in the Twentieth Century', *Theory and Society*, 27/4, Special Issue on Interpreting Historical Change at the End of the Twentieth Century (1998), 1.

[18] Carol M. Rose, *Property and Persuasion: Essays on the History, Theory, and Rhetoric of Ownership*, New Perspectives on Law, Culture, and Society (Boulder, Colo.: Westview Press, 1994), 222, John C. Weaver, *The Great Land Rush and the Making of the Modern World, 1650–1900* (Montreal: McGill-Queen's University Press, 2003), 28.

[19] 'Land in Palestine', *The Times*, 29 Feb. 1940.

[20] See C. S. Holling, Fikret Berkes, and Carl Folke, 'Science, Sustainability, and Resource Management', in Fikret Berkes and Carl Folke (eds.), *Linking Social and Ecological Systems: Management Practices and Social Mechanisms for Building Resilience* (Cambridge: Cambridge University Press, 1998). See also Weaver, *The Great Land Rush and the Making of the Modern World, 1650–1900*.

every entitlement with a kind of perfect language, a language that reflects in the present all future contingencies'.[21] Two key assumptions lay behind reducing a property right to a mechanism in a machine: one is the idea of a world populated by people acting in predictable ways, making decisions according to unchanging influences; another is the assumption of 'a radical separateness among human beings', that relationships between people are those of individual strangers, fundamentally linear in causation and reduced to one-off transactions.[22] It is a rhetoric that largely disregards any notion of a collective, or of context and background, or of the embeddedness of individuals in society or culture.

British officials were prone to draw on classical economic perspectives of well-defined property lines in individual plots of land and, as a consequence, often did not acquire a sense of the local knowledge of lived-in places. They instead saw only non-viable, non-productive use of natural resources.[23] Nowhere does this myopia feature more clearly in Palestine than in the official attempts to come to terms with a customary tenure in Palestine known as the *musha'* system—a form of collective ownership by which village lands were divided into sections of similar quality and then periodically redistributed to those inhabitants owning a share in it. *Musha'* clearly touched the colonial imagination in a vivid way, mostly since it was seen to reflect an earlier stage in the 'natural' evolution of social and economic institutions. Many officials likened *musha'* to the commons, and the perceived tragedies thereof, in an earlier period of European history.[24]

From the outset, the *musha'* system became the subject of numerous government reports which unanimously recommended that the system be abolished.[25] Such conclusions were based on a description of the system which emphasized specific features of the distribution process:

The constitution of the parent body or the basis on which that land is periodically divided varies. Thus sometimes the shares (sahm, asham) are held by the heirs of long bygone holders the origin of whose rights have been forgotten. In other cases

[21] Rose, *Property and Persuasion: Essays on the History, Theory, and Rhetoric of Ownership*, 222–3.

[22] Ibid. 222.

[23] See William Cronon, *Changes in the Land: Indians, Colonists, and the Ecology of New England* (New York: Hill and Wang, 1983).

[24] On differences between modern concepts of the 'tragedy of the commons' and concepts current in medieval times, see Susan Cox, 'No Tragedy on the Commons', *Environmental Ethics*, 7 (1985).

[25] See also Michael Fischbach, *State, Society, and Land in Jordan* (Leiden: Brill, 2000).

village clans (hamuli, hamail) share the mesha' and subdivide it again among their members: in others the mesha' shares are periodically re-apportioned among the males of the community at the moment (Zakur): in others the shares are divided among the holders of plough oxen: and there are yet further varieties.[26]

Based partly on this information and on the admittedly speculative and unreliable estimates of its widespread nature, officials immediately set out to expose the completely unredeeming value of *musha'*. 'This archaic system', wrote Lewis French, was 'the greatest stumbling block to agricultural development' in Palestine.[27] Imposing as it did 'a severe handicap . . . upon decent cultivation', and owing to 'the hand to mouth existence thereby fostered', *musha'* was condemned by Sir Ernest Dowson as 'a palpable drag upon the economic establishment of a great mass of the Palestinian peasantry and upon the financial position of the State'.[28]

It is self evident that shifting occupation of land and good husbandry are incompatible. A temporary occupant will aim at extracting all he can from the land and will put nothing into it. He will exploit and impoverish it but will not develop it.[29]

Officials throughout the government meanwhile shared in the generally positive reflection of how 'the enclosure and partition of the common fields . . . certainly assisted production'.[30] Without partition, degradation and overuse of lands were to be expected because individual users would naturally refuse to bear the full cost of further use when they could not be assured of capturing the benefits of investment or conservation. If anyone can exploit a resource then no one has an incentive to invest and conserve. Or as Dowson explained in 1925, a cultivator or grazer

cannot effect permanent improvements, such as the erection of buildings and fences, the planting of trees, etc., as he himself will move before he gets a return from them and has little prospect of being compensated for his outlay by his successor.[31]

Thus, it was commonly argued, only when rights to resources are individual, secure, and transferable will borrowers and lenders feel secure enough

---

[26] Dowson, 'Preliminary Study of Land Tenure in Palestine', CO 733/109, 179–80.

[27] Lewis French, 'First Report on Agricultural Development and Land Settlement in Palestine', 23 Dec. 1931, CO 733/214/5, 62.

[28] Dowson, 'Preliminary Study of Land Tenure in Palestine', CO 733/109, 180–4. Also 'Report of the Tithes Commission', Mar. 1922, CO 733/20, 295.

[29] Dowson, 'Preliminary Study of Land Tenure in Palestine', CO 733/109, 181.

[30] Frederic M. Goadby and Moses J. Doukhan, *The Land Law of Palestine* (Tel Aviv: Shoshany's Printing Co. Ltd., 1935), 210.

[31] Dowson, 'Preliminary Study of Land Tenure in Palestine', CO 733/109, 181.

about assets to undertake the necessary capitalization: 'When musha' is permanently partitioned and passes definitely into a man's possession he can take longer views and is naturally stimulated to do all he can to increase its productivity.'[32] Alternatively, inefficient or wasteful users would deem it more profitable to sell their rights to more efficient users who value the resource more (that is, feel that they might be able to command a higher market price for it). By reducing transaction costs, private, secure, and transferable rights to property were, in this context, key to an efficient market economy. Far from facilitating the exchange activity of individuals, *musha'* was further charged with being an ever-present cause of intrigue and quarrel.

Though publicly adhered to by government officials throughout the course of the mandate, such arguments, formed very early on and based on scant evidence, reflect more their previously held assumptions of enlightened property doctrines than they do a thoughtful and careful reading of the *musha'* system, its history, its function, its variations, and the fluid role it played in village life and economy.[33] Significantly, official arguments denuded *musha'* of any context—for example, the adaptive role played by communal governance structures in mediating the incidence of taxation, in managing and monitoring the breaking up of new lands, in generating knowledge about harvesting resources, or in regulating the cooperative working of fractional shares—and tended to ignore the significance of adaptations to the evolving market economy and to political circumstances, as its role changed over time.[34] None of this is to slight the obvious importance to the capitalization of agriculture of secure rights, but rather to be aware of the extent to which *musha'* did represent an evolved, self-consciously designed property rights system. The evident confusion among colonial officials with open access systems tells us more about British presumptions than the workings of *musha'* as actually practised.

[32] Ibid. 181–2.
[33] See analyses in: Ya'acov Firestone, 'The Land-Equalizing Musha' Village: A Reassessment', in Gad G. Gilbar (ed.), *Ottoman Palestine, 1800–1914: Studies in Economic and Social History* (Leiden: E. J. Brill, 1990), Amos Nadan, 'Colonial Misunderstanding of an Efficient Peasant Institution: Land Settlement and Musha' Tenure in Mandate Palestine, 1921–47', *Journal of the Economic and Social History of the Orient*, 46/3 (2003), Roger Owen, 'Defining Traditional: Some Implications of the Use of Ottoman Law in Mandatory Palestine', *Harvard Middle Eastern and Islamic Review*, 1/2 (1994), Birgit Schaebler, 'Practising *Musha'*: Common Lands and the Common Good in Southern Syria under the Ottomans and the French', in Roger Owen (ed.), *New Perspectives on Property and Land in the Middle East* (Cambridge, Mass.: Distributed for the Center for Middle Eastern Studies of Harvard University by Harvard University Press, 2000).
[34] Metzer, *The Divided Economy of Mandatory Palestine*, 94–6.

Villagers were more capable of cooperating and defining and redefining property rights structures that addressed shared dilemmas than officials acknowledged. Colonial officials clearly exaggerated the opportunities for improvement and development, particularly in cases of dry land farming systems with which *musha'* was most commonly associated. Sarah Graham Brown has suggested that 'for many peasants, who had no capital to invest anyway, the disincentives to invest in land and capital stock as commodities, which seemed to many people inherent in the *musha' a* system, were largely academic'.[35] As Jacob Metzer argues, the often-observed backward state of peasants in traditional societies 'reflects lack of opportunities rather than non rational behaviour'.[36]

Official conceptualizations of property rights that drew on Britain's intellectual heritage were premised especially upon the development of secure and individual rights to well-measured plots of land as part of the proper ordering of a developing economy. Though the premiss clearly reflects a utilitarian approach, such theories were characterized by the extent to which they were developed as a way of legitimizing colonial rule over the territory occupied.[37] By asserting that secure and individual rights to property constituted the basis of 'progress', British officials could point to their projected absence in colonized territory as proof of the value and necessity of imperial rule. In Palestine, officials frequently expressed their faith in the evolutionary superiority of settled cultivation over extensive agriculture, individualized property rights over communal holdings. In this regard, however, it is worth noting that concern with communal holdings generally did not tend to extend to criticism of Jewish land-holding companies specifically unless government revenue was at stake. The expected increase in corporate ownership of land by companies such as the Palestine Jewish Colonization Association demanded a special

---

[35] Sarah Graham Brown, 'The Political Economy of Jabal Nablus: 1920–1948', in Roger Owen (ed.), *Studies in the Economic and Social History of Palestine in the Nineteenth and Twentieth Centuries* (Carbondale: Southern Illinois University Press, 1982), 125. Also Charles Kamen, *Little Common Ground: Arab Agriculture and Jewish Settlement in Palestine, 1920–1948* (Pittsburgh: University of Pittsburgh Press, 1991), Roger Owen, *The Middle East in the World Economy, 1800–1914* (London: Methuen, 1981).

[36] Metzer, *The Divided Economy of Mandatory Palestine*, 96.

[37] Martin Chanock, 'Paradigms, Policies, and Property: A Review of the Customary Law of Land Tenure', in Kristin Mann and Richard Roberts (eds.), *Law in Colonial Africa* (Portsmouth, NH: Heinemann Educational Books, 1991), Thomas R. Metcalf, *Ideologies of the Raj* (Cambridge: Cambridge University Press, 1997), Timothy Mitchell, *Rule of Experts: Egypt, Techno-Politics, Modernity* (Berkeley and Los Angeles: University of California Press, 2002), Roger Owen, *State, Power and Politics in the Making of the Modern Middle East*, 3rd edn. (London: Routledge, 2004).

annual tax to compensate the government for the loss of fees on transfer and succession that would have accrued if the land remained in individual ownership.[38] As Norman Bentwich, Palestine's attorney general, explained, 'the objection to the holding of land by juridical persons is that it enlarges the system of mortmain, because a juristic person, unlike a natural person, does not die at regular intervals'.[39]

To free Palestine's agriculturalists from the stagnation in which the British found them, and set them on the road to progress and civilization in this way, Dowson's remedy was largely informed by ideas of linear progress from premodern to modern forms of property that had for a long time shaped British views of justifying empire. Sir William Fitzgerald, Palestine's last chief justice, 1944–8, captured this conviction with the following epithet:

there can be little doubt, I think, that history will record that Britain's greatest contribution to the science of the government of man is British law and British legal procedure . . . And whatever the various peoples who have been subject to British rule may think of their tutelage, I do not hesitate to mention the one thing they shall forever be grateful for, namely, that we have given to them our ideas of British law.[40]

By the time mandatory rule had come into being in the inter-war period, assumptions of a taxonomic structure which placed people everywhere on the same path to 'modernity' and 'civilization' were well ingrained. The Palestine government was following a well-established pattern of colonial governance when frustrations with the land regime they inherited were expressed as, and rather conveniently blamed upon, 'the chaos of the Turk'. 'The subject of land settlement and cadastral survey is perhaps the most important of all the problems with which the Palestine Administration is faced', minuted a Colonial Office official: 'both politically and financially it is vital that these questions be settled on a thoroughly sound basis in a mainly agrarian country which has just emerged from a long period of administrative mis-rule.'[41]

---

[38] See minute sheet, 12 Oct. 1922, CO 733/26, 174.

[39] Bentwich, memorandum, CO 733/89, 305.

[40] Sir William Fitzgerald, 'A Review of the Development of Law in Israel', in International Lawyers Convention in Israel (ed.), *International Lawyers Convention in Israel, 1958* (Jerusalem: Jerusalem Post, 1959), 324. See also Martin Bunton, 'Inventing the Status Quo: Ottoman Land-Law during the Palestine Mandate, 1917–1936', *International History Review*, 21/1 (1999).

[41] Minute sheet, 23 May 1924, CO 733/68, 482.

In addition to drawing upon their own intellectual heritage, British officers elaborated policies that drew on previous colonial experiences. J. N. Stubbs, for example, was recommended in 1922 as director of lands due in large part to his 'considerable experience in the land department in Australia'.[42] Indeed, Dowson's own thinking about the importance of secure and individual property rights reflects fundamentally his experience and knowledge of colonial contexts. This accumulated knowledge and experience then flowed back to the metropole, with mixed results. Prior to the First World War, Dowson had worked with the Egyptian survey, becoming the director of topographical survey in 1905 and succeeding Sir Henry Lyons as director-general in 1909. From 1917 to 1921 he chaired a mixed commission that looked into the settlement of land titles. With its cosmopolitan make-up, the commission sought to consider systems of registering rights to land that were in force in various parts of the world. From this experience grew Dowson's interest in the comparative study of land registration in various jurisdictions that led in the 1930s to his work in London in the Colonial Office and the establishment of 'the cadastral survey and land records office'. With his experience as adviser on land registration to the Colonial Office, Dowson advocated compulsory registration of land ownership in England and Wales on cadastral maps, maps showing boundary and ownership details of land divided into administrative units readily identifiable in a register. But he could not overcome opposition from self-interested conveyancing lawyers or government fears that a cadastral survey would prove unjustifiably expensive.[43]

What emerges in the study of colonial land policies in Palestine is a fairly clear distinction among colonial officials between the laws of England and the laws of the colonies. Discussions in the Colonial Office did not reflect an awareness of domestic reforms as much as developments elsewhere in the colonies, and inspiration for legislative activity in Palestine tended to come more from land laws that were devised specifically for the empire than they did from the laws of England. 'A long experience drawn from the greater part of the British Empire has been placed . . . freely at the disposal of this new Government,' wrote a grateful high commissioner Herbert Samuel in 1925.[44] Consider the following examples from Palestine's

---

[42] Samuel to Colonial Office, 19 Apr. 1922, CO 733/21, 91. Biographical summaries of land officials in mandate Palestine have been compiled by Mr Stephen Bank for an appendix in Dov Gavish, *A Survey of Palestine under the British Mandate, 1920–1948* (London: Routledge Curzon, 2005).

[43] I am grateful to Elizabeth Baigent for pointing this out to me.

[44] Samuel to Thomas, 25 Jan. 1924, CO 733/63, 618.

legislative activity in the 1920s. The 1921 surveyors ordinance, regulating the profession of surveyors, drew on a Nigerian ordinance, Colonial Office officials knowing 'of no similar legislation in this country'.[45] A Tanganyika ordinance was looked to in 1921 as 'a useful foundation' for the drafting of a new mining law.[46] The 1922 sand drifts ordinance, which gave the Palestine government powers to check drift of sand in coastal districts, derived from similar legislation in Cyprus, in particular the Cyprus fuel grounds law of 1901.[47] The 1924 charitable trusts ordinance was modelled on the Ceylon trusts ordinance of 1917.[48] The 1925 draft of a forests ordinance was 'knocked together' from various sources, including laws from Cyprus, the Sudan, and Nigeria.[49] The draft transfer of agricultural land bill, 1930, drew heavily from a 1923 Tanganyika law of property and conveyancing, as well from a 1913 enactment of the Federated Malay States.[50] As will be discussed in detail in Chapter 2, the 1928 land settlement ordinance drew on Sudanese land laws, and the 1931 land disputes (possession) ordinance, which allowed the district commissioner to decide, in cases of dispute, who shall exercise ownership pending a legal decision, drew on the Indian code of criminal procedure.[51]

Dowson clearly was one of the main sources for the dissemination of colonial land policies in Palestine.[52] Upon his retirement from Egyptian service in 1923, Dowson was asked to visit Palestine on his way home. He stayed for only five days but confidently furnished a report entitled 'Notes on Land Tax, Cadastral Survey and Land Settlement in Palestine'.[53] In June 1924, the Palestine government asked him to give effect to his proposals, and he returned to study the problem more fully from November to the end of March 1925, this time having the benefit of visiting all parts of the country and of discussing questions at issue with the principal officers of the government and with a number of representative members of the public. His previous concerns and conclusions were now 'confirmed'.[54]

[45] Minute sheets, 'Surveyors Ordinance 1921', CO 733/2, 565. Also CO 733/164, 26–67.
[46] Churchill to Samuel, 16 June 1921, CO 733/3/295.
[47] Official dispatch, 19 May 1922, CO 733/22, 36.
[48] Minute sheets, 'Charitable Trusts Ordinance 1924', CO 733/75, 185.
[49] Minute sheets, Sept. 1925, CO 733/97, 280.
[50] High commissioner to colonial secretary, 24 Jan. 1931, CO 733/199, 28–9.
[51] Minute sheets, 'Land Disputes Possession Ordinance 1931', CO 733/185.
[52] See also Gavish, *A Survey of Palestine under the British Mandate, 1920–1948.*
[53] Dowson, 'Notes on Land Tax, Cadastral Survey and Land Settlement in Palestine', [Oxford], St Antony's [College] Middle East Centre [Private Papers Collection].
[54] Dowson, 'Report on Progress of Land Reforms, 1923–1930', CO 733/221, 7.

These thoughts were embodied in three papers written in 1925: 'Preliminary Study of Land Tenure in Palestine', 'Covering Memorandum to Report on the Land System in Palestine', and 'The Land System in Palestine', as well as in letters and memos directed at more specific subjects. His third visit was in the spring of 1926 when he was called upon to assume general direction of working out his recommendations in practice; later that year he was, for a brief time, granted the title commissioner of lands (a post in which he was succeeded by Albert Abramson, who remained there until 1935).[55]

During this period, most discussion of the administration of land in Palestine took place under the shadow of Dowson's elaborations on the subject. 'Agriculture and Land Policy are the crying needs here,' remarked high commissioner Lord Plumer upon his arrival in Palestine in 1925, noting that 'At all turns I am met with the response "it all depends on Sir E. Dowson's report." '[56] The Colonial Office had, literally, put their money on Dowson as an expert: 'having engaged the services of an eminent expert at a very high fee, it would be unwise for [the secretary of state] to arrive at a final conclusion until he had an opportunity of studying the expert's report.'[57] Although the lengthiness of his reports made them wearisome to read, the substance of Dowson's recommendations encountered little criticism in the Colonial Office. 'I do not think that it would be possible to attempt to criticize this draft at any great length,' minuted one resigned official, 'as it is the result of Sir E. Dowson's work in Palestine and he had provided himself with a great deal of literature on the subject.'[58]

Dowson was clear about Palestine's needs: a thorough and systematic investigation and settlement of real rights from one end of the country to the other. Writing in 1925, he concluded that

we have never faced the problem resolutely as a whole or embarked upon it competently. We have had a so-called cadastral survey in half-hearted operation which was no cadastral survey in reality; we have had a so-called system of land registration which was little more than a re-entry of paper data; we have had, as I understand it, a series of Land Courts which have endeavoured to do justice in

---

[55] 'Instructions to Commissioner of Lands (Sir E. Dowson)', 22 Apr. 1926, CO 733/114, 101. Dowson would also be called upon to advise on land questions in the mandated territories of Transjordan and Iraq and, later, on agricultural indebtedness in Zanzibar.

[56] Extract from private letter from Lord Plumer to Sir John Shuckburgh, 20 Nov. 1925, CO 733/109, 224.

[57] Minute sheets, May 1925, CO 733/92, 485.

[58] Minute sheets, 29 June 1927, CO 733/142/44605, 2.

such specific cases of dispute as have been submitted to them, with which they are grievously in arrears.

Each of these three efforts to resolve the tangle of real rights in Palestine has pursued an independent path with the very natural result that after some six years occupation a systematic investigation and settlement of real rights has still to be planned.[59]

In Dowson's opinion, Palestine desperately required a comprehensive settlement of real rights by a systematic sweep of cadastral survey, investigation *in situ* with the cooperation of the villagers, and registration of results parcel by parcel, village by village. The Colonial Office found these arguments convincing and, frustrated with the lack of concrete initiatives on the part of the Palestine government, considered taking matters into their own hands. 'I do not think it is much use throwing these papers back at Palestine,' minuted one official, concluding that 'all the work done by these numerous Commissions and people who have been going around drawing traveling allowances is so much trash. It is imperative that drastic action be taken.'[60]

The legal registering of individual property rights was viewed above all as the inherent duty of the colonial government. Foundations for such an order consisted of the authoritative adjudication of all rights over immovable property with their boundaries precisely located on well-defined maps. Ever since Ireland, observes Meron Benvenisti, 'the surveyor walked beside the British officer, and sometimes has gone before'.[61] In the words of James Morris, 'Napoleon, surveying the Great Pyramids of Giza, is supposed to have cried to his veterans: "Soldiers, forty centuries look down upon you." The British, almost as soon as they arrived in Egypt, lugged a theodolite to the pyramid's summit and made it a triangulation point.'[62] In Palestine, two sequential processes were relied upon.[63] First, a cadastral survey which permanently divided and precisely measured the land in such a way that the position of any given parcel could be

[59] Letter from Dowson to undersecretary of state, Colonial Office, 21 Aug. 1924, CO 733/85, 385.

[60] Minute sheets, CO 733/68, 482; and CO 733/164, 8.

[61] Meron Benvenisti, *Sacred Landscape: The Buried History of the Holy Land since 1948*, trans. Maxine Kaufman-Lacusta (Berkeley and Los Angeles: University of California Press, 2000), 15.

[62] Quoted ibid. 15.

[63] Gavish, *A Survey of Palestine under the British Mandate, 1920–1948*, Great Britain. Palestine Royal Commission, *Memoranda Prepared by the Government of Palestine* (London: HM Stationery Office, 1937), Great Britain. Palestine Royal Commission, *Minutes of Evidence Heard at Public Sessions (with Index)* (London: HMSO, 1937).

numbered and definitely defined in relation to adjoining lands and tied to a series of triangulation points forming a national framework. Some indication of the wealth-generating role to be played by the cadastral survey is given by the ability of the Palestine government to present it to the British Treasury as a special effort of a capital nature and thus to be charged almost entirely out of expenditure on loan funds.[64] The second process was a quasi-judicial investigation, settlement, and registration of all claims to own or exercise rights over land, carried out methodically on the spot, village by village progressively throughout the whole country. Numbered and identified in this way, all references to boundaries or other verbal descriptions were omitted.

Registration of title to land is commonly associated with the South Australian reforms initiated by Sir Robert Torrens under the 1858 real property Act. Torrens's reforms drew heavily on his experience as a customs official with the registry of ship ownership, in the case of which 'instead of the record being perhaps non-existent, perhaps embedded in an unknown number of documents kept by an uncertain number of persons in a variety of places', all legal rights were being recorded in a known place, and any negotiation of those rights must conform to and be recorded in that registry.[65] The significance of the system of a ship registry is that it focused more on a tangible object; in its application to transactions in landed property, the definite, immovable, and separable patch of ground being negotiated became the focus of attention, rather than the persons temporarily possessing rights over 'it'. In Dowson's words, 'the ease and certainty with which the existing rights over any unit of landed property can thenceforth be recorded and ascertained, render this the most effective method yet devised for constructing and maintaining a simple, trustworthy, complete and up-to-date record of rights to land'.[66] Palestine's director of surveys described these features in the following terms:

---

[64] Samuel to secretary of state for the colonies, 17 Apr. 1924, CO 733/67, 256. In this regard, land settlement was compared favourably with Lord Cromer's 'famous irrigation million borrowed in the midst of Egyptian bankruptcy'. Minute sheet, 21 Feb. 1923, CO 733/60, 235. Also Dowson, 'Survey and Land Settlement Estimates: Covering Memorandum', CO 733/92, 491.

[65] Sir Ernest Dowson and V. L. O. Sheppard, *An Introductory Note on Registration of Title to Land* (London: Moore's Modern Methods, Ltd., 1929), para. 5. See also Gavish, *A Survey of Palestine under the British Mandate, 1920–1948*, 147–51.

[66] Dowson and Sheppard, *An Introductory Note on Registration of Title to Land*, para. 5.

Where the legal description of landed property involves a statement of the boundaries or abutting lands, not only does this mean much extra clerical work, but a far greater possibility of error and confusion. For this reason, even where a boundary is recognizable on the ground, it is the modern practice, in survey and land registration, to refer to a lot only by its parcel number within a block, village, survey sheet, or other unit with no topographically described boundary.[67]

Securing an individual person to an individual property through an accessible and authoritative record of land rights in this way was the key component of Dowson's vision of economic development. It led naturally enough to an approach that stressed the rational management of land. Premised on the colonial government taking upon itself the responsibility of securing personal title to specific plots of land, it drew heavily on physiocratic notions of the free working of natural economic laws and envisaged the primary task of that government to be the impartial administration of property.[68] With its insistence on straight lines of argument and a focus on utility, the approach adopted was made up of five basic, closely interrelated components. Item one was the facilitation of a market: in the absence of formal title, the major assets of the rural population were lost outside the market economy. A market approach ensured the efficient and flexible reallocation of resources, out of the hands of unenterprising owners and into those who valued it more and would thus develop it intensively. The colonial transformation of economies was widely thought to hinge on the smooth transfer of property. But a lively market in land required first that individual ownership of properties be placed on a secure and stable basis by a comprehensive settlement of title to land. Item two was the provision of credit: with a reliable system for

[67] Minute sheets, 12 July 1933, Chief Secretary's Office, ISA RG 2 L/156/33, 2089.

[68] Official arguments promoting the benefits that accrue from secure and individual rights to land can be found, *inter alia*, in: 'Report of Palestine Administration, July 1920– December 1921', CO 733/22, 464; 'Report of the Tithes Commission', Mar. 1922, CO 733/20, 294; Dowson, 'Covering Memorandum on the Land System in Palestine', CO 733/109, 235; Albert Abramson, 'Observations on the Recommendations of Land Settlement in the Report of the O'Donnell Commission', CO 733/208/5/87326; Cmd. 3686, 'Palestine: Report on Immigration, Land Settlement and Development [Hope-Simpson Report]' (London, 1930), Great Britain. Palestine Royal Commission, *Minutes of Evidence Heard at Public Sessions (with Index), A Survey of Palestine: Prepared in December 1945 and January 1946 for the Information of the Anglo-American Committee of Inquiry*. Although the survey and settlement of land was routinely defended as a necessary part of securing individual rights to property, such that registers could be deemed to be conclusive without further investigation, there was no guarantee of indefeasibility of title. See Great Britain. Palestine Royal Commission, *Memoranda Prepared by the Government of Palestine*.

ascertaining who owns what came the ability to use it as collateral. Easy access to credit allowed one to make one's land more productive. Without it, land either lay as an underexploited asset, 'dead capital', or the landholder was forced into the expensive, informal market of money-lenders. Item three was the efficient taxation of land: a record of reliable and updated information about individual property holders and individual property units was considered essential for the fair and efficient taxation of immovable property. Item four was the stimulation of long-term investment: only when individuals were confident in their tenure over their land would they invest in its development. No incentive to invest existed if the expected benefits could not be captured by those who worked on and financed them. Moreover, in the absence of secure title violent squabbles and unending litigation were thought to be more likely, further damaging the prospects of someone sinking capital into the land's 'improvement'.

Once registration was achieved, wrote Dowson in 1925, 'there is no reason why the next decade or two should not see a re-establishment of [Palestine's] ancient reputation as a land flowing with milk and honey, as striking as, if necessarily on a more modest scale than, the correspond-ing economic revival wrought by Lord Cromer in her one-time sister vilayet'.[69] In Palestine agriculture was recognized as 'the staple industry of the country', and officials there were anxious that government be seen to help and support it.[70] Officials in the Colonial Office generally agreed that 'The "land" side of an Administration such as that of Palestine is almost its most important function. It is essential that there should be security of title and this can only be effected by establishing efficient service as regards survey, settlement, and registration.'[71] Dowson's reforms offered a programme that all could buy into. By protecting and securing rights to land, Palestinian cultivators could rely on their own industry to promote their own improvement. 'The master key of economic success in Palestine is to be found,' vowed Dowson, 'as it was in Egypt and as it is everywhere else, in stimulating the individual enterprise of the mass population. It is the man behind the gun that counts most in economics as in war.'[72] A century before, James Mill had written of how a code of law would release individual energy by protecting the products of its efforts. 'Light taxes

---

[69] Dowson, 'The Land System in Palestine', CO 733 109, 252.
[70] Plumer to Shuckburgh, 19 Feb. 1926, CO 733/112, 449, 489.
[71] Minute sheets, 4 Feb. 1927, CO 733/136/44225.
[72] Dowson, 'The Land System in Palestine', CO 733/109, 252.

and good laws,' he had emphasized, 'nothing more is wanting for national and individual prosperity all over the globe.'[73] Dowson agreed, describing the ideal Palestinian peasantry as one 'whose industry was stimulated by being protected from exaction, by being taxed not only lightly but definitely and individually, whose personal and economic liberty was a matter of primary concern throughout'.[74]

So compelling was the overall logic of secure and individual rights to land, British colonial officials acted at times as though they had invented private property and at other times as though it was a natural and even timeless entitlement. Nonetheless, examinations of colonial land policy that focus attention too heavily on the rhetoric of utilitarian approaches risk projecting the desired self-image on the part of the mandate official rather than reflecting a mandate reality. It can be expected that colonial administrations would seek to champion 'enlightened' and 'progressive' policies, but such a strategy should not obscure the central features at play: that official attempts to define property relations solely in terms of a tidy set of 'rational' responses by self-interested people acting in predictable ways completely disregard any notion of a collective, or of context and background. As Huri Islamoglu has warned, the utilitarian approach 'abstracts private property from the power relations that were (and continue to be) constitutive of it'.[75] In this respect, one feature of the colonial vision of secure and individual rights to property is surely significant. This is what one Colonial Office official referred to generally as 'the dislike to be told that a man may or may not do what he likes with his own property', a position that officials were most likely to trace to a Lockian vision of secure property rights standing not only outside of the state, but as the last bastion of the individual against unfair state intervention.[76] Just how caught up the definition of property rights is with the very process of state formation can be gauged from a closer examination of the patterns and structures of the colonial state.

---

[73] Quoted in Metcalf, *Ideologies of the Raj*, 30.

[74] Dowson, 'The Land System in Palestine', CO 733/109, 252.

[75] Huri Islamoglu, 'Property as a Contested Domain: A Reevaluation of the Ottoman Land Code of 1858', in Roger Owen (ed.), *New Perspectives on Property and Land in the Middle East* (Cambridge, Mass.: Distributed for the Center for Middle Eastern Studies of Harvard University by Harvard University Press, 2000), 6.

[76] Minute sheets, 'Land Transfer Ordinance', CO 733/7, 399. See also comments by Sir John Shuckburgh before the Permanent Mandate Commission of the League of Nations, 9 June 1938.

2. LAND AND THE COLONIAL STATE

When a military occupation was established under the title of Occupied Enemy Territory Administration in the course of the First World War, British officers exercised direct rule. The League of Nations did not get around to ratifying Britain as mandatory power until 1923, but the administration of the territory passed in 1920 to a civil government, to the high commissioner in Jerusalem and the senior officers of government (mostly ex-army officers who had arrived as part of the military regime). A permanent mandates commission was established in Geneva to watch over mandatory affairs, but British colonial officials do not appear to have been overly constrained by this in their day-to-day running of Palestine. They tended to view the League's annual questionnaires as somewhat peripheral to their actual administration of the territory,[77] and representatives of the commission do not appear to have challenged the extent to which the government of Palestine was 'practically a British colonial administration'.[78] In London, control passed in 1921 from the Foreign Office to the Colonial Office, where officials of a Middle East department assisted the secretary of state in managing affairs. The exercise of legislative power was vested in Palestine in the high commissioner, assisted by his departmental officers, but the whole departmental machinery of administration was subject to the direction of the Colonial Office. Such a system was 'both bureaucratic and autocratic to the highest degree'.[79] However, it was far from monolithic. Technically, ordinances and expenditures were to be submitted for the approval of the Colonial Office, but with the rather limited resources at their disposal it was realized that it was 'undesirable to lay down rigid instructions that will inevitably be broken' and the secretary of state, 'some 3,000 miles away', was forced to defer to the men on the spot and their knowledge of local conditions.[80] The closest supervision was saved for government expenditures but there, as members of the Middle East department in the Colonial Office knew very well, they were not the sole arbiter. 'The Treasury, as the representatives of Palestine's principal

---

[77] See, for example, minute sheets, 'Report of the Administration July 1920–Dec. 1922 for League of Nations', June 1923, CO 733/46, 2. Also minute sheets, 'Annual Administrative Report for 1923', Feb. 1924, CO 733/78, 108.

[78] 'Provisional Minutes, Permanent Mandates Commission', in CO 733/78, 364.

[79] W. Basil Worsfold, *Palestine of the Mandate* (London: T. Fisher Unwin Ltd., 1925), 27.

[80] 'Discretionary Spending by High Commissioner', 2 Oct. 1922, CO 733/38, 161. See also minute sheets, Jan. 1925, CO 733/87, 35; and 24 Jan. 1928, CO 733/145/57034.

creditor, HMG, claim with justice to have the deciding vote,'[81] wrote one member, though really they hoped to shake off Treasury control. The establishment at the outset of the mandate of a grant-in-aid to cover the costs of the continued presence of a British military force in Palestine formed for many years the basis of the Treasury's claim to exercise general control.[82] In the wake of the 1929 riots, and again following the 1936 rebellion, domestic politics in Britain—and the influence of pressure groups there especially on behalf of Zionism—played a particularly important role in policy making.

While land policies flowed in part from colonial imaginations and abstract theories, they also reflected a large degree of pragmatism. Though the designs of policy were strongly supported by a logical and rational vision of property rights, any idealism was fraught with tensions and contradictions and it never assumed in Palestine the place of actual, uncontested policy. The official approach to land policies was ultimately determined by the specific contexts in which policies were implemented and adapted. Colonies could operate experimentally for only so long. When troubles were encountered, the tendency was for officials to resign themselves to the path of least resistance.[83] Colonial regimes were frustratingly tactical, changing their methods and even aims as obstacles that ought to have been anticipated presented themselves. As Roger Owen observes, given 'a certain necessary incoherence at its centre', colonial governance must be seen in large part as 'a mechanism for managing contradictions'.[84]

The contested and negotiated nature of land policies is best understood as a function of the constraints at work and inherent tensions at play in the British administration of Palestine. Three enduring tensions stand out in regard to the colonial structures and patterns that developed in Palestine.[85] One source of tension that militated against attempts to apply abstract notions of property rights in mandate Palestine was politico-economic in nature and fuelled by the overwhelming desire for social stability. Some contradictory implications followed from the focus on stability. Colonial rule focused on establishing indirect rule as

---

[81] G. L. M. Clauson, memorandum, CO 733/110, 278.

[82] Shuckburgh to Barstow, 26 July 1926, CO 733/113, 121.

[83] Cole Harris, *Making Native Space: Colonialism, Resistance and Reserves in British Columbia* (Vancouver: UBC Press, 2002), 13.

[84] Roger Owen, 'Defining Traditional: Some Implications of the Use of Ottoman Law in Mandatory Palestine', *Harvard Middle Eastern and Islamic Review*, 1/2 (1994), 117–18.

[85] On the basic features and practices of the colonial state, see Owen, *State, Power and Politics in the Making of the Modern Middle East*.

manifest through various guises such as alliances with large landowners and other conservative forces who, if sufficiently conciliated, could be useful mediators.[86] However, colonial rule invariably had to confront the ways in which liberalization of property rights contradicted such attempts for political stability. One example is the extension of British rule in tribal areas in the southern, more arid regions of Palestine. When consideration was given to how to secure the division of land into individual allotments, members of the Palestine government pressed for the compulsory partition of shares by settlement officers. But the Colonial Office in London preferred that partition be made optional rather than compulsory. 'I doubt whether it is advisable', minuted J. M. Lloyd, 'in this manner to allow an undermining of tribal custom traditions.'[87]

Another example of contradictory features of colonial processes emerged in Palestine when landlessness and displacement raised fears of a deteriorating security situation. At that point, social stability and individual title came to be seen as mutually exclusive. Of course, the deprivation of the rights of cultivators had been a long-standing and well-known risk to the liberal approach to property transactions. Europe had had its own struggle with such tensions, and colonial officials certainly carried some knowledge of this experience with them to Palestine. As Goadby and Doukhan observed, in their standard 1935 textbook on Ottoman land laws in Palestine which otherwise praised the productive benefits of enclosure and partition since the Middle Ages, such processes nonetheless usually proved 'dangerous' to the peasantry: 'Much care is needed if it is desired that the process of partition shall not have the effect of separating the peasants from the land.'[88] The historic tensions in English history (as well as Irish and Indian histories), between advocates of tenancy legislation and those of laissez-faire economics who laboured against undue interference with the rights of property,[89] would have to be worked out again in Palestine.

[86] Ylana N. Miller, *Government and Society in Rural Palestine, 1920–1948* (Austin: University of Texas Press, 1985). Kamen, *Little Common Ground: Arab Agriculture and Jewish Settlement in Palestine, 1920–1948*.

[87] Minute sheet, 22 Aug. 1927, CO 733/142/44605. The general rule was that a settlement officer might carry out the partition if two-thirds of the share owners applied to have village *musha'* land divided. Government of Palestine, 'Explanatory Note in the Form of Questions and Answers on Survey, Land Settlement, and Registration of Title', *Palestine Bulletin*, 14–17 June 1928.

[88] Goadby and Doukhan, *The Land Law of Palestine*, 210 n. 4.

[89] See Thomas Metcalf, 'Laissez-Faire and Tenant Right in Mid-Nineteenth Century India', *Indian Economic and Social Review*, 1/1 (1963).

A second set of constraints is related to the security issue but more directly financial in nature. The key feature of colonial administration on the fiscal front is that colonies were expected 'to pay their own way' and not be an imposition on the British taxpayer. Given how mindful the high commissioner had to be of the interests of the British taxpayer, and of the economies practised at home, it was at times a real problem discerning who then represented the interests of the taxpayer in Palestine.[90] Still, taxation of the colony was as high as thought to be possible without unduly agitating the local population. Combined with the tendency to place a priority on big budget items like security and administration, the result was limiting the money available to push through projects which necessarily addressed questions of individual rights, such as afforestation, marsh drainage, infrastructure development, as well as cadastral surveys and judicial settlement proceedings. The fact that proposals for such schemes often included large increases in staff on the clerical side was particularly troubling in the colonial context.[91] A Colonial Office minute in 1921 laid out Palestine's fiscal policy clearly:

> Expenditure must be worked out as a whole and be brought down to the lowest possible figure compatible with decent Government. Revenue must be collected to the greatest possible amount, in other words, the country must be taxed to the hilt and if there is anything left over beyond essential expenditure it must be decided on general principles whether the burden of taxation is to be lightened, or expenditure which is not essential, but which is desirable, should be incurred.[92]

Although consistently justified as a necessary part of the efficient functioning of economic arrangements in a colonial setting, especially in regard to the proper functioning of a taxation system, land settlement activities (that is, the settlement of title to land) lost more of their lustre in practice when it was realized that indigenous rights could be formidable obstacles to large development projects, or as it became increasingly clear that revenues were not in the end going to be as dependent upon traditional direct taxes on land as would have been expected.

A third source of tension was legal in nature and emerged from the pressure to respect the status quo. In part the pressure to respect the status quo reflected Britain's position in Palestine, sanctioned as it was by the newly invented mandate system of the League of Nations which sought to disguise colonial rule by 'entrusting' the 'tutelage' of the country to

---

[90] See Samuel to Colonial Office, 8 Feb. 1924, CO 733/64, 456.

[91] See, for example, minute sheets, 'Estimates, 1926–1927', Mar. 1926, CO 733/113, 98.

[92] Minute sheets, 15 Dec. 1921, CO 733/8, 341. See also CO 733/145/57034.

Britain. But pressure to adhere to the doctrine of the status quo also owed much to previously established patterns of military administration, which were governed theoretically by the 1907 Hague rules restricting substantial changes to the laws of an occupied territory. Formal operation of the mandate did not begin until 1923, but the civilian administration that had replaced the military one in 1920 ostensibly adhered to the convention nonetheless. Article 46 of the 1922 order-in-council, being the organic law establishing the constitution for Palestine pursuant to Britain's 1890 foreign jurisdiction Act, assured the local population that 'the jurisdiction of the Civil Courts shall be exercised in conformity with the Ottoman Law in force in Palestine on November 1st, 1914'.[93] Despite the need to maintain Ottoman laws defining rights in property, British officials nonetheless eagerly assumed a juridical vacuum wherever they thought they could, only eventually to confront, usually sooner than later, the complicated challenge of exercising their authority in conformity with existing Ottoman laws, as well as prevailing attitudes about the legitimacy of those laws. Just how successfully (or not) the Ottoman legal framework defined actual practices on the ground added another set of constraints and challenges to official designs.

To sum up, attempts to realize market ideals broke down in practice into various outcomes depending upon a host of factors that had to be negotiated between, and among, government officials and local land-holders. Government was clearly in a powerful position but negotiations were fluid and indeterminate, as the priorities of government were con-tinually reconfigured to adapt to local arrangements or take into account changing circumstances. The definition and redefinition of property rights in mandate Palestine was highly contingent upon the varying positions of participants struggling to assert their case in particular historical situations. In the chapters that follow, therefore, a premium is placed on the specifi-city of the situation, on the particular characters presenting and defining the material, and on the distinct circumstances in which they happen to do so. For example, Ottoman land laws are described (Chapter 1) in the context of the contested processes by which government sought to redefine legal and tenurial categories; the settlement process is outlined (Chapter 2) in terms of how it was actually worked out in practice in specific cases.

---

[93] Goadby and Doukhan, *The Land Law of Palestine*. For a fuller examination of the process by which British officials came to adhere to the doctrine of the status quo see Martin Bunton, 'Inventing the Status Quo: Ottoman Land-Law during the Palestine Mandate, 1917–1936', *International History Review*, 21/1 (1999).

This book aims to reveal the nature of colonial land policies in Palestine as ad hoc and makeshift, multidirectional and inconsistent, even contradictory. An attempt is made to untangle colonial land policies by specifically addressing the utilitarian set of expectations which colonial officials themselves held about the proper role secure and individual property rights were expected to play. Each component of these expectations is dealt with individually, chapter by chapter. They include: identifying and protecting the public domain; lowering transaction costs and facilitating the transfer of land to its highest value use; providing and securing of agricultural credit; ensuring the proper and efficient taxation of immovable property; and encouraging private enterprise and development.

Chapter 1 explores the ambiguous situation that developed as government championed the benefits of bringing landed assets into a market economy while at the same time asserting rights of the state to as much agricultural land as it thought it could claim—redefining Ottoman legal categories when possible, deferring to local arrangements when necessary. One of the most significant features of this confusion and ambiguity was the contested process of reinterpreting legal categories of land, and the chapter documents in particular the changing policy towards what was thought of as 'state land'. Chapter 2 scrutinizes official efforts to develop the economy through the vision of a lively market supported by a comprehensive settlement of title to land. The market approach would ensure the efficient reallocation of resources to those who valued them most. But colonial rule also hinged on stability, and so a tension was immediately revealed between the enthusiasm for the 'modernizing' ideology of the market and the anxiety for the harm done by the growing displacement of the Palestinian peasantry. Closely related to the transforming powers of the market was the liquidating of capital in order to form the basis of a system of agricultural credit, and Chapter 3 critically examines the actual relevance of credit machinery in the formulation of land policies. Chapter 4 similarly assesses the significance of taxation machinery. A primary responsibility of all colonial governments was to construct a legal and administrative system by which landed property might be easily and fairly identified, assessed, and taxed. The 1922 report of the tithes commission neatly wrapped up the whole argument: 'The need for a rapid and correct survey is urgent. Without it an absolutely defensible tithe without dispute is impossible. Nothing tends to encourage improvements and interest in land so much as a sense of security of tithe.'[94] Clearly spelled

---

[94] 'Report of the Tithes Commission', Mar. 1922, CO 733/20, 294.

out here is the normative code regulating the way property rights ought to be defined in mandate Palestine. As with all normative designs, however, what go unnoticed here are the actual prevailing complexities that need to be accommodated, often through pragmatic evasions from that simple model. Much was said in official circles about the so-called classic conversion of the downtrodden fellahin into a thriving peasantry whose 'industry was stimulated by being protected' and whose 'economic liberty was a matter of primary concern throughout'.[95] The prescription for the conversion was, again, settling title to individual plots of land. 'There is no doubt', proclaimed Lewis French, 'that survey and settlement proceedings are one of the most powerful temporary incentives to development that can be devised: because they enable a landowner, large or small, to know for the first time exactly what his rights in the land are *vis-à-vis* other landowners.'[96] The extent to which such widely held ideas were in fact as self-explanatory and as self-actuating as British officials seem to have assumed is dealt with in Chapter 5, in a way that again recognizes the need to be very specific about time and place.

To fully grasp changes in colonial land policies in mandate Palestine, one must treat with care the single, coherent generalized abstractions regurgitated in official reports throughout the period. Officials had to contend with the very real tensions and contradictions that bedevilled their abstract thinking about it. In any colonial context, the way British administrators viewed property and the meanings given to it changed with time. Colonial Office advisers in London, government officials in Jerusalem, and the administrators on the spot all had reasons to weigh these tensions differently, with the result that colonial land policies were far from consistent. To be sure, public pronouncements about the superiority of private property were continually provided by colonial officials who came into contact with the administrative apparatus in mandate Palestine. As late as 1937 Albert Abramson, formerly commissioner of lands, prefaced his remarks on the superiority of secure and individual title with an admonition from Deuteronomy cursing 'he that removeth his neighbour's landmark'.[97] But really it remained primarily a matter of faith. In practice, officials at various times either lacked the will, the capacity, or, as time went on, the interest to implement policies derived solely from an

---

[95] Dowson, 'The Land System in Palestine', CO 733/109, 252.
[96] Lewis French, 'First Report on Agricultural Development and Land Settlement in Palestine', 23 Dec. 1931, CO 733/214/5, 75.
[97] Albert Abramson, 'An Aspect of Village Life in Palestine', *Jerusalem Post*, 6 July 1937.

intellectualized consideration of the benefits of private property, or of a single set of expectations about its proper role in economy and society.

Examining the role of property in the development of British administrative policies in mandate Palestine in this way reveals that the framing of property, and the meanings given to it, were never absolute. Rather, they were subject to change with time and to the play of political and economic forces. As the challenges in administering Palestine became clearer, and even escalated, officials increasingly neither really desired, nor cared for, the securing of individual rights to property in Palestine.

1

State Lands

Despite the prevailing rhetoric around the liberalizing role played by individual rights to land—an argument that was often set against the paralysing hold of the state—official policy in the early years of the British mandate in Palestine actually aimed very much at cementing government's own role as landowner. The conviction in creating a free market in land had first to compete with the desire to guard jealously the rights of the state to whatever land it thought it could claim. Officials of an extremely budget-conscious government were vulnerable to considering public ownership of land as much a part of the national assets as the funds in the Treasury. Accordingly, the financial importance of defining and defending what could be taken to be 'state lands' took on greater financial importance. The favoured mechanism by which British officials considered disposing of rights once acquired by the state was through leases, due recognition being paid to the need for the period of the lease to be governed by circumstances so that very long leases would be considered for the intensive development of difficult areas.[1] From the point of view of increasing the public good, leasing was preferable to selling because it was assumed that the extension of British rule and good government (for example, increased security, development of infrastructure) would eventually raise property values like a rising tide. Government wanted to be sure that it received its fair share of the increased dividend.[2]

Often unfolding in the legal arena, government strategies regarding the definition of state lands throw into particularly sharp relief the highly contested process of defining legal and tenurial categories of land, in particular the ways in which Ottoman definitions were understood or deliberately misunderstood. This chapter reveals how attempts to impose new laws and procedures regarding the definition of state lands had to be negotiated and renegotiated between government and landholders.

[1] 'Report of the Land Settlement Commission', Aug. 1920, CO 733/18, 605.
[2] Minute sheets, CO 733/107, 408.

But first, this chapter will examine salient features of Ottoman rules defining property relations in the nineteenth century, and then consider the conditions under which those rules were conformed to during the mandate period.

1. OTTOMAN LAND LAW OF 1858 . . .

Until the First World War, the region of Palestine was under the rule of the Ottoman Empire, a world empire which had spent the last hundred years engaged in repeated attempts to reform administrative, military, legal, and economic structures. Driven by the need to defend against continued territorial and commercial expansion of European powers, the Ottoman state apparatus expanded in size and function as its rulers sought to extend and deepen their authority across the empire. The development of modern centralized political institutions was aimed at efficiently mobilizing the empire's resources and fostering economic growth which, in turn, would sustain the process of further expanding central authority. Overall, administrative centralization was aimed at eliminating the power of local intermediaries. More specifically, the reforms worked themselves out in such ways as controlling the production of agricultural wealth, a dominant sector of the economy: in rural areas such control, where it occurred, chiefly took the form of a government official registering titles to individual holdings in the hope that increasing numbers of industrious peasant proprietors, easily identifiable as taxpayers, would emerge. This was a desired reordering of property rights in which Ottoman elites shared a set of utilitarian goals with other state leaders around the world shaped by nineteenth-century ideas of liberalism. However, traditional pictures of 'the sick man of Europe' have tended not to recognize shared attributes. When Ottoman military defeats in the First World War led to the emergence of new political structures in the region, the British and French empires were left with what seemed to be a free hand to impose their will. Most colonial administrators tended at the outset towards universal, abstract theories of private property that in fact marginalized and dismissed the modern processes of state building previously undertaken by the Ottomans. Instead, colonial officials persuaded themselves that such features of modern statehood as the development of individual ownership, and the rule of law more generally, constituted a special part of European history.

The British administration that first occupied parts of the Ottoman Empire that would become known as Palestine was a military one, established at the end of 1917 with a staff largely made up of recruits from the available forces almost all of whom were 'new to administrative work'.[3] The choice was limited, and men had to be taken as they were found, but a level of amateurism certainly permeated governing institutions. 'There was practically nobody in the administration who had worked in an administration,' reads the testimony of a witness before the Peel Commission in 1936: 'It was the blind leading the blind.'[4] As a result of the long delays which confronted post-war efforts to reach international agreement over the future of the conquered areas of the Ottoman Empire, the ambition of British officers to create a new administration was understandably enough tempered by requirements to adhere to the doctrine of the status quo. It eventually found formal expression in article 46 of the 1922 Palestine order-in-council which aimed to assure the local population that the court system would continue to be exercised 'in conformity with the Ottoman law in force in Palestine on November 1st, 1914'.[5]

The existing law in this regard was in the main the 1858 Ottoman land code, a key part of the mid-nineteenth-century reforms—together known as the *Tanzimat*, from the Turkish and Arabic word for order—which aimed at transforming the Ottoman Empire into a modern centralized state by substituting the professional power of the Ottoman government for the influence of local interest groups that formerly challenged it at the periphery.[6] While few doubt the actual significance of the 1858 land code as an integral part of the reform process, both the actual intent of the law and its impact on landholding have been the subject of such debate that the code has been likened to 'the elephant of the blind man as it appears to scholars in different guises'.[7] For a long time, the search for a unified picture of the code's significance attempted either to locate it within broader efforts of the Ottoman government to control the peasantry or, somewhat conversely, argued that it promoted the creation of large landed estates;

---

[3] *A Survey of Palestine: Prepared in December 1945 and January 1946 for the Information of the Anglo-American Committee of Inquiry* (Washington: Institute for Palestine Studies, 1991), 15.

[4] Quoted in Great Britain. Palestine Royal Commission, *Report* (London: HMSO, 1937), 160.

[5] Norman Bentwich (ed.), *Legislation of Palestine, 1918–1925: Including the Orders-in-Council, Ordinances, Public Notices, Proclamations, Regulations, Etc.*, 2 vols. (Alexandria: Whitehead Morris Ltd., 1926).

[6] Eugene L. Rogan, *Frontiers of the State in the Late Ottoman Empire: Transjordan, 1850–1921* (Cambridge: Cambridge University Press, 1999), 4–5.

[7] Donald Quataert, 'The Age of Reforms, 1812–1914', in Halil Inalcik with Donald Quataert (eds.), *An Economic and Social History of the Ottoman Empire, 1300–1914* (Cambridge: Cambridge University Press, 1994), 856.

more recently, scholars have tended to agree that interpretations of the 1858 Ottoman land code must clearly be wary of generalizations, allow for processes of negotiation, and thus expect some significant difference in its application from one geographical region to another.[8]

A growing body of empirical studies in recent years has examined the more specific circumstances and 'moments' of land registration that actually took place under the terms of the 1858 land code, paying closer attention than before to how the categories and terminology of modernist reforms were made to relate to local knowledge and local concerns.[9] By documenting the active participation of individuals in the official land registration process, these studies have gone some distance in revising earlier judgements that described widespread manipulation by powerful individuals playing on the peasantry's fear of how taxation and conscription could be facilitated by registration. Such fears may have been real, but did not necessarily prevent registration and might have been mitigated by previous harmful experience with the vagaries of unsystematic records.

The picture that emerges is one in which the overriding demand of government is that all individuals who possessed land be provided by officials of the state with title deeds. In this respect, the land code played a key part in the process of centralizing authority in so far as it attempted to ensure that disputes over property were relegated to the administrative domain.[10] By the terms of the code itself, for example, article after article pressed that practically nothing ought to take place 'without previously obtaining the leave and knowledge of the Official'.[11] In this way, land registration can be said to have clearly helped extend Ottoman authority.

---

[8] Martha Mundy, 'Village Land and Individual Title: *Musha'* and Ottoman Land Registration in the 'Ajlun District', in Eugene L. Rogan and Tariq Tell (eds.), *Village, Steppe and State: The Social Origins of Modern Jordan* (London: British Academic Press, 1994), Huri Islamoglu, 'Property as a Contested Domain: A Reevaluation of the Ottoman Land Code of 1858', in Roger Owen (ed.), *New Perspectives on Property and Land in the Middle East* (Cambridge, Mass.: Distributed for the Center for Middle Eastern Studies of Harvard University by Harvard University Press, 2000).

[9] Mundy, 'Village Land and Individual Title: *Musha'* and Ottoman Land Registration in the 'Ajlun District', Rogan, *Frontiers of the State in the Late Ottoman Empire: Transjordan, 1850–1921*.

[10] Islamoglu, 'Property as a Contested Domain: A Reevaluation of the Ottoman Land Code of 1858'.

[11] See Stanley Fisher, *Ottoman Land Laws: Containing the Ottoman Land Code and Later Legislation Affecting Land with Notes and an Appendix of Cyprus Laws and Rules Relating to Land* (London: Oxford University Press, 1919). This version of the Ottoman land laws draws largely on the French translations in George Young, *Corps de droit ottoman; recueil des codes, lois, règlements, ordonnances et actes les plus importants du droit intérieur d'études sur le droit coutumier de l'empire ottoman*, 8 vols. (Oxford: Clarendon Press, 1900–6).

Moreover, the stress laid on identifying the sources of revenue as individual subjects, and the emphasis on locating that individual with a given property, suggests strongly that the Ottoman Empire had, as Martha Mundy puts it, 'adopted the central tenets of nineteenth century policies of government: state prosperity rests on the security of individual wealth, corresponding to individual subjecthood and tax liability.'[12]

Official expectations of increased revenue and stability were clearly bolstered by the code's effort to create 'a one-to-one correspondence between a given property and the person responsible for paying its taxes'.[13] In addition to ensuring that taxpaying cultivators were now more readily identifiable on a regular basis, Ottoman bureaucratization also allowed the opportunity for direct fiscal profit from fees paid on the issue of documents (provided upon sale, succession, mortgage, etc.).[14] Indirectly, the government could expect to benefit from the general provision of a legal context for greater investment: as Haim Gerber observes, 'land could, for the first time in Ottoman history, be owned on paper',[15] suggesting that the Ottoman government could now strike a good deal with an energetic entrepreneur willing not only to pay the price for uncultivated property but also to develop and raise production levels, and increase the flow of revenues generally. It was primarily in this way, Gerber asserts, that large estates were formed in Palestine in the wake of the 1858 Ottoman land code, not as is commonly suggested by a notable figure taking advantage of the ignorance or fear of fellahin to register their lands. The relationship between private property and economic growth lay at the heart of the Ottoman legislative effort: the main objective of the 1858 land code being the financial one of bringing as much land under cultivation as possible and, as Huri Islamoglu further argues, being driven increasingly by the conviction that the individual was better equipped to do so than the state (provided always that the registry fees and prescribed

[12] Martha Mundy, 'The State of Property: Late Ottoman Southern Syria, the *Kaza* of Ajlun (1875–1918)', in Huri Islamoglu (ed.), *Constituting Modernity: Private Property in the East and West* (London: I. B. Tauris, 2004), 216.

[13] Rogan, *Frontiers of the State in the Late Ottoman Empire: Transjordan, 1850–1921*, 83.

[14] Alexander Schölch, 'European Penetration and the Economic Development of Palestine, 1856–82', in Roger Owen (ed.), *Studies in the Economic and Social History of Palestine in the Nineteenth and Twentieth Centuries* (London: Macmillan Press Ltd., 1982), 21–2.

[15] Haim Gerber, *The Social Origins of the Modern Middle East* (London: Mansell, 1987), 72. See also Charles Kamen, *Little Common Ground: Arab Agriculture and Jewish Settlement in Palestine, 1920–1948* (Pittsburgh: University of Pittsburgh Press, 1991).

taxes were paid up).[16] A brief review of the main classifications of land under the 1858 code will help elaborate upon these efforts to enforce the claims to authority and revenue by the state, while stabilizing and securing the enjoyment of use or access by the holder (as opposed to enforcing individual ownership per se). Three categories of land most concern us here: *matruke, mevat,* and *miri.*

Matruke was a category that described land left for the general use of the public at large, like a public highway or the foreshore of the sea,[17] or land assigned for the inhabitants of a specific village or town (or several grouped together) such as threshing floors, 'set apart *ab antiquo* for the inhabitants of a place in general' (article 96), or lands on which villagers have brought animals to graze 'and shall be kept as pasturing ground for all time' (article 97).[18] The chief characteristic of *matruke* land, then, is that no possession or transfer of ownership should be allowed of land left and assigned for public utility. *Mevat* was a category that described 'dead' or waste land, unallocated and situated beyond a prescribed distance from inhabited regions (so remote from the nearest village that the voice of a speaking man would not be heard).[19] Anyone who cultivated and reclaimed land of this kind could, upon payment of a fee, be issued a title deed to the continued usufruct of the land (with the leave of an official, one could be granted the use of the land gratuitously if it was considered a question of need). Two other categories, *mülk* and *vakif,* were recognized by the Ottoman land code, but not dealt with in detail as they were placed instead under the *mejcelle,* the Ottoman civil code, and *sharia,* Muslim religious law, respectively. The owner of *mülk* land enjoyed the closest form of ownership to freehold: the law speaks of the owner of *mülk* land as having both the legal ownership and the right of use and disposal (the *rakaba* and the *hakk-i tasarruf*). With *mülk,* owners were free to use their land as they wished and were under no obligation to cultivate, but in Palestine agricultural land of the *mülk* category was rare. The *vakif* category included land which itself was dedicated to pious uses, and regulated by religious law, as well as land the revenue or usufruct of which was dedicated.

[16] Islamoglu, 'Property as a Contested Domain: A Reevaluation of the Ottoman Land Code of 1858'.

[17] In Palestine the public was deemed to have a right of way along the Mediterranean foreshore. See ISA Chief Secretary's Office, RG 2 L/85/32, 1019.

[18] See also article 13 of 'Tapu Law' in Fisher, *Ottoman Land Laws: Containing the Ottoman Land Code and Later Legislation Affecting Land with Notes and an Appendix of Cyprus Laws and Rules Relating to Land.*

[19] Ibid. 33, art. 103.

The vast majority of agricultural land in Palestine came under the category known as *miri*, land in which the usufruct, or right of use (*tasarruf*), was granted out by the state for purposes of cultivation, though the *rakaba* (legal ownership) was still vested in the state. In addition to the annual payment of taxes, the grant of a title to *miri* land was conditional on immediate payment of a fee, referred to as the 'fair price' (*bedl misl*) or 'price of the land' (*tapu misl*, frequently shortened to *tapu*) in its unimproved state. In theory, this was a sum fixed by impartial experts who knew the extent, dimensions, boundaries, and values of the land according to its productive capacity and situation.[20] The law treated the usufructuary possession of the land as a personal, hereditary, and transferable right. Finding a useful equivalent of *miri* in the English legal vocabulary poses a number of challenges. Some of these will be elaborated upon later, but the key point to note here is the extent to which the state retained the ability to negotiate the conditions upon which those rights are exercised. As Owen has written, *miri* was a category that must be seen in practice to be less about ownership per se than about the right to distribute access and prevent obstacles to its use.[21] By holding on to the *rakaba*, and thus not recognizing rights in *miri* land other than the usufruct, a dominant motive of the granting of *miri* land in these ways is understood to be such cultivation and transfer of otherwise idle land as would ensure continued enjoyment of use by its possessors and continued payment to the state of the tithes and fees owed it. In the event of land being left uncultivated for three years (without good reason) or of its possessor dying without leaving qualified heirs, the land escheated to the state in the sense that it would again be granted on payment of *tapu* either to those with a legal interest in the land and its buildings (say, as co-possessor) or to inhabitants nearby who needed it most (for example, soldiers returning home). Should such persons, within a prescribed time limit, not lay claim to the grant of *miri* land in this way, the land became *miri mahlul* and was put up to auction and adjudged to the highest bidder. In recognition of a doctrine of adverse possession, the code acknowledged the right to *miri* land of anyone who possessed and

[20] Fisher, *Ottoman Land Laws: Containing the Ottoman Land Code and Later Legislation Affecting Land with Notes and an Appendix of Cyprus Laws and Rules Relating to Land*, 21, art. 59.

[21] Roger Owen, 'Introduction', in Owen (ed.), *New Perspectives on Property and Land in the Middle East*, p. xi.

cultivated it without dispute for ten years.[22] At times, a balance had to be struck between stability and continuity of cultivation, on the one hand, and increased revenue on the other. Trade-offs and sacrifices were reflected in terms such as those which defined the concentric circles of persons with rights to the usufruct of *miri* land before a grant could be resumed by the state.[23] It was made clear that once a person with a right of *tapu* acquired the land, offers of more money coming from outside those circles would not be taken into consideration.

As the state's granting of land by *tapu* was aimed at securing its cultivation, thereby guaranteeing payment of a tithe, etc., certain prohibitions were made against activities such as building houses or planting vines that might be taken to extend personal ties of ownership to the land underneath. However, a series of laws were adopted by government in 1913, as part of the legislative activity following the deposition of Sultan Abdul Hamid II and the 1908 Young Turk revolt. These laws, though provisional in the sense that they had not received formal ratification in Constantinople, had the effect of simplifying the law mainly in the direction of erasing the differences between *miri* and *mülk*.[24] The 1913 law of disposition removed many of the previous prohibitions and tended, according to Stanley Fisher, to put the holders of *miri* land 'into the position of absolute owners'.[25] According to this law, possessors of *miri* could, without the leave of the official: plant gardens of trees and vines (despite Ottoman land code article 25); cut down timber (despite article 28); alienate or mortgage it (despite article 36); etc. According to Goadby and Doukhan, the 1913 law 'may legitimately be deemed to authorize any use of the surface of the land not incompatible with its development', a compromise that, it was argued, ended a long struggle by government to secure widespread observance of the code.[26] Such a level of compromise is an important reminder of the necessarily contested nature of property.

---

[22] Fisher, *Ottoman Land Laws: Containing the Ottoman Land Code and Later Legislation Affecting Land with Notes and an Appendix of Cyprus Laws and Rules Relating to Land,* 26, art. 78.

[23] Donald Quataert, 'The Age of Reforms, 1812–1914', in Inalcik with Quataert (eds.), *An Economic and Social History of the Ottoman Empire, 1300–1914,* 858.

[24] Frederic M. Goadby and Moses J. Doukhan, *The Land Law of Palestine* (Tel Aviv: Shoshany's Printing Co. Ltd., 1935), 14. See also Robert H. Eisenman, *Islamic Law in Palestine and Israel: A History of the Survival of Tanzimat and Shari'a in the British Mandate and the Jewish State* (Leiden: Brill, 1978), 63–9.

[25] Fisher, *Ottoman Land Laws: Containing the Ottoman Land Code and Later Legislation Affecting Land with Notes and an Appendix of Cyprus Laws and Rules Relating to Land,* 79.

[26] Goadby and Doukhan, *The Land Law of Palestine,* 34.

Modern Ottoman state administration did not, stresses Islamoglu, 'confront a society from which it was isolated and over which it sought to establish unequivocal control': attempts to mediate resistance to the code represented the very political processes which were themselves constitutive of property rights.[27]

2. . . . VERSUS 'OTTOMAN LAW IN FORCE'

Despite their official commitment to the maintenance of Ottoman laws regulating rights in property, British officials in Palestine were eager nonetheless to assume a juridical vacuum wherever they thought they could. Colonial officials made no effort to reconstruct in its entirety the Ottoman legal regime which had been officially applied to the land. Instead, Ottoman laws and practices inherited in Palestine were translated, studied, reformulated, and institutionalized (or dismissed) in ways that primarily addressed specific problems demanding the immediate attention of colonial officials. Not only did this mean that understandings of the status quo were frequently designed to meet particular circumstances, but it meant there was tremendous scope, particularly in the early years, for expression to be given to the preferences of individuals.

Completely uninterested in the intentions that might be discerned of the fathers of the 1858 land code—say, as a potential aid in determining meaning and direction of Ottoman laws—and oblivious to questions of impact—other than a general antipathy to Ottoman structures provoked by the need to discredit them as a way of justifying new interventions— British officials at the outset of the mandate appear to have approached the Ottoman land code less as blind men before an elephant than as blindfolded. Though the realities of ruling Palestine would eventually somewhat curtail their room for movement, British officials clearly did not at first feel overly constrained by the task of acting in conformity with the laws in force.[28] Remarkably, British observers reflecting back upon the mandate do not seem to have considered the question of 'Ottoman law in force' as overly problematic. The Peel Commission, for example, concluded in 1936 that 'it is true that no new system has been introduced,

---

[27] Huri Islamoglu, 'Politics of Administering Property: Law and Statistics in the Nineteenth-Century Ottoman Empire', in Islamoglu (ed.), *Constituting Modernity: Private Property in the East and West*, 280.

[28] For a more detailed description, see Martin Bunton, 'Inventing the Status Quo: Ottoman Land-Law during the Palestine Mandate, 1917–1936', *International History Review*, 21/1 (1999).

no new land code has been enacted. The Ottoman Land Code has been retained . . . several new laws have been passed to amend it, but it remains in essence the same complicated system.'[29] The existence of a legal essence was also considered by the 1947 *Survey of Palestine* which upheld that 'the Ordinances enacted by the Government of Palestine have not greatly modified the Ottoman land tenure.'[30] What is missing in these assessments is any recognition of the extent to which Ottoman law in force in mandate Palestine was a product of the interplay of a number of forces: in particular, the spread of colonial practices, the involvement of the indigenous population, and the transformation of economic forces.[31]

What highlights the important roles of colonial practices in the process of constructing a Palestinian land law during the mandate is less the overt Anglicization of 'Ottoman law in force' than its troublesome inaccessibility in official circles. In diagnosing the 'principal evils' which plagued Palestine's land system and which required immediate remedy, Dowson complained as late as 1930 that

The land law of the country was an unintelligible compost of the original Ottoman laws, provisional laws, judgements of various tribunals, Sultanic firmans, administrative orders having the force of law overlaid by a further amalgam of post-war Proclamations, Public Orders, Orders-in-Council, judgements of various civil and religious courts, Ordinances, Amending Ordinances, and Orders and Regulations under these.[32]

This confusion, noted Dowson in an earlier report,

was aggravated by the complexities, uncertainties and contradictions of the main body of the law, by the incompetence, if not corruption, of the agents who administered it, and by the concurrent toleration of important practices unknown, if not running counter, to it . . .[33]

Reference, therefore, to something called Ottoman law in force in Palestine on 1 November 1914 was 'unavoidably loose'. From the point of view of the judicial officers of the Palestine administration, such looseness might be seen as an opportunity as much as a challenge. The possibility of choosing from a variety of rules, ordinances, firmans, administrative orders, etc. gave British officials some scope in determining what would

---

[29] Great Britain. Palestine Royal Commission, *Report*.

[30] *A Survey of Palestine: Prepared in December 1945 and January 1946 for the Information of the Anglo-American Committee of Inquiry*, 228.

[31] Kristin Mann and Richard Roberts (eds.), *Law in Colonial Africa* (London: J. Currey and Heinemann, 1991).

[32] Dowson, 'Report on the Progress of Land Reforms, 1923–1930', CO 733/221/97169, 9.

[33] Dowson, 'Preliminary Study of Land Tenure in Palestine', CO 733/109, 154.

constitute 'Ottoman law in force'. Recognition should be made in this context of the process of translation. The Attorney General's Office commissioned translations on a contract basis,[34] as did judges[35] and official committees and commissions. The difficulties encountered by legal and administrative officials in procuring the actual text of a law pertaining to rights in land is indicated by the continual, often insurmountable, difficulties confronted by no less a figure than Dowson. Generally, the 1858 Ottoman land code reached the government of Palestine via a 'not guaranteed'[36] French translation, Young's *Corps de droit ottoman*. But this was not always available (though his version also forms the basis of Stanley Fisher's *Ottoman Land Laws*, which, together with translations by the Iraq government of fifteen 'provisional laws' published between 1859 and 1914,[37] was republished in 1927 by R. C. Tute). When Dowson first visited Palestine in November 1923, he was given a copy of Frederic Ongley's 1892 translation.[38] When preparing for his second visit, a 'precious' copy of Young's work was reluctantly lent him for a brief period by the Foreign Office: the Colonial Office did not have one to spare. In Palestine he faced similar difficulties, though he was able to purchase a copy of *Corps de droit ottoman* in a Jerusalem bookshop, and the lands department lent him their annotated copy of Fisher. All of this though was of limited help: Dowson complained that the latest Ottoman law Fisher could help with was dated 1883; in Young it was 1901.[39] While the absence of a complete and authoritative collection of pre-war Ottoman laws was cause for regret amongst mandate officials, the delay in putting together such a collection of ordinances and proclamations published since the occupation—'issued with historical and explanatory notes made while the actors were still on the scene'—was a source of much greater frustration.[40] The fact is that until Goadby and Doukhan undertook a preliminary study of existing laws at the end of 1927, which circulated privately before being revised and published as *The Land Law of Palestine* in 1935, no authoritative and

[34] 'Translation of Ottoman Laws', ISA, RG 3 Attorney General's Office, AG/333, box 749.

[35] See, for example: 'In the Courts', *Palestine Post*, 20 Mar. 1933, 4.

[36] Colonial Office to high commissioner Samuel, 29 Sept. 1923, CO 733/48, 373.

[37] A copy of this Iraq publication can be found in CO 733/159/2/57454.

[38] F. Ongley and Horace Edward Miller (eds.), *The Ottoman Land Code* (London: W. Clowes and Sons, 1892). The administration apparently did not own an official copy, but they borrowed a private copy for him and then supplemented it with a 'scratch collection' of post-occupation proclamations and ordinances.

[39] Dowson, 'Preliminary Study of Land Tenure in Palestine', CO 733/109, 149.

[40] Ibid.

reliable digest in English of the legislation that governed property relation in Palestine even existed. The problem apparently was twofold: on the one hand difficulty in finding someone with the necessary knowledge, experience, and time; on the other, the infuriating though typically colonial desire to minimize costs. As Dowson fumed,

If the main expense of administration, executive and judicial, of a law is justified, the relatively trifling cost of keeping it and any subsidiary instruments in print should be included, if only because it may well be considered an elementary obligation of any civilized government to keep at least the text of its current laws and public regulations within the reach of all.[41]

It is clear that land law was much less codified than commonly perceived in the literature. During the mandate, complaints were frequently heard regarding the inaccessibility of the law, especially when it had to be translated from more than one language. Add to this the fact that, until the early 1930s, there was very little attempt to organize systematically previously recorded judgements, some of which consisted at the beginning of a few words scribbled on a piece of paper, and one can readily appreciate the context that gave rise to high levels of frustration and cynicism:

the chaotic method of fighting actions meant that a litigant was in for a gamble as much as for a judicial decision. In many instances he might as well toss up than go to the expense of briefing counsel. There are lawyers who have private collections of judgements—sometimes containing contradictory interpretations of the law— and they will produce one of such judgements if briefed by appellant and the other if briefed by the respondent. The advocate on the other hand, will have his own private collection but those particular judgements may not be found in it.[42]

In considering generally the efforts of British officials to work with Ottoman law, we must of course consider the discretion given them to ensure that rules relating to property rights converged with the administrative necessities of the colonial state. For pre-mandate Ottoman law to become 'Ottoman law in force' it had to be discovered, translated, drafted, taught, and practised. And the efforts required to officially digest the 'unintelligible compost' of laws, provisional laws, administrative orders, etc. provided British officials with some scope in how they wanted to interpret it.

It is clear therefore that we need to qualify the prevailing ahistorical picture of Ottoman law during the Palestine mandate: immutable, 'out

---

[41] Ibid. 149–50.   [42] 'Legal Notes' by Justinian. *Palestine Post*, 9 May 1933.

there', and just waiting to be discovered by impartial British legislators and judges. Rather, we can conclude that Ottoman law in force during the mandate was itself very much a construct of that environment. A key role was played in this environment by British officials who continuously clarified and redrafted legislation, but the context was also defined by the assertions of the local communities. To understand how these features worked themselves out one must provide the historical contexts in which actions and reactions took place, and it is with this in mind that we now turn to a closer discussion of the importance in government circles of defining and defending 'state lands' during the mandate period.

3. THE 1920 *MAHLUL* LAND ORDINANCE AND THE 1921 *MEVAT* LAND ORDINANCE

The notion of 'state lands' as it emerged at the outset of the mandate received its legal definition from the same order-in-council that recognized Ottoman law in force. But the government's initial ideas about public domain were a potentially dramatic deviation from that law, as well as from arrangements worked out on the ground. The deviation resulted from both an unduly optimistic and unduly alarmist approach to the situation British officials encountered in Palestine. The optimism is reflected in the naively expansive terms by which *miri* (land in which the *rakaba* or ultimate ownership remained vested in the state) became in the minds of some 'a colloquial term applied to all Government land'.[43] Indeed, attorney general Norman Bentwich at one point described the holder of *miri* land as 'the tenant of the State'.[44] With the challenges of translating *miri* into an English legal vocabulary came opportunities as well. One of Dowson's early conclusions, much to the initial enjoyment of Colonial Office officials, was that public domain lay at the very heart of the inherited system of land tenure: 'fundamentally there are two main

---

[43] CO 733/120/15382, 818. The American consul in Jerusalem thought likewise, describing *miri* as 'the property of the State'. See United States Bureau of Foreign and Domestic Commerce, *Palestine: Its Commercial Resources with Particular Reference to American Trade, by Addison E. Southard, Special Consular Reports, No. 83* (Washington: Govt. Printing Office, 1922), 29. In addition to *mevat* land and *mahlul* land, a form of tenure holding known as *jiftlik*, or *mudawara*, was also included under the expansive rubric of state domain. For a discussion of the official approach to *jiftlik* land, see Chapter 2.

[44] Norman Bentwich, 'The Legislation of Palestine, 1918–1925', *Journal of Comparative Legislation and International Law*, 8 (1926), 11.

classes of land in Palestine—Mulk and the Public Domain.'[45] In a discussion of the expropriation of land for the British army, one Colonial Office official argued that

> as a matter of fact, there is little [private property] in Palestine, most of the land is Government land over which the occupiers have certain rather shadowy rights by virtue of their occupation; this should facilitate the work of 'resumption' by the authorities.[46]

In addition to the naively optimistic approach of taking the liberty to interpret the category of *miri* land in as expansive terms as possible, early efforts at legislating state control were driven also by apprehension. The official interest in bringing as much land as possible into the hands of the state, so as to 'build up and protect the public interest', was motivated by growing alarm over the apparent 'loss' of land to peasant farmers bringing seemingly unoccupied land under cultivation in the wake of the First World War. In February 1921, Sir Herbert Samuel, Palestine's first high commissioner, reflected upon a threatening 'movement' which was undertaking to 'occupy State lands hitherto uncultivated',[47] and agreed that 'it is necessary that the Administration obtain forthwith a complete record of all such lands'.[48]

As a result, the Palestine administration (prior even to becoming constitutionally operative) began formulating ways to 'conserve State Domains . . . [by] prohibiting unauthorized encroachment'.[49] Two pieces of legislation passed at the outset of the mandate, both with great potential to impact upon the daily lives of rural inhabitants, were the '1920 *mahlul* lands ordinance' and the '1921 *mevat* lands ordinance'. The terms of the 1921 ordinance repealed the last parts of article 103 of the Ottoman land code which provided that persons cultivating *mevat* land would be granted a title deed upon payment of the *tapu* value of the piece of land. In its place was substituted the following: 'any person who without obtaining the consent of the Administration breaks up or cultivates any waste land shall obtain no right to a title deed for such land and further, will be liable to be prosecuted for trespass.'[50] Not only did the person who

---

[45] Dowson, 'Preliminary Study of Land Tenure in Palestine', CO 733/109, 203.

[46] Minute sheet, 'Claims of Tireh villagers', Nov. 1923, CO 733/50, 498.

[47] Letter to Foreign Office, FO 371/6387/E1758.

[48] 'Report of the Land Settlement Commission, August 1920', CO 733/18, 592.

[49] 'Report of Palestine Administration, July 1920–December 1921', CO 733/22, 652.

[50] Goadby and Doukhan, *The Land Law of Palestine*, 46. 'Report of the Land Settlement Commission, August 1920', CO 733/18, 605–6.

cultivated *mevat* no longer have a right to a title for his efforts, he was now considered to be doing a wrongful act and would be punished as a 'squatter'. The same would, naturally enough, be applied to *mahlul* land as well. When asked for some elaboration during a meeting in 1920 with some prominent Palestinians whose counsel was briefly sought at the outset of the mandate, the legal secretary replied that

Trespass was the offence of entering on to property to which the person had no right. The penalty was five days' imprisonment and a fine of P.T. 50. The position with regard to land that a person had cultivated without permission would be that he could be turned off of it.[51]

In addition to the prescribed penalties acting as an incentive to declare cultivation of *mevat* or *mahlul* land, village leaders were liable for punishment should they even know of such 'illegal possession' but fail to inform officials.[52]

It is not entirely clear why government officials were so eager to press ahead with such an ambitious legislative agenda, with little toleration for the intricacies of Ottoman law or little comprehension of the challenges and opportunities that confronted agriculturalists. Some officials no doubt were inclined to view such measures as part of a 'forward-looking' strategy sought by advocates of the Jewish national home. British officials were indeed constantly pressed to defend their actions, in London and Geneva as well as in Jerusalem, in relation to the stipulations of the mandate document, article 6 of which called upon the administration to facilitate Jewish settlement on state lands. Not to be underestimated, of course, is the assumed financial importance that public ownership of land (particularly in urban areas) represented: 'in view of Palestine's heavy capital obligations', wrote Dowson in 1925, for example, 'it is clearly advisable to close the door as promptly as possible to such illicit drains on her capital resources.'[53] Also considered in official discussions was the need to protect government's fiscal interests by arguing the principle that the extension of British rule and good government (for example, increased security, development of infrastructure) would like a rising tide eventually raise property values everywhere, and officials were eager for government to realize its fair share of the dividend. From the point of view of increasing the public good, some simply found little virtue

---

[51] 'Advisory Council Minutes, Minutes of Meetings 1–5 (6 Oct. '20–9 Feb. '21)', CO 733/1, 434.

[52] 'Report of the Land Settlement Commission, August 1920', CO 733/18, 592.

[53] Dowson, 'Preliminary Study of Land Tenure in Palestine', CO 733/109, 208.

in the reclamation of land by individual cultivators. Such a sentiment was expressed later in the mandate by one British officer who vented his frustration with villagers' persistent claims to what he thought was *mevat* land in the following terms:

I am asked to register in the names of individuals, some of whom are poor and all of whom would be rich, land which is the property of the body corporate, that is, the State. It is a process of anti-socialism which I cannot conscientiously accept.[54]

With the passing of the *mahlul* and *mevat* land ordinances, a significant part of Ottoman law was effectively turned on its head. The terms of the 1858 land code had entitled a cultivator of *mevat* and *mahlul* who reported his occupation to a grant by *tapu*. If one of the main objectives of the 1858 Ottoman Land Code was the economic and financial one of bringing as much *mahlul* and *mevat* land under cultivation as possible, it can be concluded that the individual landholder was presented as better equipped to do so than the state: under Ottoman law, land could not be resumed by the state as against a cultivator who paid the necessary fees and taxes. There never was any question with regard to *miri* land of trespass or squatting as such. These were legal inventions of a British official, too quick with his pen in translating Ottoman legal terms into the supposed equivalent in his own legal vocabulary.[55] Gerber argues this point in the following terms:

State land, in the modern sense, is land that the state wishes to keep out of individual use, such as forest land. Such a legal category did not exist in the Ottoman Empire and came into being only in the new states. *Miri* land was not state land in this sense. There was never really a question of usurpation of such land; at the most it could be misused.[56]

By endowing the state with such a high degree of discretion as to the disposal of *mahlul* and *mevat*, the terms of the 1920 *mahlul* ordinance and the 1921 *mevat* ordinance are clearly difficult to reconcile with the terms of the 1858 land code.[57]

Whatever the nature of the deviation, this early legislation clearly reflected some serious misunderstandings of local realities, and the government's effectiveness in seeing it actualized would in fact be seriously circumscribed

[54] 'Decision of Settlement Officer, Tulkarm Settlement Area', 2 June 1938, ISA RG 22, Land Settlement and Land Registration, Habla, GP/5(4), box 3479.
[55] Owen, 'Introduction', in *New Perspectives on Property and Land in the Middle East*, p. xi.
[56] Gerber, *The Social Origins of the Modern Middle East*, 68.
[57] See discussion in Goadby and Doukhan, *The Land Law of Palestine*, 26.

by local arrangements. For a couple of years, officials would try to put a positive spin on their legislation, arguing, as they did in the 1924 annual report, that 'government's refusal to recognize claims to uncultivated areas has stimulated cultivation in many villages'.[58] But Palestinian Arab leaders immediately saw the matter differently and raised their opposition, linking it at first closely to matters of principle. General anger was expressed at the passing of legislation, especially that dealing 'with one of the most sacred rights of citizens, that is private land tenure', given that a representative parliament had yet to be convened (one never would be), nor treaty with Turkey signed, nor the mandate even officially ratified. There was mounting frustration with the growing body of laws 'which we have no share in':

Laws as such in Palestine are not derived from the spirit and conditions of the country; they resemble a plant which cannot live. They do not remain in force for long and amendments are continually introduced . . . Our land is not so fertile in crops as the Palestine government is fertile in giving us laws and legislation, which are considered as a burden by the inhabitants, who have not been used to them under the old regime.[59]

Particular criticism was levelled against the government's attempt to empower itself to appropriate uncultivated lands from their landholders. Arab leaders argued that 'there are always valid and acceptable reasons why a certain piece of land had been neglected'.[60] Reasons given included: the prevalent system of leaving sections of land fallow and the prevalent uncertainty of rainfall in some areas; the adverse circumstances resulting from the war (such as shortages of labour and cattle); the prohibitive prices for farm equipment at the time; the collapse of credit arrangements; the low market price of agricultural products; and social and political unrest emanating from opposition to many aspects of British rule. The British approach to property rights was contrasted negatively to the position adopted by Ottoman officials who 'guided by the advice of persons of experience in village conditions . . . in no case attempted to prevent

---

[58] 'Annual Report on Palestine and Transjordan Administration, 1924', CO 733/90, 141.

[59] 'Arab and Jewish Deputations to the Secretary of State during his Visit to Palestine', CO 733/92, 211.

[60] 'A Brief Statement of the Demands of the Arab People of Palestine (Moslem and Christian) Submitted to the Honourable Mr. Winston Churchill by the Arab Palestine Delegation in London', CO 733/14, 95–102. Also, 'Report on the State of Palestine during the Four Years of Civil Administration . . . by the Executive Committee of the Palestine Arab Congress', CO 733/74, 116.

any person from disposing of his land'.[61] Protesting further that no land ought to be considered *mevat* unless it fulfilled exclusive, though vague, conditions (such as lying far from the distant parts of a village), Arab representatives concluded that 'it will be impossible to find in Palestine any land which answers to these conditions'.[62]

Indeed, British officials were forced very early on to acknowledge the yawning gap between local arrangements and the legislation newly introduced. Lord Allenby had been cautious from the outset: 'it is sure that there are vast areas of waste or uncultivated land in Palestine,' he wrote upon the occupation of the country in the First World War, 'but experience has shown that an owner or tenant invariably appears when any question of ownership arises.'[63] In his 1925 final report, high commissioner Herbert Samuel arrived eventually at the same conclusion: 'On most of the State lands, Arab cultivators are settled, and possession cannot be transferred to others without injustice.'[64] When Lewis French considered the question in 1931 he reflected that 'there are no grounds for surmising that since the Occupation many valuable rights in Government lands have been squandered'.[65] The initial gap between legal doctrines and local arrangements was a reality that British officials came to terms with, but they definitely did so the hard way. In one of the government's very first attempts to dispose of what it thought of as government property, a piece of land frequently referred to as Athlit-Kabbara-Caesarea, a bruising political and legal battle ensued upon the failure to recognize the inhabitants' claims and rights. 'It is to be remembered', wrote the acting high commissioner in 1928, 'that the Government cannot again take action in land which might lead to difficulties similar to those which were consequent upon the grant of the Athlit-Kabbara-Caesarea lands.'[66] British officials in London were particularly wary thereafter of the legal positions arrived at by the Palestine government, and cautioned repeatedly that the existing interests of cultivators on 'land claimed as state domains' must be safeguarded.[67]

---

[61] 'Memorandum on Palestine White Paper of October 1930 by the Arab Executive Committee', CO 733/197, 109.

[62] Ibid. 108.   [63] Allenby to Foreign Office, FO 371/5139 E4754.

[64] 'Report of the High Commissioner on the Administration of Palestine, 1920–1925', in *Palestine and Transjordan Administration Reports, 1918–1948*, ii: *1925–1928* (Archive Editions, 1995), 32.

[65] Lewis French, 'First Report on Agricultural Development and Land Settlement in Palestine, Draft', Dec. 1931, CO 733/214/5, 49.

[66] H. C. Luke to L. S. Amery, secretary of state for the colonies, 11 Oct. 1928, CO 733/156/7, 18. See chapter 5.

[67] 'Disposal of Jiftlik Lands, August 1926', CO 733/116/17199, 346.

In 1928, the acting high commissioner of Palestine, H. C. Luke, firmly dismissed the possibility of asserting rights to state land by stating, 'it is perhaps superfluous for me to observe that this Government have a moral duty to Arab inhabitants of Palestine who in virtue of a long period of squatting have a very definite interest in lands'.[68]

Presented with the competing claims of the majority of the population, it is clear that throughout the 1920s and 1930s the colonial state had neither the will nor the capacity to push its position further. In 1924, the acting chief secretary for Palestine, Ronald Storrs, in a letter defending government policy against (*inter alia*) the charge of manipulating Ottoman land laws, reported that the *mevat* ordinance 'has only once been put into operation by the Palestine Administration, in relation to a piece of land of 198 dunoms which was needed for an aerodome in the neighbourhood of Haifa and which belonged to a wealthy Syrian landowner'.[69] Less than two years later, reflecting on various strategies available in respect of lands claimed as state domain, a Colonial Office official turned to this legislation as though dusting off an old book: 'So far as I know the Turkish Land Law provides for the State to resume possession of any State land if it is left uncultivated for, I think, three years. This is a right which is practically never exercised.'[70]

As evidenced by a memo on *bedl misl* in 1938, rather than muse about how the right to *tapu* might be taken away from cultivators, which was of course the intention of the early legislation, British officials thought themselves lucky if the government actually received any payment at all. Rather than concern themselves with legal considerations, increasing emphasis was placed on expediency and policy: 'the only remedy open to government is to sue the defaulter for non-payment of a debt, but not for the recovery of land.'[71] In increasing numbers of cases, the government was prepared to abandon a claim to *bedl misl* altogether, in order to 'make the inhabitants more willing to cooperate in the work of settlement if the change is made'.[72] As one final testament to the failure of government to

---

[68] H. C. Luke to L. S. Amery, secretary of state for the colonies, 11 Oct. 1928, CO 733/156/7, 18.

[69] Acting chief secretary Ronald Storrs to Palestine Arab Congress, 21 Nov. 1924, CO 733/75, 361.

[70] Minute by H. W. Young, 22 Sept. 1926, CO 733/116/17199, 337.

[71] 'Memo on the Extension of Period of Payment of Badl Misl', 22 Sept. 1938, ISA RG 22 Land Registration and Land Settlement, Kalandiya, GP/9/1, box 3594.

[72] H. C. Luke, officer administering the government, to Lord Passfield, secretary of state for the colonies, 25 July 1929, CO 733/174/7/67383, 17.

redefine Ottoman laws so as to assert government claims to *miri* land, it is worth turning to the *Survey of Palestine*: giving little notice overall to the whole issue, other than comparing *miri* and private freehold, it is observed that 'generally speaking land privately owned is held on what Ottoman law called the *miri* tenure'.[73]

4. COLONIAL RESOURCES AND LOCAL ASSERTIONS

As is evident in a number of encounters during the mandate period, government's initial attempts to implement a new system of public domain could not overcome the will and capacity of the cultivators themselves to assert what they saw as their rights. Government weakness in this regard hinged on two main factors: the dependence of the government on the specific knowledge of the cultivators, and government's increasing concern for their political acquiescence generally. We will consider these factors in turn.

The general lack of information about Palestine's land regime was a constant source of frustration for those dealing with the question of public domain. A great difficulty was that government simply did not know what *mahlul* or *mevat* lands were available or where they were located. As one Colonial Office official admitted, 'Surveys have been proceeding and, in some districts, have been completed; but the whole business of state lands in Palestine is a difficult one.'[74] The difficulty was commonly attributed to a general problem of information and specifically to the absence of a dependable registration of rights over land, the solution to which required the successful execution of survey and settlement proceedings. Stated bluntly by Sir John Chancellor, high commissioner for Palestine 1928–31, 'until the cadastral survey and land settlement are completed, it cannot be known exactly what areas of land are in the indisputable ownership of Government . . . it is anticipated that it will be

---

[73] *A Survey of Palestine: Prepared in December 1945 and January 1946 for the Information of the Anglo-American Committee of Inquiry*, 255. A specific example of this transformation is the registration of leases of undivided shares in *miri* land. Since one of the essential characteristics of a lease in England was that it conveyed a right to exclusive possession, 'this would have the effect of assimilating the law of miri to that of mulk'. See director of land registration to attorney general, 25 Oct. 1947, ISA Attorney General's Office, RG 3 19/90, box 716.

[74] Minute sheets, Sept. 1929, CO 733/175, 33.

many years before the survey and settlement are completed.'[75] The factor most commonly held responsible for slowing down the process was the multitude of claims that had to be negotiated when settling title. But, as is evident in the frustration of settlement officers, the negotiating of such claims incurred considerable costs in time and money:

> this judgment would run to an inordinate length if I were to attempt to make even a brief summary of all the hundreds of pages of pleadings, oral evidence and documents and to find my way through the impenetrable maze of conflicting records in the old Turkish registers with reference to areas and boundaries of all the neighbouring lands.[76]

What was envisaged for Palestine, of course, was a thorough settlement of real rights by a systematic sweep of cadastral survey. But for this to be successful a great deal of consideration had to be given throughout to the necessity of securing the cooperation of the cultivators themselves.[77] Such cooperation in the land settlement process was to be provided by the constitution of a 'village settlement committee' which would 'invariably know of [the] rights and interests, and would take steps to prevent a trespasser from obtaining title'.[78] So dependent did the process become upon the involvement of the cultivators themselves that, again and again, registration of land in the name of government proved very difficult. In 1928, a district court judge declared that 'it has been my experience that in such cases the defendant usually has little difficulty in producing a quantity of evidence that he, or his predecessors in title, have been in occupation for more than ten years, and thereupon the Government, by Article 78 of the Land Code, are bound to issue a title deed without payment'.[79]

This situation was corroborated year after year. For example, in 1933, the registrar of lands in the Gaza area, though recommending that government should press ahead with its claims to the dunes south of Gaza town, admitted nonetheless that 'the peasants will prove their possession by actual cultivation and that is very easy to them and consequently we

---

[75] Chancellor to Passfield, 23 Nov. 1929, CO 733/170, 27.

[76] 'Judgement of Settlement Officer, Case No. 8 Jaffa Sand Dunes', ISA, Attorney General's Office, AG 7/10, box 703.

[77] See, for example, discussion in 'Land Settlement Questions', CO 733/114/9490; and, Dowson, 'Report on the Progress of Land Reforms in Palestine, 1923–1930', CO 733/221.

[78] Chancellor, high commissioner for Palestine, to Lord Passfield, secretary of state for the colonies, 10 Oct. 1929, CO 733/174/7/67383.

[79] A. H. Webb, district court, Nablus, 24 Mar. 1928, CO 733/158/5, 97.

lose the case'.[80] When asked to report in 1937 on the progress of settlement in the Jaffa sand dunes, A. T. O. Lees remarked that over 40 per cent of the parcels, 'many of them directly or indirectly connected', were being disputed: 'so intricate and tortuous are the wheels within wheels of all these cases that there is in my opinion scant hope of arriving at the truth by the ordinary means, or in any one case by itself.'[81] Clearly, the lonely settlement officer was vulnerable to collusive actions among the claimants, some more intricate than others. Lees suspected that hired witnesses and ' "Gentleman's Agreements" between the parties, the main purpose of which was to defeat Government's claims', were mainly responsible for exacerbating the 'difficulty of getting down to the facts and the rights and wrongs' of each case.[82] Another settlement officer complained that

I have taken evidence, agreed upon by all parties as sufficient, for 'possession' of the unpossessable. I have had it stated on oath by every witness that land which I have seen personally to be entirely uncultivable and find described in the official cadastral survey of this country as 'rocky; uncultivable' is good cultivable land [and] that Government taxes have been paid for generations by the 'cultivators.'[83]

Yet another concern was the hearing of cases concerning unregistered land which were feared to be collusive actions brought in the courts simply with a view to obtaining a judgement under which one party (that is, the defendant, to whom judgement was given in default because the plaintiff did not appear) can then claim registration.[84] Probably less effective, though more creative, were attempts such as those described by one settlement officer 'as an amazing scheme in respect of sand dunes' which, although he had not yet visited the lands, were prima facie *mevat*: 'I am informed that an old orange grove near Tel Aviv has been completely uprooted and that the roots have been transported to the sand dunes and buried (with possibly parts of the trunks showing above the sand) in an effort to prove that old plantations existed.'[85] By the end of the mandate,

[80] Registrar of lands, Gaza, to director of lands, Jerusalem, Dec. 1933, ISA RG 22, Land Settlement and Land Registration, Gaza, GP/3(5), box 3458.

[81] Lees to commissioner for lands and surveys, 10 Nov. 1937, ISA RG 22, Land Settlement and Land Registration, LS/8(11), box 3568.

[82] Ibid.

[83] 'Decision of Settlement Officer, Tulkarm Settlement Area', 2 June 1938, ISA RG 22, Land Settlement and Land Registration, Habla, GP/5(4), box 3479.

[84] Bentwich, legal secretary, to president land court, Jerusalem, 21 June 1922, ISA RG 22, Land Settlement and Land Registration, Jaffa, G 180/2, box 3526.

[85] Camp to central settlement office, Jaffa, 26 Mar. 1934, ISA RG 22, Land Settlement and Land Registration, LS/8(9), box 3568.

one officer lamented that 'It has become practically a matter of course among land-grabbing circles that Vacant State Lands are free for the taking if only one knows how to set about it, and that Government is always amenable to threats in the event of a show down. There is no longer any respect for Government rights in land.'[86]

The representation of government claims in the settlement process was further complicated by the fact that, according to the way the settlement process was at first structured, it was the settlement officer himself whose duty it was to record government's claim. This resulted in a number of problems. On the one hand, the settlement officer was ostensibly responsible for 'impartially enquiring into and disinterestedly recording rights without regard as to whether they pertain to this or that body or person';[87] on the other hand, the settlement officer was also supposed to be 'doing [his] best to safeguard any land that [he] might think to be government land'.[88] Dowson in particular was vexed by this contradiction, convinced that one person could neither fairly nor effectively maintain the impartial registration of all rights over land while maintaining in a partisan way the state's rights against counter-claims of private property. He described the association of these two responsibilities in the same officer as 'vicious in principle and inexpedient'.[89] One of the roles would naturally enough be subordinated. Settlement officers admitted to there being few resources and little interest left for pursuing government's case, once the arduous effort of recording all claims and counter-claims for a block of parcels had been completed.[90] In 1942, the director of land settlement, worried that government claims were being ignored or forgotten about, even in areas to which no claims by private individuals could be fully established, felt compelled to draw the settlement officers' attention to this trend and remind them 'to take all necessary precautions to ensure that Government rights are protected and no Government lands are alienated to individuals'.[91] Given

---

[86] M. Alhassid, 'Memo for Attorney General, Secret and Very Important', 2 Feb. 1946, ISA Attorney General's Office, RG 3, 12/46, box 707.

[87] Dowson, 'Preliminary Study of Land Tenure in Palestine', CO 733/109, 208.

[88] 'Judgment of Settlement Officer, Case No. 8 Jaffa Sand Dunes', 1 Nov. 1940, ISA Attorney General's Office, RG 3, 7/10, box 703.

[89] Dowson, 'Land Tenure and Taxation in Palestine', 733/136/4425, 61.

[90] Settlement officer, central settlement office, to commissioner of lands and surveys, Jerusalem, 30 Dec. 1935, ISA, Land Registration and Land Settlement, RG 22, LS 8/14, box 3568.

[91] Maurice Bennet, director of land settlement, to settlement officer, Tiberius settlement area, 7 Feb. 1942, ISA RG 22, Land Registration and Land Settlement, Tiberius, GP 12, box 3498.

the discretion evidently handed them, and given how close the settlement officers were to actual practices and how significant was the pressure to expedite the process of land settlement, accusations eventually emerged from other departments about the extent to which settlement officers made the law up as they went along. For example, settlement officers were criticized sharply by the Attorney General's Office in 1946 for continually demarcating areas of land as 'communal grazing reserves'. Of course a reaction could be expected from some official quarter to the alienation of land in which the state was still thought to have some rights: 'it spells disaster for the agricultural development of the country. It amounts to putting the clock back, in my estimate, at least a thousand years from the point of view of land husbandry.' But the condemnation of the actual behaviour of the settlement officer, one who sought above all 'an amicable settlement of claims', was equally intense:

My long experience has shown that the practice of giving a free hand to Settlement Officers (with all the respect I have for them) of defining areas as Communal Grazing Reserves is to be deplored . . . It has been my unpleasant duty on several occasions to draw the attention of the authorities concerned to the fact that Settlement Officers, perhaps unconsciously and possibly with a genuine belief that they were acting strictly in accordance with the law and with common sense, have arbitrarily taken to themselves the power to allocate Vacant State Lands as Communal Profits-a-Prendre reserves. Not only have the Settlement Officers no right to take these powers, but they have used them to the detriment of Government and the public interest. The duty of Settlement Officers is *to determine existing rights in land,* including those of the Government, and to record these rights.[92]

Even allowing for some cheating on the part of claimants, the fact is that government's attempt to empower itself to appropriate the land it sought was not on solid ground, either legally or practically. So complicated and involved were the disputes, government representatives clearly found it difficult to establish their claims, reliant as they were on the information and goodwill of the local claimants. It was a process that had to operate with, and be legitimized by, the participation of the cultivators themselves. A settlement officer could not afford to risk alienating the local inhabitants, when the active assistance of local cultivators, as well as the sharing of their local knowledge, was so essential to the success of his work.

In this respect, it is worth considering the situation with regard to the management of forests and sand drifts. In his 1923 review of the

---

[92] M. Alhassid, 'Memo for Attorney General, Secret and Very Important', 2 Feb. 1946, ISA Attorney General's Office, RG 3, 12/46, box 707. Emphasis in original.

agricultural situation, the director of agriculture, E. W. Sawer, revealed clearly the need for afforestation of sand dunes which, spreading largely from the coastline of Palestine, were feared as a threat to fertile land and village infrastructure.[93] The ordinance he drafted the following year provided for the extension of government management by taking over the largest forest area possible, thus reflecting more the idealism of early land legislation than the fiscal constraints typical of colonial administration. The minute sheets of the Colonial Office were highly critical of such steps. As one minute put it, 'Mr Sawer is an idealist who if let have his way would have half Palestine preventing the goats of the other half from grazing among forests.'[94] A rather heavy-handed government management had been envisaged by the 1922 sand drifts ordinance, which aimed at reclaiming dunes by forcing the village *mukhtar* to supply the resources requested by a government officer.[95] The provisions of this ordinance were intended to confront the challenges created by an Ottoman proclamation that where *miri* land was not cultivated by reason of it being covered by sand 'it was not to be liable to confiscation'.[96]

But the fact was that government could only afforest to the maximum that its relatively meagre financial resources would permit. It was thus highly dependent upon the cooperation of local cultivators so as to relieve public funds as far as possible of the necessary costs.[97] Steps were also taken, for example, to ensure that individuals or villages as a whole who undertook to cooperate in the work of reclamation would be rewarded with a recognition of their right to the land (say, as *matruke*). Local property rights systems can be seen in this way to have gained increased recognition from official authorities in need of economizing on development and monitoring costs. As explained in a note on the 1925 draft forest ordinance, 'the senior staff of the Department of Agriculture and Forests is much too small to enable it effectively to supervise the protection and management of all areas of potential forest throughout Palestine'.[98] By 1946, the sand drift ordinance had been invoked on only two occasions, neither very successfully.[99]

[93] 'A Review of the Agricultural Situation in Palestine', CO 733/46, 187. See also 'Forestry Operations', CO 733/68, 166.

[94] Minute sheets, 'Forests Ordinance, 1924', CO 733/75, 207.

[95] 'Minutes of the Eighteenth Meeting of the Advisory Council', CO 733/18, 242.

[96] Official dispatch, 19 May 1922, CO 733/22, 36.

[97] See 'Forestry Operations', 8 May 1824, CO 733/68, 173.

[98] Dowson to chief secretary, 12 Mar. 1925, CO 733/97, 311.

[99] Roza El-Eini, 'British Forestry Policy in Mandate Palestine, 1929–1948: Aims and Realities', *Middle Eastern Studies*, 35/3 (1999), 124.

The effective protection and management of forest area depended, therefore, on 'the confidence and sympathy between district officers and people'. In Dowson's view, the main obstacles to the development of forests were the initial suspicions that government was really aiming at establishing state ownership, and the concern of villagers for what they considered communal rights and privileges relating to grazing and wood-cutting.[100] However, once fears of government motives were mitigated, the villagers would share in recognizing the benefit of protecting the forest resource: 'In practice, there seems little doubt that, exercised with sympathy and discretion the protection of potential forest areas can, and should, be effected not only without detriment, but with positive benefit, to the inhabitants of adjoining villages.'[101]

Therefore, what he proposed, in contrast to the exclusive tone informing previous pieces of land legislation, was 'generous recognition of existing beneficial practices . . . subject only to such regularization as the prevention of abuse requires'. The probability of villagers adapting to and supporting decisions—say, with accurate information about forest boundaries and the resource system generally—was greater when they were included in the decision-making process than when ultimate decisions about ownership were decided by a centralized government. By ignoring local arrangements, governments risked losing credibility, and thus capability, in the formation of desired property rights systems.

It has to be recognized that the responsibility for the failure of people to register rights to immovable property lies primarily with the government for providing a bad service, and that the only proper and defensible course is for Government to put its service on a sound footing, when registration would be sought . . . It was not justifiable for a State to provide a bad service and attempt to make use of it obligatory.[102]

In addition to the dependence of government on local knowledge and cooperation, government weakness in pressing their case for expanded rights to state land also hinged on the increasing concern for the political

[100] Dowson to chief secretary, 12 Mar. 1925, CO 733/97, 307.
[101] Ibid. 308.
[102] 'Note by Ernest Dowson on draft Correction of Land Registers Ordinance', 10 Apr. 1925, CO 733/97, 212. Dowson continued: 'Thus if the postal service were bad, other means of conveying letters would be devised and resorted to by the people; and there would neither be justification for, nor success in, attempting to enforce resort to the bad State service while it remained defective. The only defensible and only sensible course would be to substitute a good postal service for the bad, when the people would gladly use and pay for it.'

acquiescence of the local population. An important constraint on government action, which will be elaborated upon in following chapters as well, emerged in the early 1930s with the increasingly politicized nature of the land question in mandate Palestine. In the wake of the brutal violence of the 1929 riots, concern over the political repercussions of an increasing class of displaced Arabs had a huge impact on land policies. From 1930 on, a heavy emphasis was placed on checking 'the present tendency towards the eviction of peasant cultivators from the land'.[103] Wholly abandoned was the official position with regard to land that a person who had cultivated without permission could be turned off of it. Anxious about the feelings of disaffection and unrest that 'political exploitation tends to create in the landless class', the policy of the government had shifted significantly in the 1930s and some officials found it hard to deny that government was guilty of failing to give property owners (including itself) protection against unlawful encroachment 'which every citizen has a right to expect'. Whatever the origins of occupancy, the practical point, as the department of land settlement put it, 'is what is to happen to the Arabs should it be decided to turn them off the land'.[104] When provisions were drawn up for the 1933 protection of cultivators ordinance, concern was expressed about whether the definition of the 'statutory tenant', who henceforth would be looked after, ought to include 'a mere trespasser who manages to remain on a piece of land for twelve months'. The discussion quickly ended in the affirmative: 'we should make no attempt to exclude trespassers from the definition.'[105] As finally explained in a 1933 memorandum by the secretary of state for the colonies, 'full power [is] reserved to take all steps necessary to protect the tenancy and occupancy rights, including the rights of squatters, throughout Palestine'.[106]

Despite, or perhaps even because of, early attempts to enlarge and protect state domains, the subjects of trespass and squatting caused the government of Palestine, and the department of land settlement in particular, great concern.[107] In the absence of a trespass bill, continually held

[103] Great Britain, *Report of the Commission on the Palestine Disturbances of August, 1929* (London: HMSO, 1930), 166.

[104] 'Settlement of Kuskus Tabun', ISA, RG 22, Land Registration and Land Settlement, LS 8/16, box 3568.

[105] 'Note for the Secretary of State on the Draft Protection of Cultivators Ordinance', CO 733/234, 26.

[106] 'Policy in Palestine', Feb. 1933, CO 733/234, 55.

[107] Attorney General's Office to R. F. Jardine, director of land settlement, 9 Apr. 1947, ISA, Attorney General's Office, RG 3, 12/18 Vol. II, box 706.

up in government circles, reference frequently was made to Hailsham's *Laws of England*, and debate centred around when exactly trespass was an offence: for example, discussion revolved around the need to prove criminal intent (not easily done), and the extent to which police action depended on the crucial issue of timing (authorized use of force limited to cases of expulsion immediately after actual entry; once trespassers were on the ground for any length of time, no direct action could be contemplated and recourse would have to be made to the courts). By the late 1930s, representatives of Jewish land-purchasing agencies such as Abraham Granovsky were outraged by authorities acting as though they were 'more interested in protecting the supposed rights of the Beduin to make mats out of the reeds which grew in the swamps' than in protecting legally acquired rights. Granovsky was particularly vexed by 'the interests of the Beduin families squatting on these lands' carrying more weight with the government than the future development of areas of particular economic value around the new port, and pipeline terminal, of Haifa.[108] As an example of the limited progress made over the course of the mandate, the director of land settlement described in late 1947 an inspection he made of forest areas demarcated as state domain in which 'trespassers had recently constructed massive walls'.[109] Court proceedings had been undertaken against those charged, but the inability of government to represent itself and to challenge the defendants' recourse to arguments based on *tapu* rights had become 'most alarming'. As stated by the director, 'One trespasser told me that he had a good claim to the land based on the recording of his name as a trespasser in the Magistrates Court.'[110]

5. CONCLUSIONS

Official attempts to conserve and expand (having first invented) notions of state land fizzled in the face of a yawning gap between the government's own intentions and the inhabitants' practices on the ground. In part this failure is a reflection of the limited capacity of colonial governments to effect and legitimize radical interventions in the land regime. Its approach was based on misapprehensions of the situation, and reinforces the view

---

[108] Abraham (Avraham Granott) Granovsky, *Land Policy in Palestine* (New York: Bloch Publishing Company, 1940), 157.

[109] R. F. Jardine to attorney general, 11 Oct. 1947, ISA, Attorney General's Office, RG 3, 12/18 Vol. II, box 706.

[110] Ibid.

of the administration in these early years as experimental and amateur. The extent to which the gap in Palestine reflected the inexperience of those British officials who found themselves in positions of legislative responsibility in the wake of the First World War came to be recognized by colonial officials,

> The great difficulty is that we do not know what state lands are available. When the Civil Administration took over the Government of Palestine, it found the position chaotic. The Turkish system of Land Registration had been far from satisfactory, and had been thrown into further confusion by the war. The Government was thus faced with the necessity of setting up Survey and Land Registration organizations, which, themselves consisting largely of raw and inexperienced personnel, had to cope with every imaginable difficulty.[111]

As for the hopes of the Jewish Agency that, as per the articles of the mandate document, close settlement of Jewish immigrants upon state lands would be encouraged, British officials would frequently acknowledge that it had reason to complain. British officials admitted how unrealistic the articles were in the first place: 'in the excitement of the moment difficulties and obstacles were ignored. The presence of more than half a million Arabs, owning most of the soil, was forgotten.'[112] But officials also came to resent the extent to which 'it was argued over and over again'.[113] As far as the Colonial Office was concerned the Jewish Agency learned as well as it did that 'State land in Palestine was of doubtful area'.[114] British officials began to resent the somewhat tendentious nature of the charges levelled against them and the extent to which, as Warwick Tyler has suggested, 'the state lands issue provided a convenient stick with which to beat the British dog'.[115]

---

[111] Minute sheets, Sept. 1929, CO 733/175, 31.

[112] 'Report of the High Commissioner on the Administration of Palestine, 1920–1925', in *Palestine and Transjordan Administration Reports, 1918–1948*, ii: *1925–1928*, 25.

[113] This was particularly so when they had to 'go into the "dock" in Geneva' and be cross-examined by the permanent mandates commission. See specifically discussion in CO 733/175/67411.

[114] Ibid.

[115] Warwick P. N. Tyler, *State Lands and Rural Development in Mandatory Palestine, 1920–1948* (Brighton: Sussex Academic Press, 2001), 48. Everyone seems to have been playing politics with this issue: representations of Arab politicians have already been discussed (see n. 39); for their part, British officers admitted that one high-profile effort to rebuild the Gaza area after the First World War by actually selling off land registered as *mahlul* was nothing more than 'one big bluff' meant to position them better in political debates 'so that if the Arabs complain saying Jews get better treatment we can turn around and say to them "we have offered you a considered scheme and you have rejected it"'. See minute sheets, 'Rebuilding of the Town of Gaza', CO 733/65, 610; also CO 733/54, 347.

As Goadby and Doukhan attempted to clarify in their 1935 text on Palestine's land laws, the fundamental characteristic of public domain is that it is subject to the control of government, and thus includes 'only such land as the State exploits or is free to exploit in such way as it pleases, uncontrolled by any law or custom determining the methods of exploitation'. State land, in this sense, is therefore land which the government wants reserved for itself—say, an aerodrome or perhaps a special forest—and kept out of the hands of individuals. Even then, government found itself having to move with extreme caution:

the Ottoman Land Code prescribes in several Articles that land which escheats to the State because of failure of heirs or of failure of cultivation and is not redeemed by persons who have what is called a right of 'tapu' and similarly land which is reclaimed from the sea or a river or a lake must be put up for sale by auction. It not infrequently happens that land which so reverts to the State is useful for some public purpose, e.g. an agricultural station or Government building and it is unreasonable in those circumstances that the Government should have to sell the land. It has been found, also, that frequently the price obtained at a sale by auction conducted according to the present Regulation is altogether inadequate. It is proposed, therefore, that the Government should have the right of occupying such land itself for any Government purpose.[116]

The failure of government to intervene radically in local property systems through the implementation of new *mevat* and *mahlul* ordinances passed at the outset of their rule may be seen to be in line with those arguments in the literature on property rights which emphasize the intensely contextualized nature of property. British colonial officials in Palestine found out the hard way that attempts to intervene in property rights regimes necessarily took place on an already structured and highly contested field, and could not be entirely disconnected from other debates, political, social, economic, nor from the discourses that informed and supported them.

[116] 'Note on an Ordinance to Make Certain Amendments in the Ottoman Land Law', CO 733/159/1/57447.

2

Free Market

Few features of Britain's administration of Palestine in the inter-war period were more central than that of defining a market in land, but the policy-making process was riddled with contradictions and ambiguities that had serious consequences for both Palestinian landholders and the establishment of a Jewish national home. This chapter explores the multi-faceted ways officials attempted to realize the 'modernizing' ideology of a Palestine transformed by the free working of natural economic laws, above all the smooth transfer of property, while at the same time negotiating relations between Arabs and Jews. One of the early official land commissions, vexed by what it saw as uncultivated lands through-out Palestine, emphasized the role played by 'the free flow of money' in making land productive. It concluded 'that every encouragement should be given to landowners to sell their excess areas and that there should be no restriction on sales'.[1] The market approach to the formation of colonial land policies was expected to ensure that land in the hands of 'unenterprising' owners would be transferred to those who would develop it more intensively. 'Anything that will assist towards easy and rapid transactions in land', wrote high commissioner Samuel in a dispatch defending the 1921 budget for land registry expenditures, 'will be a great benefit to all concerned.'[2] But widespread rioting in 1929 impressed upon colonial officials the extent to which the question of land was bound up with Arab feelings of hostility and fear towards Zionism, and thus exposed dramatically the adverse consequences of a market in land. There was increasing tension between the general desire to facilitate transactions in land and the fear that individualization of title was in fact leading to social dislocation and the growth of a politically active class of displaced cultivators. This tension was present very early on and reflected the weight of colonial experience with peasant dispossession. Although the land

[1] 'Land Settlement Commission's Report, 1920', CO 733/18, 610–20.
[2] Samuel to Curzon, 16 Feb. 1921, Co 733/1, 124.

commission assured that 'as [the peasant] is dependent on his cultivation as his means of livelihood having no other regular method of supporting himself and his family and as he is an intelligent person and a keen agriculturalist he is not likely to part with all his lands',[3] the approach officially adopted by the government was much less laissez-faire. Indeed, it was described aptly by Dowson as 'an attempt to exercise administratively a beneficent control over all land transactions in Palestine'.[4]

As elsewhere, attempts to realize the market ideal broke down in practice into various outcomes depending upon a host of factors that had to be negotiated between government and landholders. Negotiations were fluid, as the priorities of government were continually reconfigured to adapt to local arrangements. Policies and laws were defined and then redefined through the interplay of a number of forces that came together most vividly during the settlement process itself. In addition to addressing such issues generally, through an analysis of changing policies and key pieces of legislation, this chapter focuses on the way such tensions worked themselves out in small-scale, historically specific events. Particular attention is paid to a comparison of the official process of settling claims to land in the so-called *jiftlik* village of Beisan in the 1920s, with that in the *jiftlik* villages of Sajad and Qazaza in the 1930s. These were former estates of the Ottoman Sultan Abdul Hamid II, the inhabitants of which enjoyed a 'special sort of tenancy'. How this tenancy was understood, interpreted, and used by the government offers a useful window into the twists and turns of colonial land policies in mandate Palestine.

In Palestine there of course existed the added impetus of facilitating a Jewish national home, and to be sure Jewish land purchases had a huge impact on the policy-making process in the 1930s especially. But it was economics more than politics that drove the initial attempts of British officials to stimulate an active land market despite the protests raised in the post-war period by the Zionist Organization (which was particularly worried that a renewed land market would lead to speculation, dedication to religious endowments, and to the promotion of loans to Arab fellahin, all of which would harm the Zionist cause).[5]

[3] 'Land Settlement Commission's Report, 1920', CO 733/18, 610.
[4] Dowson, 'Report on the Land System in Palestine, December 1925', CO 733/109, 256.
[5] Dov Gavish, *A Survey of Palestine under the British Mandate, 1920–1948* (London: Routledge Curzon, 2005), 37, Kenneth W. Stein, *The Land Question in Palestine, 1917–1939* (Chapel Hill: University of North Carolina Press, 1984), 41–2.

1. LAND TRANSFER ORDINANCE, 1920/1921

Necessary background to the promulgation of the 1920 land transfer ordinance can be found in the troubled conditions under which British officials operated after 1917.[6] Land registers were regularly described as being in a state of complete chaos, but the heavy emphasis on the loss of papers seems exaggerated, possibly reflecting the hopes of a new regime for a clean slate or, more benignly, a useful way of excusing the slow progress of post-war reconstruction. Some registers evidently were destroyed or had disappeared, while others were transferred to safer premises for protection by concerned Ottoman officials. Ongoing military operations throughout 1918 no doubt affected the immediate British assumption of the Ottoman land registration system: the fact that the line of fighting did not coincide directly with the administrative borders of each land registry office meant that British forces would have controlled territory the registers for which were still behind enemy lines. All in all, it is somewhat difficult to untangle the official record regarding the status of the files of the thirteen district land registries the British authorities succeeded to in the wake of the First World War. But whatever the reasons for the confusion in Palestine, most of the registries were subsequently recovered and Ottoman land records certainly played a very important role in the British administration of Palestine.[7] This importance can in part be measured by the fact that for six months in early 1948 hundreds of 'Turkish Registers' were photographed when the decision was made by the commissioner of lands to microfilm all land records, and send the copies to England for safe keeping for the duration of the civil war.[8]

Also adding to the chaotic situation in Palestine during the First World War was the fact that many of the inhabitants had mortgaged their

---

[6] The 'Palestine Censorship Record 1918/1919' estimated that 'only about one-third of the original population of the occupied territory now remain'. FO 371/4229/83544.

[7] Judge Williamson, 'Note on Land Law', Spry Papers, Private Papers Collection. Middle East Centre, St Antony's College, Oxford. See also: 'Report of Palestine Administration, July 1920–December 1921', CO 733/22, 644–6; Frederic M. Goadby and Moses J. Doukhan, *The Land Law of Palestine* (Tel Aviv: Shoshany's Printing Co. Ltd., 1935), 299. *A Survey of Palestine: Prepared in December 1945 and January 1946 for the Information of the Anglo-American Committee of Inquiry* (Washington: Institute for Palestine Studies, 1991), 238.

[8] See J. F. Spry, 'Appendix II: Note on the custody of the records on the termination of the Mandate'. Spry Papers, Private Papers Collection, Oxford, St Antony's College, Middle East Centre.

properties during the course of the war in order to provide money for all sorts of reasons, ranging from the purchase of basic necessities at a time when the currency had depreciated to the purchase of exemption from military service. Following the war, people were not able to redeem their mortgages. In view of the concern that courts would order the sale of land in execution of mortgages, and in light of the confusion in land administration generally, the British authorities decided to close the land registries and prohibit any transaction of immovable property. In June and November of 1918, proclamations similar to those of the government of Iraq in the previous year were issued to officially close the land registries, explaining that time was required to re-establish and reorganize them.[9]

In 1919, Judge Williamson, formerly director of land registries in the Sudan, attempted to patch together a functional land registration system.[10] The situation which he confronted was certainly messy, but apparently redeemable. Although the records were ostensibly in a state of confusion (and were, moreover, out of date and, given the absence of a cadastral survey, imprecise regarding measurements of land) it was felt that the Ottoman administrative apparatus could be reconciled with British practice. Williamson devised a series of forms and a procedure of registration by which transactions between parties that met with the approval of government could be issued a certificate, provided taxes were paid up and documents proving evidence of title, and the approval of the *mukhtar* of the village, were in order.

It remained however a registry primarily of transactions between persons (registry of deeds), and not of transactions with reference to defined plots of land (registry of title). That is, although each devolution of land was by law required to be completed by recourse to the land registry, it was not considered necessary to locate precisely on the ground the area of land to which the transaction referred and index all transactions by reference to a suitable map defining the area. Such a course could not be adopted in the absence of a reliable cadastral survey maintained up to date and this did not exist, though the department of land registries did undertake for itself the survey of some properties 'with a view to preventing future

[9] See Norman Bentwich (ed.), *Legislation of Palestine, 1918–1925: Including the Orders-in-Council, Ordinances, Public Notices, Proclamations, Regulations, Etc.*, 2 vols. (Alexandria: Whitehead Morris Ltd., 1926).

[10] Great Britain. Palestine Royal Commission, *Memoranda Prepared by the Government of Palestine* (London: HMSO, 1937), 38–40, *A Survey of Palestine: Prepared in December 1945 and January 1946 for the Information of the Anglo-American Committee of Inquiry*, 238–40.

boundary disputes and to enable registration to be reasonably accurate'.[11] A cadastral survey was initiated with a view to remedying this defect, but proper measures were not instituted to ensure cooperation between the departments of survey and of land registry.[12] 'If the survey was abolished tomorrow', wrote Dowson disparagingly in 1925, 'the procedure of land registration would not be affected.'[13] Independent surveys were being carried out at the same time under the direction of various land registry offices, and even courts had recourse, when deciding on land cases, to their own surveyors.[14]

Such imperfections as still existed in the system as revised by Williamson unnerved advisers in London. The preference had been to continue to defer regulations permitting land transfers until it was certain that the land registration offices were working well enough. This was also connected to the progress of peace negotiations with Turkey, which would regularize their legal position to authorize such changes.[15] Taking the lead from experience in Iraq, one suggestion was that new registrations be permitted on a trial basis at first, in municipal areas only. But the administration in Palestine was determined to go ahead with the re-establishment of the land registration system sooner rather than later and, as a result, was content with registration remaining personal, not territorial, and with no official guarantee being attached.[16]

Many factors contributed to the rush in 1920 to re-establish the land registration system, however imperfect. In large part it was due to the

[11] 'Report of Palestine Administration, July 1920–December 1921', CO 733/22, 646.

[12] A cadastral survey was begun around Gaza in early 1921 to provide a reliable basis for the registration of rights over land, but the work was rarely utilized: surveys used by the land registry were independently commissioned, and courts dealing with land cases made their own recourse to surveyors. 'Report on the Land System in Palestine', CO 733/109, 239. Gavish and Kark state that 'a type of cadastral inventory was begun by the Ottoman Empire in Palestine, and consisted of maps drawn up for lands held by the Sultan, state lands put up for sale, and lands subject to large development projects'. Dov Gavish and Ruth Kark, 'The Cadastral Mapping of Palestine, 1858–1928', *Geographical Journal*, 159 (1993).

[13] Dowson, 'Report on the Land System in Palestine, December 1925', CO 733/109, 257.

[14] Dowson, 'Covering Memorandum to the Report on the Land System in Palestine', Dec. 1925, CO 733/109, 239.

[15] Minute by O. A. Scott, 9 Dec. 1919, FO 371/4226/160011.

[16] The 'increasingly large number of transactions' recorded in the registry was, however, viewed as some indication of the large measure of public confidence the system continued to enjoy. See Great Britain. Palestine Royal Commission, *Memoranda Prepared by the Government of Palestine*, 39, *A Survey of Palestine: Prepared in December 1945 and January 1946 for the Information of the Anglo-American Committee of Inquiry*, 240.

widespread recognition that the land market was, as Barbara Smith describes it, 'a private sector area in which a laissez-faire approach was the golden rule'.[17] The urgent need felt in Jerusalem for a resumption of land transfers was primarily a response to the widely held belief that the prevention of land transactions was shackling the transformative powers of the free flow of money and thus having a 'serious effect on economic conditions of the country'.[18] As explained in the official telegram from general headquarters, then located in Cairo, the hastened re-establishment of a functioning land registry would be 'a provisional measure to meet immediate needs of military administration and remove hardship from which large proportion of inhabitants are suffering'.[19] A year later, Herbert Samuel would again emphasize the importance of reopening the land registers, saying that 'the resumption of land transactions is the first condition of economic revival'.[20] According to Samuel, 'the relations between creditor and debtor are very unsatisfactory, and the prohibition of forced land sales tends to a certain demoralization of the debtors'.[21] Accordingly, in mid-1919 the military administration drafted an ordinance to provide for land transactions in accordance with Ottoman law (that is, what they knew to be Ottoman law) though on a limited scale and under official control. By taking the initiative in this way, the proposals of the local officials risked undermining the land policy of the Zionist Organization, which at the time was wary of the legal definition of land titles and feared both speculation in land, and its dedication into *vakif*.[22]

The general principle behind the drafting of a new ordinance, which came to be known as the 1920 land transfer ordinance, was that all transactions other than leases for a term of not more than three years required an individual to obtain the written consent of the administration. There were two stated reasons for requiring written consent; both reflected previous experience in Iraq and were reinforced by concerns expressed by the Zionist Organization.[23] First, it was hoped that consent would regulate land transfers by checking speculation which,

[17] Barbara J. Smith, *The Roots of Separatism in Palestine: British Economic Policy, 1920–1929* (Syracuse, NY: Syracuse University Press, 1993), 92.
[18] Telegram Clayton to FO, 27 June 1919, FO 371/4171/94476, 159.
[19] Telegram from GHQ Cairo to WO, 12 Aug. 1918, FO 371/4226/118896.
[20] Samuel to FO, 23 Aug. 1920, FO 371/5139/E10569.
[21] Samuel to Churchill, 1 Mar. 1921, CO 733/1, 209.
[22] Gavish, *A Survey of Palestine under the British Mandate, 1920–1948*, 37, Stein, *The Land Question in Palestine, 1917–1939*, 42.
[23] FO 371/4151/127607.

if ignored, would cause an excessive rise of prices and prevent development. Secondly, it was hoped to prevent the aggregation of large estates. Consent, then, would technically be withheld if the administration was not certain that the person purchasing the land intended to cultivate it immediately.

But consent was also to be withheld, by the terms of article 6 of the land transfer ordinance, if the administration was certain that the person transferring the property (or the tenant in occupation, if the property was leased) was not retaining sufficient land for the maintenance of his family. In its executive instructions, the Palestine government explained to the officers concerned that, while it sought to promote in every possible way the creation of a market in land and the closer settlement of the country, it was also anxious that the interests of the present tenants and occupants of the land should be properly protected.[24] It was an anxiety born from years of experience with peasant dispossession throughout the empire, and was described as a measure 'to protect the Arab "in spite of himself" in matters where he is perhaps none too well fitted by nature to protect himself'.[25] 'In Palestine', warned Goadby and Doukhan, 'the peasant needs to be protected against his own lack of foresight.'[26]

The 1920 land transfer ordinance, passed in an effort to kick-start a market in land in the wake of the economic disruptions of the war, sought also to protect the status of agricultural tenants. This condition represents the most significant, if unsurprising from a colonial point of view, departure from Ottoman laws which did not themselves provide directly for the protection of agricultural tenants. The amendment was achieved by the inclusion of provisions which, as one colonial official minuted, were 'prompted by considerations similar to those that made Lord Kitchener enact the "Five Feddan Law" in the Sudan'.[27] Following their occupation of Egypt in 1882, the British worked hard at consolidating a free market in land, but in 1912 found themselves having to pass a law—itself modelled on measures that had been taken in north-west India—that prevented credit institutions from seizing, in the event of foreclosure, the last five acres of a mortgaged property.[28] There may well

---

[24] Great Britain. Palestine Royal Commission, *Memoranda Prepared by the Government of Palestine*, 56.

[25] Minute sheets, 24 Nov. 1921, CO 733/7, 399.

[26] Goadby and Doukhan, *The Land Law of Palestine*, 233.

[27] Minute by Mills, Nov. 1921, CO 733/7, 399.

[28] Timothy Mitchell, *Rule of Experts: Egypt, Techno-Politics, Modernity* (Berkeley and Los Angeles: University of California Press, 2002), 71–2.

also have been considerations closer to home, and it is worth drawing attention to the fact that special legislation 'to give greater protection to the tenant than the Common law afforded' was being considered and developed concurrently in England.[29] It was recognized from the beginning in Palestine that the development of a market in land would in its train raise the question of landlessness and peasant dispossession. Colonial officials knew this from experience and there was no reason to think that the particular circumstances of Palestine, the limited cultivable area of which was home to a rapidly growing population as well as the target of the Jewish national home, would be any different.

Fundamentally linked to these departures from Ottoman law was another recognized change: the very special powers granted by article 8 to the high commissioner (the draft ordinance empowered the military governor) to give or withhold sanction to sales up to any extent and without giving any reason. Although article 36 of the 1858 land code had contained certain limitations on the validity of a transfer made without the leave of an official, the 1913 provisional law of disposal was understood to have abolished the necessity of consent.[30] Generally, the series of provisional laws issued by the Ottoman government after the Young Turk coup of 1908 represented to the British administrator a helpful 'simplification' and 'modernisation'.[31] These laws were, strictly speaking, provisional in that they had no parliamentary authority. Nonetheless, they proved to be a fruitful source for British legislators (but only when deemed necessary).

The claiming of such powers by the high commissioner met with some criticism from the local population. To be sure, of approximately 2,000 petitions evidently presented to the administration up to May 1921 for the disposition of immovable property, only twenty-five were refused.[32] Nevertheless landowners were reported to have unanimously demanded the removal of necessary consent to all land transactions and desired the *status quo ante bellum*. It was noted that widespread suspicion regarding the supreme powers of the high commissioner, and the possibility that they would be used to help develop a Jewish national home, contributed

[29] For example: the Agricultural Holdings Act, 1923; the Landlord and Tenant Act, 1927. Cited in Goadby and Doukhan, *The Land Law of Palestine*, 236.

[30] R. C. Tute, *The Ottoman Land Laws [Microform]: With a Commentary on the Ottoman Land Code of 7th Ramadan 1274* (Jerusalem: Greek Convent Press, 1927), 4–42.

[31] Goadby and Doukhan, *The Land Law of Palestine*, 13–14. See also Dowson, 'Preliminary Study of Land Tenure in Palestine', CO 733/109, 157.

[32] Samuel to Churchill, 14 May 1921, CO 733/3, 205–8.

to the overall hostility shown towards the government.[33] Such grievances grew stronger 'when it is seen that Zionists can buy from Mr. George Sursock over 15,000 dunams of land in the Galilee District near Jezreel. The restriction clauses then become a farce . . . Villages do not grow by accident—and in dealing with any land question we really act in a matter that possesses continuity from times prior to the dawn of history.'[34]

As Smith has observed, the political representatives of Palestinian Arab society were themselves often owners of large tracts of land who no doubt were looking after their own economic interests.[35] Still, opposition was represented in official communications as strong and widespread. 'The Ordinance is objected to on religious grounds,' one enquiry noted: 'The Sharieh Law states "A possessor may dispose of his possession as he pleases" and the Land Transfer Ordinance is in direct contradiction to this.'[36] It was clearly a difficult issue for British officials to take sides on. 'It is a question', wrote the authors of the earliest official report on government's role in the definition of property rights in Palestine, 'if it can dictate to individuals regarding the disposal of their property.'[37] A Colonial Office official elaborated

It has always been a matter of amazement to me that the Arabs never appreciated the benefits of these restrictions towards themselves . . . I have always suspected that the real reason for the objection is the dislike to be told that a man may not do what he likes with his own property.[38]

As a result of these negative reactions, the 1920 land transfer ordinance was amended the next year.

The 1921 land transfer ordinance removed the restrictions that had allowed the administration to object to speculative purchases (which was proving very difficult). Also, instead of the high commissioner, the

[33] See 'Administrative Report for July 1921', CO 733/5, 282. Samuel to secretary of state for the colonies, 22 Nov. 1921, CO 733/7, 399. 'A Brief Statement of the Demands of the Arab People of Palestine (Moslem and Christian) Submitted to the Honourable Mr. Winston Churchill by the Arab Palestine Delegation in London', CO 733/14, 102. Also 'Report on the State of Palestine during the Four Years of Civil Administration . . . by the Executive Committee of the Palestine Arab Congress', CO 733/74, 116.
[34] Minute by Mills, Nov. 1921, CO 733/7, 399.
[35] Smith, *The Roots of Separatism in Palestine: British Economic Policy, 1920–1929*, 94.
[36] 'Report of Land Commission', CO 733/18, 610–11.
[37] Ibid. 630.
[38] Minute by Mills, Nov. 1921, CO 733/7, 399. Added G. L. M. C. Clauson, 'Before we leave, or before the Zionist Organisation has finished with their land development policy in Palestine, we shall have really ghastly difficulties over the land, and not improbably bloodshed, but these difficulties are not in any way connected with this ordinance.'

director of land registries was henceforth charged with the responsibility of assenting to any particular land transfer. The legislation still required the director to withhold consent to any transfer of agricultural land if he was not satisfied that tenants retained sufficient land, but the provisions were wholly inadequate. Despite attempts to exercise administratively 'a beneficent control' over all land transactions in Palestine, the interest in a lively market clearly outweighed at the outset of the mandate the fear of peasant dispossession. This is particularly evident in the lack of concern over the patent failure of the legislation to achieve its purpose, particularly in regard to land transfers to the principal Jewish land-purchasing bodies. 'In practice', high commissioner Chancellor explained in January 1930, 'the Land Transfer Ordinance, 1920 (Amendment Ordinance, (no. 2), 1921), did not, save possibly in one individual case, secure, either for "tenants in occupation" or for persons "exercising customary rights" sufficient land for the maintenance of their families.' Instead, government allowed such persons to 'contract out' of the law and to accept monetary compensation in lieu of their statutory right to land.[39] Jewish purchasers at the time adopted a policy of not buying land unless it was delivered free of tenants, and tenants did not avail themselves of the provisions of the ordinance. In practice, government consent became a mere formality. Tenants disappeared with monetary compensation, or were evicted, before government officials were even informed of the transaction. Furthermore, the ordinance gave no protection in the case of an enforced sale.[40]

In 1929, section 8(1) of the land transfer ordinance was repealed and the protection of cultivators ordinance enacted. Among the official reasons given for these changes were:

(a) that the law could be evaded by the purchaser refusing to purchase the land except with vacant possession and so compelling the vendor to remove all tenants from the land before the sale took place;

(b) that to require a landlord, who wished to sell a block of his property, to procure land in a different area for tenants whom he proposed to evict was an

[39] Chancellor to Passfield, 17 Jan. 1930, CO 733/182/8/77050, 82. See also Norman Bentwich, 'Report of the Committee to Advise on the Protection of Agricultural Tenants', published in *Palestine Bulletin*, 13 Dec. 1927, 1–2. Also, 'Protection of Agricultural Tenants Ordinance: Explanatory Note', *Palestine Bulletin*, 2 Sept. 1928, 2. And Kenneth W. Stein, *The Land Question in Palestine, 1917–1939* (Chapel Hill: University of North Carolina Press, 1984), 52–6.

[40] See, for example Great Britain, *Report of the Commission on the Palestine Disturbances of August, 1929* (London: HMSO, 1930), Stein, *The Land Question in Palestine, 1917–1939*.

extraordinary impediment on the landlord's right to dispose of his land and was calculated to prove a great obstacle to the close settlement of land; and

(c) that tenants who are removed from one area can usually find for themselves other land to cultivate in a different area without great difficulty and that they are better able than their former landlord to obtain the land they want and that the payment of money is, therefore, likely to be of greater assistance than the provision of a piece of land.[41]

Based on these arguments, the 1929 protection of cultivators ordinance essentially tried to bring the law in line with common practice on the ground and provided for the payment of compensation to the tenant in respect of termination of tenancy, disturbance, improvements, and so forth. Tenants were now technically entitled to a year's notice, but the previous requirement that a cultivator retain a subsistence area elsewhere was simply dropped. Officials either accepted that there was a surplus of agricultural land available on which evicted persons could obtain a new area, or were resigned to the fact that the absence of a record of tenancies in Palestine, as was thought to have existed in India, made it extremely difficult for a tenant to in fact establish a right.[42] It is worth noting that the legislative protection afforded to cultivators at the outset of the mandate had been further eroded by the 1928 mortgage amendment ordinance which allowed companies to buy mortgaged properties upon the default of the borrower. The Palestine government had wanted to maintain the Ottoman prohibition on the buying in by companies out of fear that it would encourage speculation or that the land would fall into mortmain, but the Colonial Office was adamant about generally 'knocking off some of the shackles on Companies'.[43]

An important factor that lay behind the new amendments to the land transfer ordinance was that, until this point, landlessness was not considered a grave problem.[44] Rather, the focus was on creating a market in land so as, on the one hand, to ensure that the land of unenterprising owners would soon enough be transferred to those who would develop it more intensively. This would also fulfil the obligations made regarding the establishment of the Jewish national home. But it obviously cannot be assumed that only Jewish land purchasers were active in the land market. The reports by Lewis French in the early 1930s make it clear that

---

[41] Cited in Chancellor to Passfield, 17 Jan. 1930, CO 733/182/8/77050, 83.

[42] Sir John Hope-Simpson, *Palestine. Report on Immigration, Land Settlement and Development*, Cmd. 3686 (London: HMSO, 1930).

[43] Minute sheets, 13 Aug. 1928, CO 733/159/2/57454.

[44] Stein, *The Land Question in Palestine, 1917–1939*, 50.

Arab buyers (and not just brokers) constituted a significant part of the market. In 1932, French referred to a 'severe land hunger' due in part to 'considerable buying by Arab capitalists, partly speculative and partly investment'.[45] Accordingly, throughout the 1920s, the process of the displacement of tenants and cultivators from the land went on practically unchecked. The 1929 amendments simply constituted legal recognition of this reality.

2. SETTLEMENT OF TITLE TO *JIFTLIK* VILLAGES

The crucial question of how to respond to the growing assertion of individual proprietary rights, while at the same time preserving, or possibly even inventing anew, the stability of communal bonds, provided the context for the battle over legal interpretations of so-called *jiftlik* lands. As a category of land, *jiftlik* frequently was included by officials in the redefinition (and attempted invention) of *miri* under British rule as 'state land'. Comparison between the categories was often made by officials, the tendency being to ignore the legal particulars and casually group them under the rubric of lands which, in the words of the legal secretary, 'are at the disposal of the Government'.[46] The fact that *jiftlik* was not in Ottoman law a legal category as such (that is, the Sultan's personal estates could not actually be shown to have been redefined as *mülk* when he assumed ownership of them, and were therefore always held as *miri*), but rather more like a customary form of tenure, did not prevent the Palestine government from immediately trying to assume ownership as landlord.

Thus, government's initial attempts to define its position regarding *jiftlik* land followed roughly the same pattern in the 1920s established for *mahlul* and *mevat* land, that is to guard whatever control over land it thought it could before in the end deferring to local arrangements on the ground and recognizing the rights of the cultivators as they saw them. However, the increasing concern over the political repercussions of a growing class of displaced Arabs had a huge impact on government's attempts in the 1930s to settle title to *jiftlik* land. Whereas ownership of land in the Beisan *jiftlik* was registered in the 1920s in the names of the cultivators, settlement operations (and prolonged court proceedings) for

---

[45] Lewis French, 'Supplementary Report on Agricultural Development and Land Settlement in Palestine', CO 733/214/97049, 14.

[46] Bentwich, legal secretary, to Major Abramson, chairman of land commission, 19 Aug. 1920, CO 733/18, 586.

the *jiftlik* villages of Sajad and Qazaza by contrast declared the cultivators 'tenants and merely tenants' of the Palestine government.

As defined by the Ottoman land code, *jiftlik* was a term used to describe 'a tract of land such as needs one yoke of oxen to work it, which is cultivated and harvested every year'.[47] But, ordinarily, it came to mean the whole outfit of a farm, including the land of which it was comprised, the buildings, the animals, the stock, the implements, etc. It came into use in Palestine to refer particularly to the landed estates farmed by the Sultan. Also known as *mudawara*, *jiftlik* was a classification which referred to lands throughout Palestine that, at various points in the early 1870s, were 'turned over' to the Sultan, and later to the Ottoman Treasury.[48] It was not well understood by the British administration how these lands actually came to be registered in the name of the Sultan. Samuel felt that 'there was a certain measure of oppression in the means by which the ownership of the lands was transferred from the Arab cultivators to the Sultan Abdul Hamid'.[49] But, in 1925, Dowson concluded that 'it seems that at one time this Sultan was keen on being a good farmer and landlord, and that the peasantry in various parts of Palestine recognising the better regime then prevailing on the Sultan's private estates applied that the land they held and cultivated on miri tenure should be thus "turned over" to him'.[50] What was clear was that the original holders, and their descendants, stayed on the land and continued throughout to regard themselves as *de jure* owners. The only practical difference in their situation was that beyond payment of the ordinary tithe, they owed the state an additional 10 per cent—regarded by the government as rental, but by some cultivators as a payment 'under duress',[51] or by others as a payment in lieu of certain privileges, for example exemption from military service.

Responsibility for defining the relationship between government and the cultivators of *jiftlik* land was first assigned to the 1920 land commission. The role of the commission in this case was threefold: first, it was required to report upon what steps should be taken to obtain an accurate record of *jiftlik* lands and on how to make the best disposition of them in

---

[47] Goadby and Doukhan, *The Land Law of Palestine*, 62.

[48] In fact, not all *jiftlik* property was re-registered in the name of the Treasury in 1908 and, throughout the mandate, the Palestine government was pestered by legal actions instituted on behalf of the heirs to the Sultan. See, for example, CO 733/44, 389. See also discussion in Naomi Shepherd, *Ploughing Sand: British Rule in Palestine 1917–1948* (New Brunswick, NJ: Rutgers University Press, 2000), 121–5.

[49] Samuel to Churchill, 23 July 1921, CO 733/4, 514.

[50] Dowson, 'Preliminary Study of Land Tenure in Palestine', CO 733/109, 178.

[51] Samuel to Churchill, 23 July 1921, CO 733/4, 514.

the interests of the country; second, it would report on what measures could be taken to ensure the greater productivity of the soil; and, finally, it was expected to make recommendations to protect the interests of the 'tenants or occupants of Government lands'.[52] The land commission was not a legal body and therefore did not attempt to advise on the legal basis on which the cultivators claimed ownership of their land. Rather, it aimed to formulate policy, based on the directions issued to it as above. In May 1921, it recommended (as a matter of policy) the 'non-alienation' of *jiftlik* land, actually referring to it specifically as 'state land'. But it also recommended that the tenure of the occupants of all *jiftlik* land, on account of its peculiar history, be settled in perpetuity. For reasons already noted, the commission suggested long leases, the period of which should be governed by circumstances.

In the case of *jiftlik* land in the region of Beisan, this strategy was compromised somewhat by the suggestion that the cultivators be offered very long leases (say, ninety-nine years). Long leases were recommended for two reasons. First, it was thought that agricultural development would entail expenditure which only very long leases would secure. Secondly, it was conceded by the commission that the 'tenancy' of *jiftlik* cultivators was somewhat special in that 'these cultivators did not part with their lands willingly but by force of circumstances' and were not therefore 'ordinary tenants'. Implicit in official discussions over the Beisan *jiftlik* from the start was the idea of a statute of limitations. Evidence to support the state's claim had decayed over time, making it more difficult for the government to be certain that it could settle legal title in its favour. British officials were never altogether convinced that the process by which ownership had been transferred to the Sultan was entirely consolidated in law in the first place.[53]

Be that as it may, the cultivators of the Beisan *jiftlik* simply declined outright the idea of leases.[54] Claiming they had been 'ousted by force',[55] the cultivators refused to admit to the legality of any alleged prior transfer of ownership to the state, and demanded to be treated as owners. In the end, the government agreed and, by the terms of the Ghor Mudawara Agreement, legally registered the cultivators of the Beisan *jiftlik* as individual

---

[52] Bentwich to Major Abramson, 19 Aug. 1920, CO 733/18, 586.

[53] 'Land Settlement Commission's Report', 10 Feb. 1922, CO 733/18, 624.

[54] Lewis French, 'First Report on Agricultural Development and Land Settlement in Palestine', 23 Dec. 1931, CO 733/214/5, 147.

[55] Great Britain. Palestine Royal Commission, *Memoranda Prepared by the Government of Palestine*, 194.

owners of *miri* land.[56] The nature of this agreement is best described by the care with which the terms for the indenture were chosen: 'Now this is to witness that this Agreement has been made between the Government of Palestine and the cultivators of the land as a permanent settlement of their respective rights.'[57] Words such as 'purchaser' or 'purchase price' were avoided since the cultivators refused to admit that this agreement stood for a 'sale and purchase' of their land. The Ghor Mudawara Agreement regulated the area of land which each head of a family should be entitled to have transferred and registered in his name as *miri* property. It further provided that where the transferee was a member of a tribe the lands transferred to each member would constitute a 'tribal area' and that additional area for such tribes living principally on their flocks and herds, to be known as tribal grazing areas, would be determined. The provision of grazing land contradicted the government's drive towards intensive cultivation, but it was noted that the Ottoman government had allowed for it and that 'to summarily disallow this would be a harsh measure and even if legally defensible would be politically inexpedient'.[58] The transfer price to be paid to the government was fixed at 150 Egyptian piastres per dunam of irrigable land and 125 Egyptian piastres for non-irrigable land payable with the tithes in fifteen annual instalments. Each title deed granted to a cultivator indicated that the land was held subject to these terms. It also provided that if the transfer price was not fully paid at the end of the fifteenth year the transferee was then deemed to have forfeited his right to title and to have all along been a tenant of the government.[59] Although the Ghor Agreement prohibited any sale of land before the instalments of the 'transfer price' had been paid in full, there was nothing to affect the rights of creditors who could attach the lands and have them sold in satisfaction of their claims.[60]

---

[56] Certain provisions of the agreement provoked much criticism: in particular, those that dealt with the amount of land to be allotted to each cultivator. Nonetheless, the legality of the transfer does not appear to have been questioned by officials. A list of lands claimed as state domain, produced by the Palestine Land Registry in 1926, described all *jiftlik* lands as 'occupied by Arab cultivators of long standing and should, presumably, be treated on the same basis as, but different in detail from, the lands affected by the Beisan Land Agreement of 1921'. CO 733/170/2.

[57] The actual agreement between the cultivators of the Beisan lands and the government of Palestine is set out in Lewis French, 'First Report on Agricultural Development and Land Settlement in Palestine', 23 Dec. 1931, CO 733/214/5, appendix IIIB, 153.

[58] 'Land Settlement Commission Report', CO 733/18, 629.

[59] Plumer to Colonial Office, 20 May 1926, CO 733/114, 423.

[60] 'High Court no. 18 of 1932', Sir M. McDonnell (et al.) (eds.), *The Law Reports of Palestine . . . : [1920–1946]*, 14 vols. (London: Waterlow and Sons, 1933–47), i. 774.

Given the tendency of the Palestine government until this point to guard assiduously whatever rights in land it thought it could, why did it admit the Beisan cultivators' claims to *ab antiquo* rights as deserving of legal recognition? There are good reasons for attributing this change of heart to the recognition by the government of the relevance of a sort of doctrine of adverse possession. The occupiers of the land, while perhaps not benefiting from having been legally registered as the true owners, nevertheless ought to acquire a prescriptive title to the land because they had continuously cultivated it for at least several decades. The cost of developing the land and the idea of a statute of limitations (as mentioned above) were certainly contributing factors. Political considerations also played an important part when deciding upon the future of the Beisan *jiftlik*. Writing ten years later, Lewis French explained that 'considerations of law possibly, considerations of equity and policy certainly, forbade the Government in such a wild and unsettled locality to terminate the leases of these tenants'.[61] In this context it is also worth noting the concern expressed by Samuel when he made a personal visit to the area only to be greeted by a hostile demonstration. It was in fact shortly following this organized reception that government proceeded with the allotment of territory along the lines of the Ghor Mudawara Agreement. No doubt the government hoped that confirming the local population in the occupancy of their lands would reap political rewards: The Peel Commission, for example, also spoke of the extent to which the government needed to 'placate' this 'wild and unsettled locality'.[62]

One of the most common reasons put forth publicly by British officials in support of securing the cultivators' tenure to the land was that by settling the question of ownership, the Palestine government could thereby institute cadastral survey operations immediately and thus eliminate any confusion over claims to property and this, of course, facilitated market exchange. 'The Administration has been anxious to come to an equitable arrangement with the present cultivators of the land', Samuel wrote in 1921, 'in order to facilitate the colonization of the larger parts of the lands which are now uncultivated.'[63] In 1923, Samuel again noted the benefits of market transactions:

---

[61] Lewis French, 'First Report on Agricultural Development and Land Settlement in Palestine', 23 Dec. 1931, CO 733/214/5, 145.

[62] Great Britain. Palestine Royal Commission, *Report* (London: HMSO, 1937), 260.

[63] Samuel to Churchill, 23 July 1921, CO 733/4, 511.

the Baisan Land Settlement . . . has converted the customary, but uncertain, tenure of the cultivators into a new legal tenure on terms satisfactory both to them and to the Government. Portions of the land so allocated to the cultivators, which are surplus to their real requirements, are about to be sold by some of them to an American Zionist Group, and the payments that are in prospect have had a marked effect upon local politics.[64]

The 1920/1 annual report described the benefits of the Ghor Mudawara Agreement in similar terms, noting moreover that 'one of the first conditions of agricultural progress is . . . the settlement of land titles'.[65] In later years officials were certainly keen to argue the point that 'cultivation in the Beisan area has been very much stimulated as the result of security arising out of the agreement'.[66]

By 1926, British officials were coming to the realization that the allotment of such areas to cultivators and to tribes as tribal grazing areas in fulfilment of these obligations would render in the end very little surplus land available for others to develop.[67] Particularly severe criticism of these results came from the Jewish Agency, which had hoped from the beginning that *jiftlik* could be equated to the 'state lands' referred to in article 6 of the mandate.[68] Later, this criticism focused less on the question of rights and more on the logistics of demarcation: 'while the Jewish Agency has always fully recognized the right of the Beisan settlers to the lands worked by them,' argued a 1930 memorandum, 'it considers that there is a case for an investigation of the working of the Agreement in practice.'[69] Criticism was not levelled here against the Ghor Mudawara Agreement recognizing the legal rights of the Beisan cultivators accruing from long occupation of land wrongfully appropriated by Sultan Abdul Hamid.[70] Rather the Jewish Agency objected to the units of allotment which appeared to be surplus to the actual requirements of the cultivators, and to the fact that much land was then left uncultivated (though this was a condition probably made worse by several years' poor rainfall, lack of labour, machinery, and capital).[71] Assertions were made that the state of cultivation was

---

[64] 'Notes on the High Commissioner's Tour: October 21st to 25th, 1923', CO 733/50, 517.

[65] 'An Interim Report on the Civil Administration of Palestine, 12 Months Ending June 1921', CO 733/22, 464.

[66] Minute sheets, 22 Sept. 1926, CO 733/116, 327.

[67] Plumer to Colonial Office, 20 May 1926, CO 733/114, 423. Also CO 733/133/4.

[68] Letter from Weizmann, 15 Feb. 1924, CO 733/62, 642.

[69] 'Summary of Proposals', CO 733/192/2/77275, 16.

[70] 'Memorandum on Policy in Palestine', CO 733/192/77275, 32.

[71] See, for example, minute sheets, 'Disposal of Jiftlik Lands', CO 733/116, 322.

'deplorable' and that tribal lands were 'merely grazed over by a few wandering goat herds'.[72] The British officer in charge of the land settlement process in Beisan disagreed, reporting that 'considering the short time that has elapsed since the parcellation of the lands, the development of a few of the villages has been remarkable', and concluding that 'where such partition had been longest in existence, improvement in cultivation was most noticeable'.[73] The Palestine Zionist Executive further contended that the terms of the agreement, whereby a transferee could only dispose of his land if the purchaser was prepared to pay the whole of the balance due to the government, placed them at a disadvantage as compared with land speculators who, they complained, could command larger sums of ready money than they could. High commissioner Plumer disagreed:

It is not immediately obvious that the exercise of the right of free disposition on the part of the cultivators has contributed largely to undue speculation. The facts are that since the Agreement became operative in 1922, approx 80,000 dunums have been allotted; of this amount only 8,803 dunums have been sold, and these sales were by two villages out of eleven villages in which allotments were made. Moreover, only in two cases were lands resold after having been so acquired from the cultivators. While there is ground for supposing that a portion of the land sold is held by the purchasers for purposes of speculation, the figures reveal that at the present date speculation has not reached such dimensions as to justify the argument of the Zionist Organization.[74]

But, so dissatisfied was the Jewish Agency with the general rate of progress in the delimitation of state lands, it suggested that officers of the Palestine administration were deliberately slowing down the process of land settlement in the Beisan area. Such accusations tended, however, to take little account of the technical difficulties regarding land tenure and survey of the lands in question.[75]

Already very sensitive about Zionist complaints that the obligation under article 6 of the mandate to facilitate Jewish settlement on 'state lands' was not being pursued actively enough, the Colonial Office eventually agreed that changes to the Ghor Mudawara Agreement were necessary.[76] As one Colonial Office official minuted:

---

[72] See Lewis French, 'First Report on Agricultural Development and Land Settlement in Palestine', 23 Dec. 1931, CO 733/214/5, 152.

[73] Quoted ibid.

[74] Plumer to Colonial Office, 20 May 1926, CO 733/114, 423.

[75] Minute by O. G. R. Williams, 9 Dec. 1929, CO 733/170/2/67027, 4.

[76] Minute by H. W. Young, 30 July 1925, CO 733/107, 408.

We have to deal with a very small country in which a comparatively large number of settlers may be expected to enter until saturation point is reached. We are bound by an international instrument to encourage in this country the close settlement of Jews on the land. We are all agreed that the future of Palestine lies more in its potentialities as an agricultural than as a manufacturing country. This being so, are we justified in allowing occupancy tenants who have acquired a moral title under entirely different conditions and a corrupt system of administration to remain in occupation of holdings which are far beyond their capacity to cultivate?[77]

High commissioner Plumer at first demurred, worried that to modify one article of the agreement might give rise to undue apprehensions on the part of the Beisan inhabitants. However, Plumer did agree that it was desirable for economic reasons to enable transferees to dispose of part of their (surplus) property, and it was noted, as a sort of quid pro quo, that the transferees themselves were eager to modify the terms of repayment which were proving onerous, many of them already in arrears.[78]

Eventually, a solution was found in the modification of article 16, which had required payment of the full purchase price to the government before any disposition was allowed. This article had aimed at ensuring the transferees settle on the land rather than speculate with it. In 1928, it was decided that the agreement should be modified to enable a transferee to dispose of a holding or a part of it on two conditions, showing once again colonial tensions in sharp relief.[79] First, only once purchasers had obtained approval by government for a scheme of intensive cultivation could they then assume responsibility for paying the annual instalments due upon the lands. This, it was hoped, would both assist in preventing speculation and at the same time promote development by inducing the Beisan cultivators to put more of the land on the market. By permitting the transferee to more freely dispose of his property, this first condition reflected a market approach. In contrast, the second condition tended to reaffirm the principle of protection that had fallen off the political radar in recent years. It obliged the cultivator to retain such land as would 'in the opinion of Government suffice for the maintenance of himself and his family'.[80] The

---

[77] Minute by H. W. Young, Sept. 1926, CO 733/116, 322.

[78] Letter from Plumer to Colonial Office, 7 Oct. 1927, CO 733/133/4/44072.

[79] See correspondence in CO 733/170/2/67027, and ISA Chief Secretary's Office, RG 2 L/179/32, 1739.

[80] The 'Statement of Policy' was published in the *Official Gazette* on 16 Sept. 1928, and is reprinted as appendix IIIC in Lewis French, 'First Report on Agricultural Development and Land Settlement in Palestine', CO 733/214/5, 165–8.

legal adviser of the Colonial Office determined that such amendments could be secured by a statement of policy which, issued in 1928, extended the period of payment to a maximum of thirty years and sparked endless discussions on what actually constituted a sufficient subsistence area, referred to as the 'lot viable'.

When, under the terms of the 1921 Ghor Mudawara Agreement, ownership of land in the Beisan *jiftlik* was registered in the cultivators' names, their *ab antiquo* rights were officially admitted. The reasons behind this agreement lay chiefly in the broader economic and legal context which, particularly in the earlier part of the mandate, informed the colonial approach to the question of land: mainly, the conviction that systematic settlement of secure and individual rights to land was essential for economic development. To be sure, many British officials would come to believe that the mechanics of this first essay in dealing with settlement in Beisan were not very satisfactory. In a confidential letter, dated 21 October 1926, for example, the Colonial Office informed high commissioner Plumer that

Agricultural development is a matter of primary concern to the future of Palestine. It is an object which, apart altogether from any specific obligations imposed by the mandate, the Government is bound to pursue with all the means at its disposal. The Beisan settlement may have been the best obtainable in the special circumstances of the case; but its terms ought not to be regarded as a precedent for adoption elsewhere, if they do not conduce to the best interests of agricultural development.[81]

What is clear nonetheless is that criticisms so levelled in the 1920s focused on the limits that were placed on transactions, but did not question the general importance of the market approach. In fact, the Colonial Office was particularly anxious in this regard to hear from Plumer about the possibility of acquiring land in the Rafah *jiftlik* that could be sold on the open market to Jewish land companies.

By the early 1930s however, many British officials were in a very different state of mind about the virtues of the market. The settlement processes of the *jiftlik* villages of Sajad and Qazaza at that time shed light on the evident confusion and contradiction surrounding the nature of rights that the British administration was willing to recognize in Palestine.

---

[81] Letter from Colonial Office to Chancellor, 21 Oct. 1926, CO 733/116.

3. PROTECTION OF CULTIVATORS ORDINANCES, 1929 AND 1933

Within months of the promulgation of the 1929 protection of cultivators ordinance, the August Wailing Wall riots crushed the widespread optimism in market transactions, and the problem of landless Arabs abruptly emerged into official view. The issue of landlessness had been highlighted in the 1920s by the Arab press, which found in Jewish land purchases perhaps the most concrete example of the threat posed by the Zionist movement.[82] In 1925, the Arabic newspaper *Filastin* directed the government's attention to the potential ramifications, warning that 'if [the fellah] now sells his land, he will in future be one of the causes of public insecurity in the country'.[83] But it was the Shaw Commission, sent out to report on the 1929 disturbances, that was chiefly responsible for the changing emphasis in colonial policy. Larger structural changes in the economy were putting pressures on the fast-growing Arab population on the land, but the Shaw Commission highlighted the resulting dispossession of Arab tenants, emphasizing that it had reached an 'acute' level. Since there was no alternative land on which persons evicted could then settle, the commission concluded, a displaced and discontented class was being created in Palestine, a potential cause of future disturbance. The possible consequences of not taking adequate steps to prevent further displacement were described in the Colonial Office as including 'an increase in crime . . . in particular in the activities of armed gangs and the making of political capital out of the Government's failure to take effective action'.[84]

The situation was seen as increasingly threatening, with the 'gap between the landless cultivator and the vagrant or criminal' increasingly narrowing.[85] In the opinion of the 1930 Shaw Commission, Palestine simply could not support a larger agricultural population than it then carried unless methods of farming were radically changed. Meanwhile, they regarded it as of vital importance that, pending the results of a careful investigation, ways should be found of checking 'the present tendency towards the eviction of peasant cultivators from the land'.[86] On this

---

[82] Raya Adler, 'The Tenants of Wadi Hawarith: Another View of the Land Question in Palestine', *International Journal of Middle East Studies*, 20/2 (1988).
[83] Quoted in 'Palestine Press', *Palestine Bulletin*, 12 Oct. 1925, 3.
[84] Minute sheets, 11 Apr. 1930, CO 733/185/1/77072.
[85] High commissioner to secretary of state, 11 May 1933, CO 733/234/17272, Part 1.
[86] Great Britain, *Report of the Commission on the Palestine Disturbances of August, 1929*.

recommendation, Sir John Hope-Simpson was sent out to Palestine to examine on the spot the questions of immigration, land settlement, and development. In October 1930, he summarized the situation in the following terms:

It is the duty of the Administration, under the Mandate, to ensure that the position of the Arabs is not prejudiced by Jewish immigration. It is also its duty under the Mandate to encourage the close settlement of the Jews on the land, subject always to the former condition. It is only possible to reconcile these apparently conflicting duties by an active policy of agricultural development, having as its object close settlement on the land and intensive cultivation by both Arabs and Jews. To this end drastic action is necessary.[87]

Hope-Simpson recommended that government undertake an agricultural development scheme aimed at improving farming methods, thereby providing sufficient land for the Arab fellahin as well as for additional Jewish settlement. An essential element of this scheme was that until the actual mechanics were worked out, all disposition of land should rest with the authority in charge of the development scheme. That is, land transfers should only be permitted provided they did not interfere with the agricultural development scheme. As for the 1929 protection of cultivators ordinance, Hope-Simpson was particularly critical: 'what is eminently required is, not compensation for disturbance, but a provision against disturbances.'[88]

Hope-Simpson's main ideas were embodied in the 1930 White Paper which contemplated three specific measures to combat the threatening problem of landlessness: first, the establishment of the development scheme which, when initially discussed, was to involve a guaranteed loan of 2.5 million Palestine pounds; second, an investigation into the number of 'landless Arabs' (specially defined); and, third, the introduction of legislation with the object of closely supervising land transfers so as to prevent increases in the displacement of the indigenous agricultural population.

The first two projects did not do well. Initially, money was found to appoint Lewis French as director of development. The author of two reports on the prospects of agricultural development, French confirmed for the Colonial Office the fears expressed by the Shaw Commission: 'it is perhaps not irrelevant to speculate at long range as to whether the Arab

[87] Hope-Simpson, *Palestine. Report on Immigration, Land Settlement and Development.*
[88] Ibid.

effendi will eventually sell his lands at a profit to the Jews, and leave Arab cultivators or tenants to become serfs of the Jews (if they care to employ them on the land), or merely hewers of wood or drawers of water in the towns.'[89] His development plans were ambitious, and certainly challenged the prevailing laissez-faire approach of the Colonial Office. As Downie minuted,

a scheme of this kind, under which the improvement of the land (e.g irrigation etc.) is carried out by the Govt, renders unnecessary the institution of a Land Bank for the provision of long term credit for the cultivators . . . as regards Arabs, what we now have in view is a scheme of land development to be undertaken by the GOVT, thus obviating any necessity for private long-term credit facilities to individual Arab cultivators for the purpose of improving their land. There can be no doubt that in view of the character of the Arab cultivator and of the physical aspect of the problem (i.e. large scale irrigation is the main requirement) advances to individual Arabs for improving each his own little patch would be a sheer waste of money. Under Mr French's proposals the Govt would take over the whole business of settlement and development. When a suitable area had been found, and at a suitable opportunity, the Govt would establish a settlement of, say, 50 Arabs. For this purpose it would acquire the land (at present devoted to extensive cultivation) and would not pay cash compensation to the existing occupiers, but would compensate them by giving them in exchange a smaller area developed for intensive cultivation (Thus the existing occupiers would become members of the new settlement.) All the work of irrigation, tree planting, etc., would be carried out by the Govt, which would recoup itself (so far as possible) by charging rent to the colonists. Govt would also pay a subsistence allowance to the colonists during the waiting period while the land was being prepared for intensive cultivation. Under such a scheme as this there would be no necessity for private long term credits to Arab cultivators by means of an Agricultural Bank or otherwise, since the work of development would be done by Government.[90]

Whether such a vision would ever have been supported in London, officials there and in Palestine soon had to take into account rapidly changing financial conditions. The economic condition of Palestine was actually showing some signs of improvement in the early 1930s, but world economic conditions remained uncertain and financial stringency in London remained acute. As a result, the development scheme was repeatedly, and indefinitely, 'postponed'.

    [89] Lewis French, 'First Report on Agricultural Development and Land Settlement in Palestine, Draft', CO 733/214/5, 92–3.
    [90] Minute by Downie, 12 Dec. 1932, CO 733/223/97248.

As for the landless Arab inquiry, it was rendered ineffectual by the terms under which it was structured. In order to absolve any Jewish responsibility for the creation of a landless class, the Jewish Agency worked hard at ensuring that the investigation define landlessness in narrow terms. As Kenneth Stein puts it, 'the number of claims submitted was neither representative nor reflective of the number of Arabs displaced . . . nor was the final tally of 899 demonstrative of anything except a Jewish Agency political victory'.[91] The inquiry's usefulness can be partly surmised by the fact that among the number of cultivators who, although displaced from lands acquired by Jewish purchasers, were not covered by the special definition of what made for a 'landless Arab' were individuals who obtained employment in towns. In the event of any severe economic downturn, these were the very individuals who would lose their means of livelihood and constitute a political danger.[92]

With the development scheme shelved, and the landless inquiry suitably emasculated, the urgent problem facing the Palestine government was how to prevent future displacement. At the permanent mandates commission of the League of Nations, Britain's accredited representative Drummond Shiels explained the situation in the following terms: 'the main point was not so much the actual number of persons who had been dispossessed of their land . . . but the fears for the future'.[93] Accordingly, 'the best action to take was to guard against such a grievance being allowed to exist or increase rather than to consider the exact measure of what had happened in the past'. In response, members of the permanent mandates commission likened the situation in Palestine to the problem of the sale of land elsewhere: 'It existed everywhere . . . The natives, attracted by the prospect of being paid for it in hard cash, and of receiving what seemed to them to be considerable sums of money, often sold their land. It was desirable to put them on their guard against their own impulsiveness. Certain Administrations, moreover, required that no land should be sold by the natives to foreigners without their previous approval.' Observers in Palestine tended to agree: 'The conditions are closely analogous to those with which the governments in India have had to contend in several provinces, and that obtained at one time in Ireland,

---

[91] Stein, *The Land Question in Palestine, 1917–1939*, 157.

[92] See Charles Kamen, *Little Common Ground: Arab Agriculture and Jewish Settlement in Palestine, 1920–1948* (Pittsburgh: University of Pittsburgh Press, 1991).

[93] League of Nations, Permanent Mandates Commission, Minutes of the Seventeenth (Extraordinary) Session, Tenth Meeting, 9 June 1930.

namely, a growing population, no adequate outlets in industry, and increasing pressure on the soil,' wrote Sir Samuel O'Donnell, head of a 1931 commission set up to examine the financial situation of the Palestine administration. 'The only solution is the grant of fixity of tenure, coupled with provision for the regulation of rents.'[94] To this Lewis French added the argument that 'nothing is so fatal to progress as want of security of tenure—a want which can be supplied by protecting the small proprietor and the occupancy tenant from eviction'.[95] French was harshly critical about 'the past policy of *laissez-faire*' and submitted that 'for the future the truth that prevention is better than cure should be held up as the guiding principle'.[96]

In this context, the government reserved the power to take necessary steps to protect the tenancy of Arab cultivators throughout Palestine.[97] As outlined in 1931,

In giving effect to the policy of land settlement as contemplated in article 11 of the Mandate, it is necessary if disorganisation is to be avoided, and if the policy is to have a chance to succeed, that there should exist some centralised control of transactions relating to the acquisition and transfer of land during such interim period as may reasonably be necessary to place the development scheme upon a sure foundation. The power contemplated is regulative and not prohibitory, although it does involve a power to prevent transactions which are inconsistent with the tenor of the scheme . . . Any control contemplated will be fenced with due safeguards to secure as little interference as possible with the free transfer of land.[98]

The last important consequence of Sir John Hope-Simpson's Report and the 1930 White Paper, therefore, must be seen to be the 1933 protection of cultivators ordinance, which replaced all former legislation and was substantially the law until the end of the mandate.[99] As Goadby and Doukhan point out, the provisions borrowed heavily from Acts passed in England, notably the 1923 agricultural holdings Act and the 1923

---

[94] O'Donnell to Passfield, 4 July 1931, CO 733/196/1/87033/File C.

[95] Lewis French, 'Supplementary Report on Agricultural Development and Land Settlement in Palestine', 20 Apr. 1932, CO 733/214/8, 81.

[96] Ibid. 48.

[97] For example, para. 12 of the 'MacDonald Letter', 13 Feb. 1931: 'what [the 1930 White Paper] does contemplate is such temporary control of land disposition and transfers as may be necessary.'

[98] As stated in para. 12 of the 'MacDonald Letter', but repeated thereafter as a policy guide line. See discussion in CO 733/234/17272.

[99] *A Survey of Palestine: Prepared in December 1945 and January 1946 for the Information of the Anglo-American Committee of Inquiry*, 290.

increase of rents Act.[100] The object of the ordinance was to more carefully protect tenants from eviction by requiring that 'statutory tenants' who had not neglected their holdings be provided with a subsistence area if ejected. Under this ordinance, a landlord was prevented from selling tenanted land without first relocating the tenants.

A great deal of consideration would continue to be given to the question of whether it was necessary to protect small owners—'against themselves' as it were—as well as tenants.[101] Restrictions on dispositions by owner-occupiers was the Rubicon that the Colonial Office—ever protective of the cherished rights of individuals to engage in whatever commercial transactions they want with their own property, and conscious of its obligations under the mandate to facilitate Jewish settlement —was desperately trying to avoid crossing. The idea of having every disposition of agricultural land coming before the high commissioner to be approved or rejected was more than alarming to officials in the Colonial Office: as one minute asked, 'Is this a possible course? Or would it create such an amount of work and such a clog upon the free transfer of land as to render it either impracticable altogether, or to make the cure worse than the disease?'[102] In 1933 the Colonial Office reaffirmed that 'the right of the owner-occupier to sell his land should remain unrestricted, at any rate for the present'.[103] But in Jerusalem the high commissioner in particular watched the situation closely, and within two years, as will be discussed in the following chapter, the Palestine government finally prepared legislation which would prevent a landowner from selling his 'lot viable', i.e. the minimum area necessary for a family's subsistence.

4. LAND SETTLEMENT IN THE *JIFTLIKS* OF SAJAD AND QAZAZA

Increased anxiety in official circles with peasant displacement provides the key to understanding why, in 1921, the Beisan inhabitants' claim to *ab antiquo* rights in *jiftlik* land was deserving of official recognition whereas in 1931, the process of land settlement of *jiftlik* villages of Sajad and Qazaza produced no such admission.

[100] Goadby and Doukhan, *The Land Law of Palestine*, 236.
[101] For example, minute sheets, 17 Jan. 1931, CO 733/199/87072.
[102] Minute sheets, 25 Apr. 1930, CO 733/185/1/77072.
[103] 'Memorandum by the Secretary of State for the Colonies', 1 Feb. 1933, CO 733/234/17272.

As land settlement operations in the *jiftlik* villages of Sajad and Qazaza were undertaken in accordance with procedures laid down by the 1928 land settlement ordinance, its provisions are worth considering in some detail. The ordinance, drafted by Dowson and drawing on Sudanese land laws, provided for 'the best known and only effective practice' of recording rights to land.[104] The whole of Palestine was not made subject to the provisions of the new ordinance at once. Government policy was to apply it to rural lands only,[105] specifically to well-defined 'settlement areas' which were systematically declared 'whenever it appears expedient'.[106] The programme of defining settlement areas was determined by the need to advance settlement operations 'fan-wise' from certain centres, initially around Gaza and Jaffa.[107] This was described as conforming to 'a programme of minimum expenses and maximum efficiency'.[108] Survey and settlement in the coastal plain required fewer staff, less transport, and less supervision than a programme of a more sporadic nature. Any interruption of these procedures by taking up a particular village outside of the prescribed schedule was avoided because it would have involved delay and increased expenditure. As Dowson explained, 'any sporadic investigation of rights and privileges in advance of regular settlement has evident and serious disadvantages. Such a patchwork settlement cannot be thorough; and it will distract and squander the effort of the Survey and Settlement parties.'[109] The centres were first located along the coast and in the plains because the greatest amount of progress at the least amount of cost could be achieved by concentrating there. Land settlement in the hill areas was not so straightforward and simple. A 1922 report by the director of surveys, for example, estimated the cost of surveys in the plains to be PT 3 per dunam and PT 4.75 per dunam in the hilly regions.[110] In 1932, the progress of settlement work in the hills was estimated at 50 to 60 per cent

---

[104] Goadby and Doukhan, *The Land Law of Palestine*, 271.

[105] Minute sheets, ISA Chief Secretary's Office, RG2 L/91/31, 0429.

[106] Section 3(1), land settlement ordinance 1928. See Palestine, *The Laws of Palestine in Force on the 31st Day of December 1933*, rev. edn. prepared by Robert Harry Drayton (London: Waterlow, 1934).

[107] Abramson to chief secretary, 19 July 1932, ISA, RG 22, Land Registration and Land Settlement, LS 8 (11), box 3568. Also Abramson, 'Observations on the Recommendations on Land Settlement in the Report of the O'Donnell Commission', CO 733/208/5/87326.

[108] See 'Interview with the Acting High Commissioner', *Palestine Bulletin*, 6 Sept. 1928, 2.

[109] Dowson to chief secretary, 12 Mar. 1925, CO 733/97, 311.

[110] 'Minutes of the Seventeenth Meeting of the Advisory Council', 1 Apr. 1922, CO 733/18, 253.

less than in the plains.[111] The hill areas were more densely inhabited and as a result of long-standing cultivation patterns the size and shape of holdings varied much more than in the plains.[112] It could also be that progress in settlement could be demonstrated more rapidly in the plains because various formal or informal arrangements had already been made to divide *musha'* land in villages there.[113] The fact that Jewish land-purchasing agencies had since the late nineteenth century focused their resources on the agricultural opportunities in the plains has drawn attention to the political ramifications of adopting a land settlement programme that focused efforts on that area. But officials at the time were adamant about the professional concerns involved. The director of surveys insisted on a clear and deliberate plan in 1922: 'an odd surveyor or two monkeying about in advance of regular operations is much more likely to be harmful than otherwise, and will not hasten matters in the end.'[114] In 1936 the commissioner of lands and surveys proclaimed his aversion to departing from the settlement programme in order to take up 'scattered' areas by explaining: 'the difficulty is that if we tackle too many areas where there are likely to be complicated disputes, we shall bite off more than we can chew . . . I want to make it clear that we cannot settle the odd cabbage-patch.'[115]

Introduction of this land ordinance added a new layer of registration in Palestine.[116] In terms of Palestinian cultivators holding a title to land which, say, would be readily acceptable to a credit institution as collateral, there now existed the following: cultivators registered as owners through Dowson's 1928 land settlement scheme; cultivators who had been assigned title to land by the Beisan lands commission; and, persons registered as owners in the existing registers in accordance either with the 1919 system devised by Judge Williamson or with the 1920 provisions of the land transfer ordinance (the titles of which would be subject to revision under the terms of the 1928 ordinance).

[111] Abramson to chief secretary, 28 July 1932, ISA LS 8/1. box 3558.

[112] See also Haim Gerber, *The Social Origins of the Modern Middle East* (London: Mansell, 1987), Gershon Shafir, *Land, Labor, and the Origins of the Israeli–Palestinian Conflict, 1882–1914* (Cambridge: Cambridge University Press, 1989).

[113] Kamen, *Little Common Ground: Arab Agriculture and Jewish Settlement in Palestine, 1920–1948*, 97. 'Report by Mr. C. F. Strickland of the Indian Civil Service on the Possibility of Introducing a System of Agricultural Cooperation in Palestine' (Strickland Report) (Jerusalem, 1930).

[114] C. H. Ley to J. N. Stubbs, 18 Jan. 1922, ISA LD 53/3/6, Beisan, box 3395.

[115] Abramson to Lees, 17 Feb. 1936, ISA RG 22, LS 8/11, box 3568.

[116] *A Survey of Palestine: Prepared in December 1945 and January 1946 for the Information of the Anglo-American Committee of Inquiry*, ch. VIII.

Once a settlement area was declared, the official procedures of the 1928 ordinance followed along four stages. The first stage consisted of dividing the lands of the village into block plans of convenient size and shape, and preferably of equal value, and of tying them definitively to a triangulation point: 'no good settlement can be carried out without a good survey and no good detailed survey can be carried out without a good triangulation framework,' testified Salmon in 1937, remarking also on how reliable and how well marked the triangulation survey should be.[117] This division into blocks satisfied fiscal, as well as registration, purposes. The urban property tax had been promulgated in 1928 and the intention was to replace the tithe in rural areas with a land tax as soon as possible. British officials relied heavily at this stage on village subdivisions that already existed. As Dowson had observed, 'the expedient of constituting blocks of land of approximately equal value is familiar to people and has long been used by them as an equitable basis for the apportionment of *mesha*".[118] These block plans were prepared by survey officers in the field who roughly sketched on a topographical map such visible features as hedges and fences, wadis and roads, as well as boundaries already defined by villagers. In the circumstances, the survey officer usually completed some of the settlement himself, as was described to the Peel Commission:

If you went out and saw the surveyor doing his work you might think that there was a riot on, because there is a tremendous amount of shouting and argument, but really it is a fairly peaceful business and after wasting a great deal of time they decide where so-and-so's angle iron is to go in.[119]

The survey work was all recorded in field books and then sent to the head survey office where plans were prepared which listed against every parcel of land, the number, the area, and the reputed owner, i.e. the name of the man who says 'this is my land'. By surveying land in this way, the expectation was that the register of titles would no longer need to describe boundaries by verbal references to neighbours, or to geographical features: 'the fixing of the boundaries, marks and features on the ground can be accurately done,' explain Goadby and Doukhan, 'so that it is no longer possible for any one to trespass secretly on the land of another.'[120]

---

[117] Great Britain. Palestine Royal Commission, *Minutes of Evidence Heard at Public Sessions (with Index)* (London: HMSO, 1937), 19–20. See also C. H. Ley, 'An Outline of Cadastral Structure in Palestine' (Government of Palestine, 1931).

[118] Dowson, 'The Land System in Palestine', CO 733/109, 269.

[119] Great Britain. Palestine Royal Commission, *Minutes of Evidence Heard at Public Sessions (with Index)* (London: HMSO, 1937), 20.

[120] Goadby and Doukhan, *The Land Law of Palestine*, 270.

The plans, and accompanying information, were then handed over to the settlement branch who appointed an officer to initiate the second stage: the process of recording claims. The settlement officer would proceed to the village and set up a 'camp' from which he would issue notices, provide the appropriate claim forms, and entertain the villagers with coffee and cigarettes.[121] In any matter of common interest the villagers were represented by a committee which was chosen from persons nominated by the inhabitants. The village settlement committee was empowered in its own name to bring and defend actions, and it was its duty to protect the interests of the absentees, minors, and incapacitated persons. In this process of recording claims, the settlement officer would as a first step record all rights of ownership, mortgages, leases for a period of more than three years, rights of way, and such other interests as may be registrable. Such claims had to be made on the proper claim forms obtained on application at the camp. During this process, the settlement officer would also ascertain from claimants the grounds on which claims were based and obtain the necessary supporting documents with names of witnesses. Schedules of claims were then prepared and posted for a prescribed period of time (not less than fifteen days), during which additional claims or counter-claims might be lodged.

The settlement officer could then commence the third stage of settlement operations: the final investigation and settlement of claims. If there were conflicting claims, the settlement officer had the judicial power to decide the dispute. If he thought that a person who had not presented a claim was in fact entitled to any right in land, he could proceed as if such a person had made a claim. Once the final schedule of rights for each registration block was completed, it was posted in the village. Appeals against a settlement officer's decision could be filed in the land court or the district court, but it appears that on the whole appeals were not very frequent.

The fourth, and final, stage was the forwarding of the schedule of rights, with its accompanying registration block plan, to the registry office of the sub-district in which the village was situated. The information could then be entered into a new land register which, loose leaf in form, 'conforms to the best modern practice':

A parcel of land is taken as a unit of registration. The ownership in this land and all the interests to which it is subject, the charges cautions and easements

---

[121] Director of lands, 11 Dec. 1922, ISA RG 22, G 41/9, box 3542.

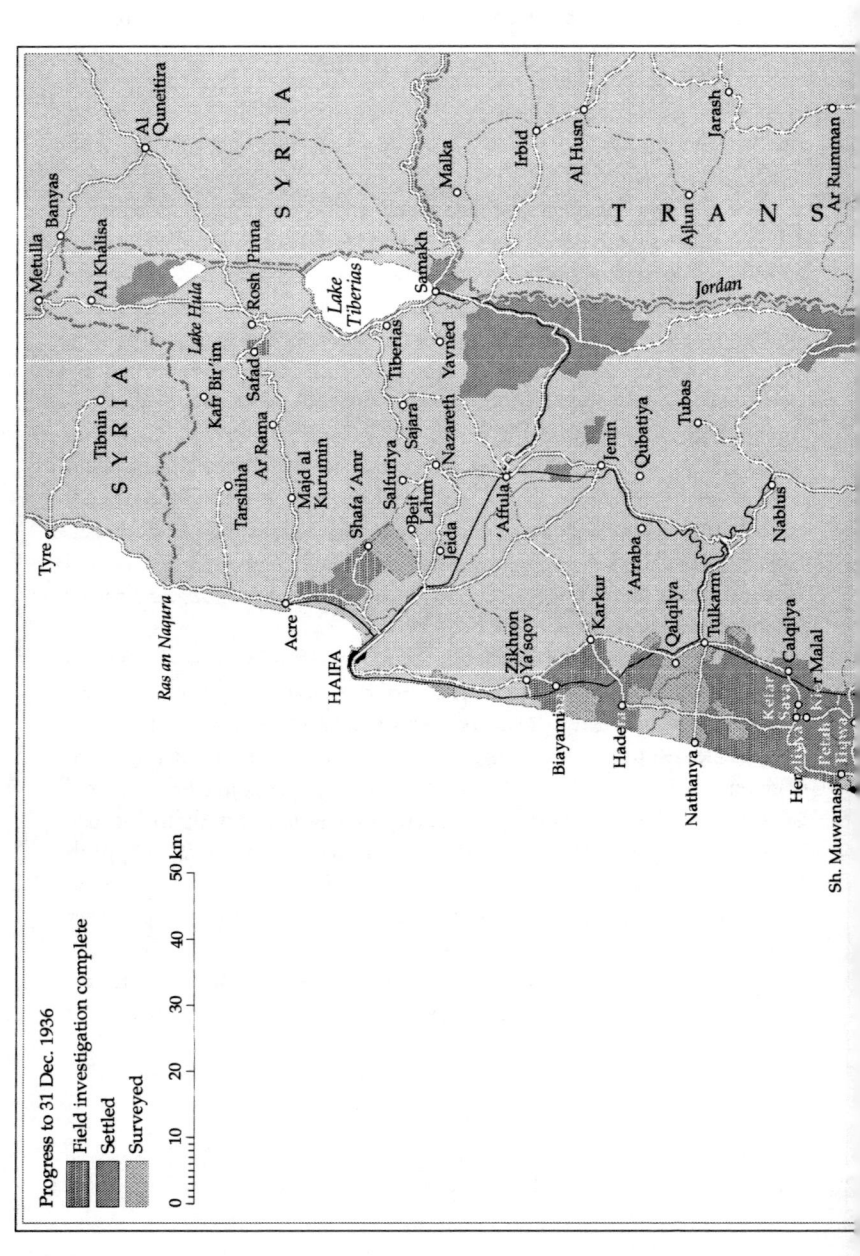

Progress to 31 Dec. 1936

Field investigation complete
Settled
Surveyed

0 10 20 30 40 50 km

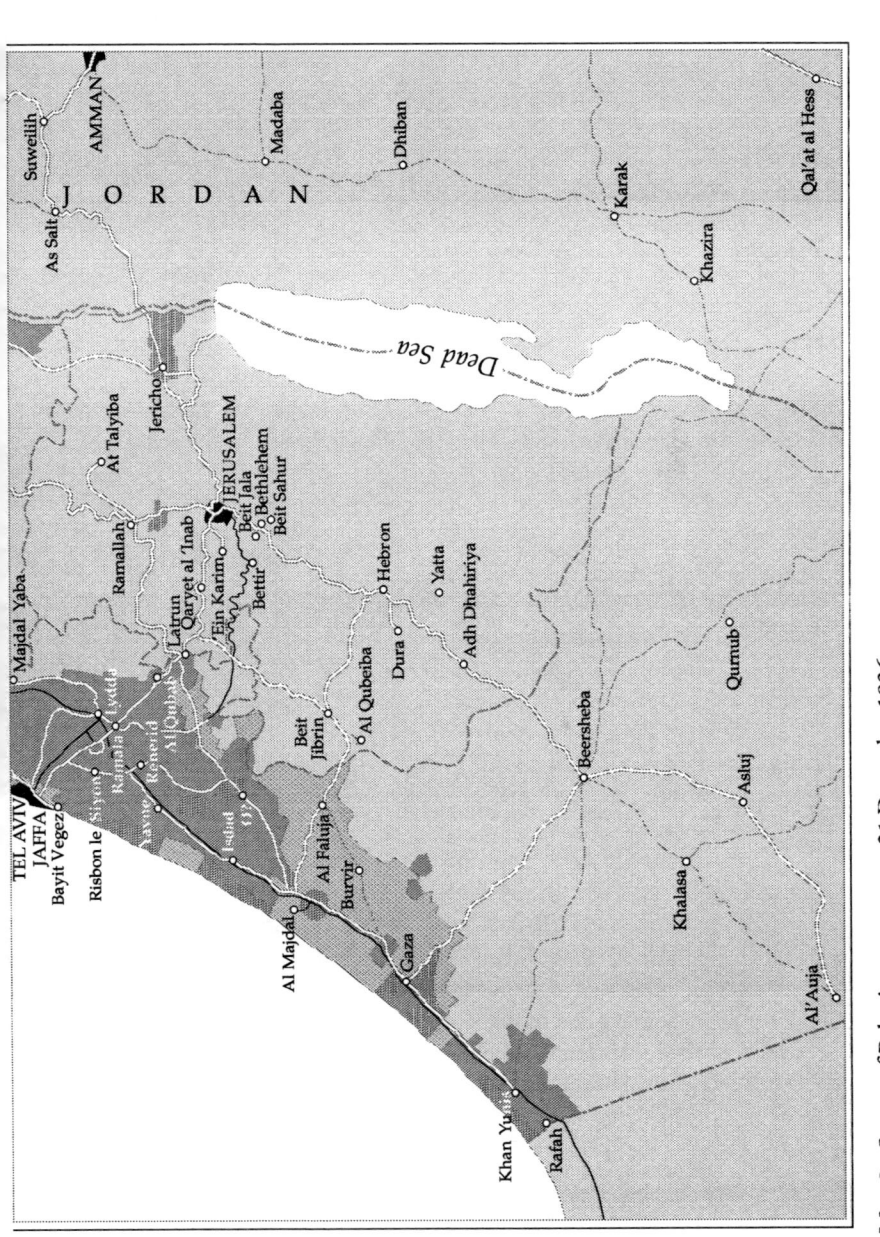

Map 2. Survey of Palestine, progress to 31 December 1936

affecting it are all recorded in the registration. Every subsequent dealing with the land is recorded in the Register of Title. To the holder of a Title a certificate or an extract from the Register is issued.[122]

The whole of Palestine was not automatically made subject to the provisions of the new ordinance: rather, they applied only to well-defined 'settlement areas' which were declared 'whenever it appears expedient' in the *Official Gazette*.[123] Any interruption in the programme by taking up a particular village outside of the prescribed schedule was to be avoided because it would have involved delay and increased expenditure. It was therefore significant that the villages of Sajad and Qazaza were not actually included in the 'normal' progress of settlement operations for the year 1931/2. Land settlement was (reluctantly) scheduled in the autumn of 1931 by the commissioner of lands and surveys in advance of the normal operations only because it was urgently required by the director of development, Lewis French. At first, the commissioner hesitated and explained that staff simply could not be spared for any settlement in advance of normal operations. He eventually agreed to take the highly unusual step of rearranging the schedule to include forthwith these *jiftlik* villages in the programme of settlement, but he also expressed strong reservations. In a letter to the chief secretary, he recalled the 'intractability' of the Beisan inhabitants during the attempts made ten years earlier to confirm the position of the government in *jiftlik* lands. And he concluded by expressing the concern, somewhat prophetically as it turned out, that settlement operations in Sajad and Qazaza might 'possibly bring about a situation which Government might not wish to be faced with at the present juncture'.[124]

Once declared 'settlement areas', the official procedures for Sajad and Qazaza proceeded along three of the four established stages of the settlement process. The first stage consisted of dividing the village lands into registration blocks of convenient size and shape and preferably of equal value; second, claims to the land were recorded with the help of a village settlement committee; and, third, the claims were investigated and any that conflicted were resolved judicially by the settlement officer. Normal procedure would then have seen the completed schedule of

[122] Goadby and Doukhan, *The Land Law of Palestine*, 282.

[123] Section 3(1), land settlement ordinance 1928. In Robert Harry Drayton (ed.), *The Laws of Palestine* (London, Waterlow and Sons Ltd., 1934), 854.

[124] Abramson to chief secretary, 25 Sept. 1931, ISA, Land Registration and Land Settlement, RG 22, LS 1/10, box 3776.

rights forwarded to the registry office. In this case, however, an appeal was lodged against the settlement officer's decision by none other than the attorney general.

After completing his investigations of claims to rights and interests in the *jiftlik* lands of Sajad and Qazaza, the settlement officer had made two significant decisions concerning the nature of the rights enjoyed by the cultivators. On the one hand, he decided that title to the ownership of the land, which had previously been registered as *miri* land in the name of Sultan Abdul Hamid, should now be vested in the name of the high commissioner in trust for and on behalf of the government of Palestine. This was of course in contrast to the decision made in the Beisan *jiftlik*. But it was argued by the settlement officer that such registration ought to be done by virtue of the action of the Ottoman government in September 1908—in the wake of the Young Turk revolution—in transferring to itself the properties of the Sultan, who himself was deposed. However, the settlement officer went on to say that cultivators of Sajad and Qazaza should be legally registered in the schedule of rights as having 'heritable and assignable rights of occupancy and tenancy'. In practical terms, this decision resulted in the cultivators being registered as having something very close to the rights granted to the Beisan cultivators. By the terms of the Ghor Mudawara Agreement, as we have seen, the land was distributed to the cultivators on *miri* tenure—that is, with the understanding that the *rakaba* or 'ownership' technically remained vested in the state, while the cultivators were granted the *tasarruf,* or usufruct possession.

Around the time of the settlement officer's decision, contemporary observers of legal issues pertaining to land tenure were not sure what to make of this. Lewis French, for example, noted the decision in an aside in his reports, and it warranted an uncertain footnote in Goadby and Doukhan's *Land Law of Palestine,* also published shortly after the decision was made. At any rate, the decision did not stand for long. In a rather unusual move, the attorney general quickly appealed the decision, arguing for a much more circumscribed and limited form of tenancy for the *jiftlik* cultivators. It is worth reviewing with some care the reasons behind the granting of such occupancy rights by the settlement officer, before considering the possible reasons which lay behind the attorney general's appeal.

Prior to reaching his decision, the settlement officer of Sajad and Qazaza discussed the matter of *jiftlik* lands thoroughly with the settlement officer of the Gaza area, where settlement of *jiftlik* lands was concurrently undertaken (in line also with Lewis French's request). Together the two settlement officers had no difficulty arriving at the same conclusions regarding 'heritable and assignable rights', both on matters of principle and on the exact phraseology to be used. In fact, the Gaza settlement officer drew up a similar schedule of rights for the inhabitants of the *jiftlik* villages of Muharraqa, Kaufakha, Jaladiya, and Rafah.[125] In appreciating why the settlement officers decided in favour of recognizing heritable and assignable rights in *jiftlik* lands, it is important to consider several factors. On the legal side, it is significant that article 10(3) of the land settlement ordinance made it mandatory, and not merely discretionary, that the settlement officer had regard to equitable rights. It is also significant to note that an important difference existed between actions conducted during the established procedure of land settlement and those instituted before the land courts. Actions before the land courts were voluntary and were confined to the points at issue. In contrast, the settlement officer was undertaking a settlement of all relevant facts and interests pertaining to land on a comprehensive and territorial basis. A brief perusal of the legal records makes it clear that settlement officers were widely of the opinion that the 1928 land settlement ordinance gave them the fullest powers to carry out an investigation into any claims.[126] If there were conflicting claims, the settlement officer had the judicial power to decide the dispute. In doing so, he was required to 'apply the Land Law in force at the date of the hearing of the action, provided he shall have regard to the equitable as well as legal rights to land'.[127] Even if interested parties did not lodge a claim themselves, a settlement officer, if he was satisfied that they had rights, proceeded, by virtue of section 27(4), as if they had lodged a claim.

Such appears to have largely been the case for the cultivators of Sajad and Qazaza who, in the words of the settlement officer himself, 'are illiterate and ignorant of the meaning of legal terms . . . [and] unable to properly state or define their claims'.[128] In defining their rights, equitable and legal, the settlement officer had to take into consideration the following interests: cultivators of the *jiftlik* had previously disposed of rights to one another; cultivators had erected buildings and planted trees on the land

---

[125] Commissioner of lands and surveys to district commissioner, southern district, 27 Nov. 1936, ISA, Land Registration and Land Settlement, RG 22, LS 1/10, box 3776.

[126] As an example, see records in CO 733/204.

[127] Goadby and Doukhan, *The Land Law of Palestine*, 276.

[128] I. N. Camp, settlement officer, 'Memorandum on Decisions by Settlement Officer, Sajad and Qazaza Jiftlik', 15 Mar. 1932, ISA, Land Registration and Land Settlement, RG 22, LS 1/10, box 3776.

on their own volition; when a cultivator died, his heirs were entitled to inherit. Moreover, similar interests had on several previous occasions given rise to disputes which settlement officers had in fact decided judicially. It is also notable that the settlement officer had himself already gained a great deal of knowledge about *jiftlik* lands through several years of experience in Beisan where, as we have seen, registered ownership of land had in fact been transferred to the cultivators under the terms of the Ghor Mudawara Agreement. Following that agreement, settlement officers commonly assumed that other *jiftlik* properties would be handled in the same way. Indeed, a list of 'state domains' was provided by the lands department that marked all *jiftlik* properties with an asterisk, explaining that 'those villages marked x are occupied by Arab cultivators of long standing and should presumably, be treated on the same basis as, but different in detail from, the lands affected by the Beisan Land Agreement of 19.11.21'.[129] In understanding the settlement officer's decision, it is worth drawing attention to the nature of similar interests in England at that time, of which the settlement officer would surely have been aware: as Goadby and Doukhan explained, 'it is natural that persons familiar with the working of the leasehold system in England should assume that the lessee has an heritable and assignable interest'.[130] Also of note is that no distinction between *miri* land and *jiftlik* or *mudawara* land was made in the 1930 Syrian land code.[131]

When forced to defend his decision before the attorney general, the settlement officer argued that 'the practical and political objections to such a bare registration in the name of the Government alone without mention of any rights of tenants or even their existence on the Land (or of the existence of their houses and trees on the land) are so apparent as scarcely to need mention'.[132] But, if indeed so apparent, why then did the attorney general refuse to register heritable and assignable rights of cultivators in *jiftlik* lands? Shortly after being informed by the director of development of the decision by the settlement officer, the attorney general on behalf of government appealed to the land court, sitting as a court of appeal. He appealed against the registration of such tenancy

---

[129] CO 733/116.   [130] Goadby and Doukhan, *The Land Law of Palestine*, 184.

[131] Abdallah Hanna, 'The Attitude of the French Mandatory Authorities towards Land Ownership in Syria', in Nadine Méouchy and Peter Sluglett (eds.), *The British and French Mandates in Comparative Perspectives* (Leiden: Brill, 2004), 459–60.

[132] I. N. Camp, settlement officer, 'Memorandum on Decisions by Settlement Officer, Sajad and Qazaza Jiftlik', 15 Mar. 1932, ISA, Land Registration and Land Settlement, RG 22, LS 1/10, box 3776.

rights on the ground that there was nothing in the legislation of the country which could justify the existence of such rights. In fact, he argued, the decision of the settlement officer created a form of tenure which was legally unknown in Palestine, and was contrary to the land code. Judges Copland and Shehadeh, sitting as a land court, allowed the appeal and decided that the settlement officer had indeed 'misdirected himself' and that equitable or customary rights as claimed were not in fact such as could be legally recognized 'since they have not been exercised from time immemorial'.[133] The judgement is worth quoting at length:

Section 10(3) of the Land Settlement Ordinance, 1928, states that the Settlement Officer shall apply the Land Law in force at the date of the hearing of the action, provided that he shall have regard to equitable as well as legal rights in land. If it were not for this provision, I should have no hesitation in holding that such hereditary and assignable occupancy and tenancy rights did not exist, and that they were a form of tenure unknown to the law, as being contrary to Article 23 of the Land Code. They are certainly not a legal right . . . Can they be said to come within the description of equitable rights? . . .

Equitable rights arise in many ways and are of varying descriptions. The only phase of them which it is necessary to consider in the case before us is whether such a right should be recognised as regards these lands on the ground of customary user—that is to say, whether the undisputed user for a period of something over fifty years is such that the Courts should, in the course of their equitable jurisdiction, recognise this customary tenure and give effect to it. I think that there is no doubt that . . . the lands have been held by the tenants on the customary basis of hereditary and assignable occupancy and tenancy rights, without hindrance or objection, since the establishment of the Jiftlik, and on no other basis. But a custom, in order to obtain the force of law, or a customary right, in order to be enforced as an equitable right, must be both ancient and invariable. In this case it is undoubtedly invariable, and the point that requires determination is whether it has been exercised over such a sufficiently lengthy period, that it may be described as ancient.

Very little help is to be obtained from any Ottoman Law . . .

I think that the correct rule is that a custom with regard to a right or interest in land, in order to be clothed with the force of law, must have existed for such a period, that its origin has been lost sight of, so that it may be said to have existed ab antiquo, or as the English expression goes, for such a period that 'the memory of man runneth not to the contrary'. And that cannot be said to be the case here.

---

[133] Settlement Appeal, No. 18/32. ISA, Land Registration and Land Settlement, RG 22, LS 1/10, box 3776.

Based on this reasoning, the land court allowed the appeal and decided that, as a result, the village cultivators were 'tenants, and merely tenants' of the government, and had not acquired any legal or equitable rights as against it. The observations made by the settlement officer with regard to the hereditary and assignable rights of occupancy and tenancy were consequently deleted from the schedule of rights for Sajad and Qazaza. When reference later was made to those *jiftlik* registrations that did occur in the name of the occupiers (for example, in the Nazareth area), they were described as having been taken 'on grounds of expediency and not of law'.[134]

The question that needs to be considered in greater detail is why the Attorney General's Office was so uncomfortable with the settlement officer's provision of heritable and assignable rights and so decided to lodge an appeal against this judgement. The possibility that this was a purely legal matter—that is, disagreement over the procedure required to clothe custom with the force of law or concern over a new class of tenancy being *eo ipso* created—is possible, though government was known to have had the option of considering an amendment to the land code in order to provide for rights along the lines of the settlement officer's decision.

In determining the government's position (that of the attorney general) against the registration of such rights, there are two matters of some importance. One is a question of policy: at the beginning of the mandate, the task of maintaining the claims of the state to ownership of land was charged, as under the Ottoman system, to the land registry. But, on grounds of principle, it was gradually accepted that the registry ought properly to be regarded only as the strictly impartial recorder of rights to land, and that its position was therefore compromised by the fact that it was also charged with the incompatible duty of maintaining the claims of the state. So in 1927, it was decided that the attorney general should take over responsibility for the presentation and defence of such claims. Thus, in 1931, when rights and interests in the lands of Qazaza and Sajad were being settled, it was the attorney general's 'job', as it were, to push for the claims of the state.

A more significant clue to the attorney general's appeal however is the link to particular historical circumstances after 1929. It is important to bear in mind that the reason for Sajad and Qazaza being prematurely settled resulted from the urgent request of the director of development,

---

[134] 'Note to Director', 24 Apr. 1947, ISA LS 1/10, box 3776.

Lewis French, whose major responsibility was the resettlement of those Arabs compendiously named 'landless'. We have seen that concern over an ever-increasing number of displaced cultivators, and over the political repercussions of its continuous growth, was particularly acute in the wake of the 1929 riots. This mounting anxiety led British administrators to become more and more fearful that the expansion of secure and individual rights in land, if uncontrolled, could lead to an undermining of communal bonds and thus result in social dislocation. Had land settlement in Sajad and Qazaza resulted in the cultivators being secured in assignable and hereditary rights over land, there was the fear that they might be tempted to sell their holdings and so become landless, thus creating new obligations which the development department would have to deal with in the future. One thing appears certain: in appealing the decision of the settlement officer, the 'state' was not interested in securing its rights to the land in order to participate more liberally in the market as a landowner secure in his title. The Palestine government had no intention whatsoever to evict its 'tenants' from the land in order to bring it into the market. Rather officers of the government were more likely of the opinion that had the court upheld the decision of the settlement officer that the cultivators of *jiftlik* land had hereditable and assignable rights, nothing could have prevented the cultivators from assigning their rights to others and thus becoming landless. Peasant cultivators, with rights subject to the state, were viewed as much more politically docile.

In 1921, it might have made good economic sense to British officials to provide the occupants of the Beisan land with the necessary security of tenure to develop their land; but in 1931, individualization of land tenure was no longer being encouraged as a mark of progress. The commissioner of lands stated it bluntly when he warned in the early 1930s that 'it is unwise to give any Arab cultivators an alienable title', a sentiment elaborated upon by the district commissioner in Jerusalem:

what safeguard will there be that the recipients of jiftlik lands under an agreement will not immediately speculate with their holdings and complicate the problem by bringing into existence absentee landlords, landless Arabs, landowners without water rights, etc.[135]

Though settlement officers were left uncertain as to how to register rights in *jiftlik* land, there was agreement with the new policy: 'I am inclined to

---

[135] District commissioner, Jerusalem district, to chief secretary, 26 Feb. 1936, ISA, Land Registration and Land Settlement, RG 22, LS 8/14, box 3568.

recommend that the tenants should remain as tenants,' wrote the settlement officer in 1936 when considering the Huleh *jiftlik*, 'and that no land should be transferred to them, as, if it were, they might be tempted to sell their holdings and so to become landless.'[136]

Such reconsideration of the merits of a free market in land has also been posited as a way of understanding changing attitudes towards *musha'*. As with *jiftlik*, by the 1930s the partition of *musha'* 'must have seemed roughly equivalent to digging up a hornet's nest'.[137] The Peel Commission in their 1937 report noted that 'in certain areas, the Arabs regard this system of tenancy, destructive as it is of all development, as a safeguard against alienation . . . the Administration have been reluctant for political reasons to abolish it by legislation'.[138] Indeed, Sir Thomas W. Haycraft, formerly chief justice in Palestine, likened *musha'* to the Jewish system 'of tying up the land of agricultural colonies so as to prevent any part falling into the hands of strangers'. *Musha'* he argued, 'may not be a good system for the most profitable use of the land, but it prevents these lands passing away from the villages by sale and the growth of a large number of landless Arabs liable to drift into a proletariat population likely to become an element of social and political instability'.[139] Jewish land-purchasing agencies acquired title to undivided shares in village lands, and until partition actually took place Arab cultivators usually remained on the land. Such was also the prevailing situation with those cultivators of *musha'* who, indebted to creditors, were pressed to sell their shares at increasingly high prices in order to be able to discharge their liabilities.[140]

5. CONCLUSIONS

In addition to providing an overview of British legislative efforts both to define property transactions and to regulate government's rights with regard to certain categories of land, this chapter has concurrently sought to ground its analysis of the market in land in Palestine in particular historical contexts, the settlement operations of *jiftlik* villages in 1921

[136] Camp to commissioner for lands and surveys, 16 July 1936, ISA LS 8/2, box 3558.
[137] Roger Owen, 'Defining Traditional: Some Implications of the Use of Ottoman Law in Mandatory Palestine', *Harvard Middle Eastern and Islamic Review*, 1/2 (1994), 127.
[138] Great Britain. Palestine Royal Commission, *Report*, 219.
[139] Sir Thomas W. Haycraft, 'Palestine under the Mandate', *Journal of the Central Asian Society*, 15 (1928), 174.
[140] See Chancellor to Passfield, 17 Jan. 1930, CO 733/182/8/77050.

and 1931. Taken together, the dual approaches reveal how the colonial desire to facilitate economic development through the creation of a market in land, though cautious from the outset, proved increasingly problematic. The settlement processes described here also give a sense of the various consequences for Palestinian cultivators of the changes in British thinking about property.

By the early 1930s, British officers were in very different states of mind about the virtues of the market, and the settlement processes in Sajad and Qazaza offer useful glimpses into the evident confusion surrounding the nature of rights that the British administration was then willing to recognize in Palestine. As expectations changed, property became a controversial subject, and there was much confusion over the purposes that the institution of property ought to serve. The government was neither coherent nor single minded in its formation of land policies. In the early 1930s it appears that for the experienced settlement officer the recognition of individual rights was still considered proper and fair. For others in the colonial administration, however, the notion of property as entailing a control over its disposition had become politically dangerous. The idea of private property came to be regarded as much as a problem as it was a solution.

Finally, the successful appeal by the attorney general itself raises an interesting point about the formation of colonial land policies in Palestine, particularly as it unfolded in the legal arena. The court system, as distinct from other judicial elements of the settlement process, must be viewed as an important, though not unproblematic, instrument of British land policy. So broad was the term 'equitable rights' that the phrase should be recognized for the extent to which it granted courts a wide degree of discretion in the interpretation and application of Ottoman law. One must be wary of generalizations, and always attempt to provide the context in which the judicial process took place. Still, in deciding the significant issue of whether customary practice or Ottoman laws were to prevail, the courts do seem to have been allowed some flexibility. In the case presented here, adherence to legal rules prevailed over maintaining custom. At other times, however, custom was allowed to prevail over law. One example, provided by R. C. Tute's commentary on the Ottoman land laws in mandate Palestine, is in the preservation of customary forms of inheritance in certain villages.[141] Where the custom was that a woman

---

[141] Tute, *The Ottoman Land Laws [Microform]: With a Commentary on the Ottoman Land Code of 7th Ramadan 1274*, 56–7.

who marries outside her community forgoes her interest in communal or tribal land, it was considered that 'the enforcement of a Statutory scheme of inheritance is a legal as well as a practical impossibility in the areas for which these ancient customs obtain'. The risk in interfering with such traditions was that all rights would be thrown into confusion and 'a great increase in violent crime may be anticipated'. One can conclude that a fair degree of discretion was given in the regular court system to ensuring that the rules relating to property rights converged with the changing necessities of the colonial state.

3

Credit

Colonial officials commonly argued that securing legal title to land would open up possibilities for treating it as a commodity. One of the most important features of the commoditization of land was its use as collateral against loans that could be invested into its further development. In Palestine the development of a credit system based on the mortgaging of land was repeatedly described as one of the chief incentives behind land settlement. 'The foundations for an era of prosperity for the cultivators of the land', high commissioner Lord Plumer stated, 'cannot be either stable or permanent unless the cultivators have an assurance of the security of their tenure and title and it is only when this security is assured that a satisfactory credit system, without which agriculture cannot prosper, can be established.'[1] The 1920 land commission had already raised alarm at the monopolistic and injurious role of the moneylender who charged exorbitantly high rates of interest: 'it is beginning to be realized that registration of property does carry with it certain privileges. At present an Arab cannot obtain a loan from a Bank on his land and he cannot produce a title deed.'[2] But what bank? Although British officials recognized early on that long-term credit facilities for the provision of investment capital could not emerge without active government sponsorship, the role played by government remained a very cautious one. 'There can be no possible doubt as to the desirability of providing better credit facilities for Palestinian cultivators,' minuted a Colonial Office official in 1930: 'The question is what is the best means of providing such facilities.'[3] While British officials unanimously disparaged the usury of the moneylenders, described on one minute sheet as 'the curse of the country',[4] they failed

---

[1] 'Statement to Arab Deputation', reprinted in *Palestine Bulletin*, 23 Feb. 1926. On the significance of secure title to obtaining credit, see enclosures in CO 733/164/4/67019 and CO 733/184/10/77067.

[2] 'Report of the Land Settlement Commission', Aug. 1920, CO 733/18, 619.

[3] Minute by Mayle, 23 Jan. 1930, CO 733/184/77067, 2.

[4] Minute sheets, Dec. 1923, CO 733/61, 547.

properly to understand the role played by the informal market.[5] This chapter takes a closer look at the importance of the relationship between security of title and investment in land as it worked itself out on the ground in mandate Palestine. This will allow for a more concrete assessment of the actual role played by credit provision in the formation of British land policies.

1. AGRICULTURAL LOANS, 1919–1923

Under Turkish rule, agricultural credit was made available in Palestine by thirteen branches of the Ottoman Agricultural Bank (OAB). Agencies of the bank were evidently accommodated in government offices in every *kaza* of Palestine. The assets of the Ottoman Agricultural Bank were comprised of the assets of the Caisse d'Utilité Publique, the institution which it succeeded in 1898, and the receipts from an additional 0.5 per cent on the tithe (one of many increases which together brought the rate to 12.63 per cent). The object of the bank was to grant loans for agricultural purposes, secured by mortgages on immovable property 'or other suitable security'. Long-term loans were issued to persons who were still debtors to the Caisse d'Utilité Publique, and debts to usurers were liquidated by the bank on the transfer of the mortgages. Loans were issued at an initial charge of 1 per cent for administrative expenses, and interest at 6 per cent per annum was charged.[6]

But the system collapsed during the war. Its funds were either looted or removed by retreating forces, and its records completely disrupted. Upon occupying Palestine, British military officers showed little interest in trying to reconstruct the operations of this semi-official institution, despite their adherence to the doctrine of the status quo and despite widespread recognition of the importance of the bank's achievements in 'providing the cultivator with seasonal credit necessary to avoid recourse to usurers'.[7] In 1921, British officials took the necessary measures to wind

[5] See Amos Nadan, 'Competitive Advantage of Moneylenders over Banks in Rural Palestine', *Journal of the Economic and Social History of the Orient*, 48/1 (2005), Roza El-Eini, 'The Agricultural Mortgage Bank in Palestine: The Controversy over its Establishment', *Middle Eastern Studies*, 33/4 (1997).

[6] Minute by W. S. Edmonds, 27 Sept. 1919, FO 371/4226/133761. Also Donald Quataert, 'Dilemma of Development: The Agricultural Bank and Agricultural Reform in Ottoman Turkey, 1888–1908', *International Journal of Middle Eastern Studies*, 6 (1975).

[7] Great Britain. Palestine Royal Commission, *Memoranda Prepared by the Government of Palestine* (London: HMSO, 1937), 45.

up the bank's operations. All the property of the bank was officially vested
in the public custodian of enemy property who, as liquidator, proceeded
to reconstruct the accounts from whatever documentation was available.
Two 'acts of grace' were offered. On the one hand, properties foreclosed
by the bank were to be restored to their former owners on payment of
the principal and interest due. The former owners of these lands had contended that, since the inability to pay off the debt was due solely to the
temporary financial stringency caused by the war, the foreclosures were
invalid.[8] On the other hand, it was decided that no interest would be
charged on outstanding debts due to the bank until after 1 September
1921.[9] The work of administering the liquidation was stated as 'heavy'
owing to the labour entailed by obtaining facts:

Great difficulty has been experienced in arriving at the true financial position
of the Palestine branches of the Bank, as the Turkish authorities took away or
destroyed many of the books before they evacuated Palestine. The loss of these
books has entailed a great labour in investigating Land Registries, Tithes Books,
the registers of the Notary Public, and a large number of receipts, discharges of
mortgages and other papers, which have been collected from all over Palestine
in order to obtain reliable figures.[10]

As of 30 September 1929, the sum reported by the Palestine treasurer to
have been paid over was EP 20,512, although an estimate was also given
of estimated outstanding assets (EP 66,000) and of bank-owned property
(EP 15,000). The treasurer concluded that 'we are not in a position to
estimate the amount which will ultimately be collected'.[11] In liquidating
the OAB, it was provided that 'the assets resulting from the liquidation
shall be disposed of as the High Commissioner shall direct, regard being
had to the purpose for which the O.A.B. was founded'.[12] The implication
was that the PP 20,000 would be employed in the institution of a new
agricultural bank. In fact nothing was done until, thirteen years later,
funds were offered as loans to Arab cooperative credit societies.

Despite the bank's liquidation, the Palestine government continued
to levy the additional 0.5 per cent on the tithe which was raised by the

      [8] 'Report of Palestine Administration, July 1920–December 1921', CO 733/22, 681.
      [9] Frederic M. Goadby and Moses J. Doukhan, *The Land Law of Palestine* (Tel Aviv:
Shoshany's Printing Co. Ltd., 1935), 178.
      [10] 'Report of the Palestine Administration, July 1920–December 1921', CO 733/22,
681.
      [11] Treasurer to chief secretary, 22 Nov. 1929, CO 733/184, 73.
      [12] See 'Memorandum', by Trusted, attorney general, 8 Apr. 1933, CO 733/233/
17264, 16.

Ottoman government on behalf of the agricultural bank. The surplus was simply buried in general revenues. In 1921, high commissioner Samuel considered the appropriateness of utilizing for the purposes of general administration funds that were earmarked for the purpose of providing agricultural credit. But he was consoled by the attorney general who advised that the government was at liberty to do whatever it wanted with it.[13] In the Colonial Office, attempts were made to defend the action of absorbing the extra tithe into general revenue by expressing doubt as to whether the Ottoman hypothecation of revenues ever actually took place ('it was not of course used for this purpose during the war, if it ever was').[14] As a general principle, the utilization of certain revenues for specific expenditures was to be avoided in colonial administrations. All proceeds were in the first place to be used to discharge state liabilities: 'Adam Smith enunciated this doctrine many years ago and it has not been seriously confronted since.'[15] No separate entries were ever kept for accounting purposes by the Palestinian Treasury, but some idea of the amount which this extra revenue constituted is provided in pieces of official correspondence. When high commissioner Chancellor raised the question of an agricultural bank in 1930, he recalled that

in 1921 Sir Herbert Samuel considered the question whether such additional tithe should be utilised for purposes of the administration of the country or should be earmarked for the purposes of an agricultural bank. . . . The additional tithe, approximating £76,000, was in fact collected and paid into general revenue.[16]

Nonetheless, British officials in Jerusalem always felt guilty enough to admit to a 'moral obligation, if not legal obligation' to allocate a share of revenue for purposes of agricultural credit.[17] This concern led at an early point to the somewhat spurious contention that the government actually 'continued to carry out this obligation through the system of Government Agricultural Loans made at a low rate of interest'. In fact, the system which was worked out by the military administration with regard to agricultural loans was quite separate from anything to do with

[13] See Norman Bentwich, 'Legal Position Regarding the Ottoman Agricultural Bank', CO 733/27, 504. He advised that: 'The Government of Palestine would appear to be clearly entitled both under the Rules of International Law and the provisions of Article 240 of the Treaty of Sevres to these debts owing to the Bank.'

[14] Minute by G. L. M. Clauson, 27 Feb. 1925, CO 733/110/12721, 232.

[15] Minute sheets, 22 Feb. 1922, CO 733/19, 256.

[16] Chancellor to Passfield, 11 Jan. 1930, CO 733/184/77067, 65–6.

[17] See Norman Bentwich, 'Legal Position Regarding the Ottoman Agricultural Bank', CO 733/27, 510.

the Ottoman Agricultural Bank. During the latter months of 1918, the military administration attempted to deal with the chaos left by the war. The cessation of credit, in particular, was viewed as 'a considerable setback to the agricultural prosperity of the country, and consequently to the development of its revenues'.[18] Given the impoverishment of the people in the summer of 1918, military officials realized that, if taxes were to be collected, the facilitation of credit in cash would be necessary to restore in some degree the condition of agriculture.[19] With meagre resources at their disposal, British military officers tried to confront some of the more urgent cases, particularly in the Jaffa district, by issuing a few short-term loans. In addition, provision was made for the issue of what widely came to be referred to as 'mule loans', the sale on credit of army mules which were no longer serviceable for military purposes but which could, it was thought, still be of use for general agricultural work. Though seemingly well intentioned, the whole endeavour proved futile: 'many of the mules . . . never became acclimatized to their new conditions of life and a number of them died shortly after their purchase by the cultivators.'[20] The tendency to confuse the system of agricultural loans, 1919–23, with the institution of the Ottoman Agricultural Bank may have been due to the need to pacify the Zionist Organization, which objected to the scheme on the grounds that it represented a departure from the status quo which the British had pledged to maintain. When the issue was debated in the House of Lords, the Earl of Crawford responded that the Foreign Office could assure the Zionist Organization that 'the Administration was not introducing new legislation but was operating a Turkish institution under the laws and usages of war'.[21]

None of the initial measures on the part of the military administration came close to meeting the needs and demands of cultivators generally and by 1919 some officials were pressing the urgency of additional credit facilities. As the chief administrator complained, 'loans for a much longer period than was warranted by the political circumstances of a temporary military administration were called for'.[22] In this regard, Major General

---

[18] Money, chief administrator OETA(S), to GHQ, Cairo, 9 May 1919, FO 371/4226/127920.

[19] Money to General Staff, GHQ, Cairo, 9 May 1919, CO 733/48, 45.

[20] Great Britain. Palestine Royal Commission, *Memoranda Prepared by the Government of Palestine*, 45–8.

[21] Quoted in Barbara J. Smith, *The Roots of Separatism in Palestine: British Economic Policy, 1920–1929* (Syracuse, NY: Syracuse University Press, 1993), 113.

[22] Money, chief administrator, to GHQ, Cairo, 9 May 1919, CO 733/48, 45.

Sir W. Lawrence, who actually had previous experience in the provision of credit facilities elsewhere, played a crucial role in the setting up in Palestine of a rather informal arrangement (later presented to the Foreign Office as a fait accompli) between the financial adviser of Occupied Enemy Territory Administration (South) and the Anglo-Egyptian Bank Ltd. (AEB) (later amalgamated in Barclays Bank (Dominion, Colonial & Overseas)) for the widespread grant of agricultural loans in Palestine. In the beginning, it was anticipated that not more than EP 80,000 would actually be required but, in the terms of the agreement dated 18 June 1919, the AEB undertook to advance, as and when required, a sum of EP 500,000 for the issue of loans by the administration, and on its responsibility. The rate of interest charged by the bank was 6 per cent, that by the administration 6 per cent (raised to 9 per cent as a penal measure if instalments fell into arrears)—a rate which, it was noted, reflected the administration of similar loans in India and elsewhere.[23]

By the terms of the agreement between the administration and the cultivator, all mortgages were supposed to be made in general accordance with the Ottoman provisional law for mortgage of immovable property, 2 March 1915.[24] When pressed by the Zionist Commission to defend these arrangements at a time when the land registries were, after all, supposed to be closed, an official with the Palestine government emphasized that 'no question arises of land titles'.[25] It was necessary to spell this out for the Foreign Office since they were almost immediately fielding complaints from the Zionist Commission who expressed the fear that the Anglo-Egyptian Bank would thereby accumulate title to foreclosed mortgages. Rather than basing it on land titles, the system arrived at by British officials divided agricultural loans into two categories: long-term loans, which included loans over EP 60 and were repayable within five years; and short-term loans, loans less than EP 60 and repayable within three years. The number of applications for long-term loans was small, but the applications for short-term loans amounted to several thousand. For the purpose of security, a loan of over EP 20 required a mortgage on immovable property, though 'a mortgage on a share of musha'a land less than one quarter of the whole is rarely accepted'.[26] In practice, this meant that the mortgagor had to produce a certificate signed by the *mukhtar* and

[23] Ibid.
[24] Copy of the exact terms can be found in FO 371/4226/127920, 76–81.
[25] Telegram from general officer in command, Egypt, to Foreign Office, 2 Aug. 1919, FO 371/4225.
[26] 'Report on Agricultural Loans', Mar. 1924, CO 733/70, 399.

two notables stating that he was the owner of the land offered as security and that there were no encumbrances on it. Also, the personal examination of a British officer was necessary to ascertain whether the projected improvement would yield a sufficient return to justify the loan applied for. For a lesser amount, the security of future crops was accepted subject to certain collateral guarantees, for example, the willingness on the part of two 'men of standing' who were able to refund the loan in the event of default by the borrower. Such guarantees were to be certified by a notary public, a cost which, on a loan of less than PP 20, actually consumed an appreciable proportion.[27] These arrangements were designed to be of a temporary character. But they were continued by the civil administration under Samuel, partly because of the guilt felt over absorbing the revenue that was meant for an agricultural bank, and partly because of the fear about the political consequences of discontinuing the loans. By 1923, however, a number of factors contributed to the cancellation of the agricultural loans scheme. It is worth considering these factors in some detail, because they would have an enduring impact on the provision of agricultural credit in general.

By 1923 the question of advances from the Anglo-Egyptian Bank for agricultural loans in Palestine was entangled in the question of appointing official bankers. During the military administration, official banking business was conducted through the AEB, an arrangement that was inherited by the civil administration.[28] In addition to undertaking the agricultural loan advances, the AEB also advanced sums of money to tide the administration over temporary shortages. In return for this, the AEB early on pressed that it should be recognized as the official bankers. In May 1921 the bank threatened to discontinue supplies unless the government undertook to recognize it as official bankers and 'make all financial arrangements for the State through it, or at any rate in consultation with it'.[29] Officials in the Colonial Office understood this demand to refer especially to the flotation of the Palestinian loan, which was being proposed at the time, and to the question of note issue. While there was general acceptance in Palestine and in the Colonial Office of the need for official bankers, and likewise of the AEB's financial strength in the region and suitability for the job, there was deep resentment at being 'held up' by a bank. General satisfaction was at any rate expressed with the Crown Agents

---

[27] 'Report on Agricultural Loans', See also Goadby and Doukhan, *The Land Law of Palestine*, 179.

[28] Minute by Clauson, 23 Oct. 1921, CO 733/6, 220.   [29] Ibid.

carrying out many of the banking functions for Palestine (including the flotation of loans) and Colonial Office officials were reluctant to share the substantial profits involved in the matter of note issue.[30]

It was in this context of worsening relations between the Palestine government and the Anglo-Egyptian Bank that the matter of the EP 500,000 advance for agricultural loans was revisited in April 1922. At issue was the formal undertaking on the part of OETA (South) in 1919 to give the bank what was in effect a guarantee by the British government for repayment of the loans. When the British Treasury (which was never asked for approval of the scheme in the first place) was finally informed of this, they immediately charged that no such guarantee could actually have properly been given without an Act of Parliament. So, as far as the Treasury was concerned, no guarantee existed.[31] The fear widely expressed in London was that there was nothing to prevent the AEB from demanding repayment in full at any time, thus placing the Palestinian government in 'a position of serious embarrassment'.[32] For their part, the AEB responded by refusing to carry on advancing the agricultural loans money to the Palestine government without an imperial guarantee.[33] As no accompanying moves were made to make the AEB Palestine's official bankers, the writing was on the wall for the agricultural loans scheme, 1919–23.

The balance outstanding as of 31 December 1923 amounted to EP 358,062 and was repaid to the bank by the government as regularly as instalments were collected from borrowers.[34] Sums collected were transferred periodically to the bank, and in January 1928 the Palestine government paid the balance outstanding at that date and retained the subsequent collections. This course was dictated by considerations of economy, since the bank charged interest at 6 per cent, whereas their surplus balance was invested in London at an average rate of 4 per cent. Despite the palpable frustration felt in London, the repayment of the loans caused relatively few problems in the end.[35] 'Of the total of LP 576,319 issued by Government as Agricultural loans directly to cultivators in the years 1919–23,' wrote Palestine's attorney general in 1933, '538,108 has already been recovered and it has only been necessary during the period to write off as irrecoverable loans aggregating 18,000.

[30] Telegram from secretary of state to high commissioner, 2 Dec. 1921, CO 733/7, 347.
[31] See minutes in CO 733/61, 132.
[32] Secretary of state for the colonies to Samuel, 24 Aug. 1923, CO 733/48, 341.
[33] Mr Foa to Colonial Office, 10 Apr. 1923, CO 733/61, 132.
[34] Clayton, OAG, to Duke of Devonshire, 17 Aug. 1923, CO 733/48, 222.
[35] Minute sheets, 9 Nov. 1923, CO 733/51, 41.

There is therefore good reason to hope that future loans will be equally recoverable.'[36]

Without lessening the importance of the nagging imperial guarantee issue, it is nonetheless necessary to underline the extent to which this issue conveniently provided the Colonial Office with a timely and desirable foil behind which to hide its deep antagonism to the whole scheme of agricultural loans. When one colonial official described the reason behind halting the issue of agricultural loans as 'owing to the attitude of the Anglo-Egyptian Bank', Clauson noted revealingly in the margin of the minute sheet that their discontinuation 'was regrettable but inevitable'.[37] More than anything, what made cancelling the loans inevitable was the growing anxiety in the Colonial Office at the prospect of the Palestine government being held liable for any irrecoverable losses by the terms of the informal nature of the agreements made by officials in the military administration. Colonial Office officials were worried that Palestine would be faced with too many bad debts to make good to the Anglo-Egyptian Bank, and was thus likely to lose seriously over the long run.[38] This fear can be traced directly to a personal letter sent from the Palestine treasurer to the Colonial Office in December 1922:

I feel somewhat uneasy as regards Agricultural Loans, of which there are some 12,000 accounts. Inadequate security appears to have been taken in the past, and I fear that there may be considerable losses. I doubt very much whether any bank would take over these assets. I am causing the accounts to be thoroughly investigated with a view to submitting a full report. It would be helpful if you called for a report from me. In my annual financial report, I stated that the arrears approximated E.P. 40,000. At the end of October they amounted to E.P. 62,991.[39]

The Colonial Office was horrified. In a stern dispatch to the high commissioner, the situation was described as 'exceedingly serious' and they demanded 'to see a substantial improvement in regard to these loans'.[40] The previous month, the Palestine government had sent a breakdown of collections, district by district, and the Colonial Office proposed that disciplinary measures be taken against the local officials where collections were slow; where collections were good, it was proposed that the officials

---

[36] Trusted, officer administering the government, to Cunliffe-Lister, 25 May 1933, CO 733/242/17448, 62–4.

[37] Minute sheets, 8 Feb. 1924, CO 733/64, 442.

[38] Minute sheets on 'Estimates', 2 May 1924, CO 733/68, 43.

[39] Davis to Vernon, 15 Dec. 1922, CO 733/38, 278.

[40] Devonshire to Palestine, 19 Sept. 1923, CO 733/48, 228.

responsible should be commended. Furthermore, the Colonial Office asked that the district revenue inspectors 'be warned of their responsibilities in this matter'.[41] In response, Palestine confirmed that no more loans would be issued, and assured the secretary of state that priority would be placed on the collection of arrears and that additional collectors would be appointed, during and just after the harvest time, to expedite recovery.[42]

In October, Samuel set up a committee to consider fully the question of agricultural loans. The written report that emerged described a number of the very features which the Colonial Office had found particularly unattractive and concluded that most of the problems attached to the issuing of loans were due to the lack of subsequent control.[43] It was demonstrated that the loans were frequently misapplied, the money either being spent on unproductive measures (thereby only increasing the individual's indebtedness) or being lent out again at exorbitant rates (thereby increasing others' indebtedness, while at the same time cheating the government). Moreover, to recover the sums which were due, the Palestine government's only recourse was to go to the courts, who could then direct the execution officer to seize the property. But this caused a great many problems, among them: the delay this entailed; the fact that, as one official pointed out, 'if loans are repaid, tithe will not be paid';[44] and, perhaps of greatest concern, the anger felt by cultivators at being foreclosed on by the government. Not surprisingly, therefore, the report found that 'in practice, partly through leniency, partly owing to the vast amount of clerical work involved, partly owing to the paucity of execution officers, legal seizure has comparatively rarely been made. Consequently large amounts are due from many borrowers.'[45] The committee expressed the view that the sheer logistics of administering the agricultural loans were worthy of a special department. There were so many details to be supervised, and so many possibilities of fraud, that ordinary administrative officials could not exercise adequate control. The committee was unanimous in recommending the establishment of a new agricultural bank, but it was divided as to whether to continue the system of agricultural loans. The majority held that agricultural loans must continue until such a bank was set up, arguing that

[41] Ibid.
[42] Clayton, officer administering the government, to secretary of state, 3 July 1924, CO 733/70, 392.
[43] 'Report on Agricultural Loans', Mar. 1924, CO 733/70, 399.
[44] Minute by Keith-Roach, 3 July 1923, CO 733/70, 388.
[45] 'Report on Agricultural Loans', Mar. 1924, CO 733/70, 399.

as Palestine was an agricultural country and its prosperity depended almost entirely on agriculture, it was essential at all costs to render financial assistance to the cultivator. They further held that, though many borrowers had doubtless misapplied the loans granted to them, a great many others had made great use of them. In any case only a small section of the population had as yet benefited by Agricultural Loans and a large proportion still needed the benefit derived from them.[46]

The Colonial Office was quick to respond. 'It seems to me', minuted Clauson, 'that the report gives sound reasons for discontinuing the system of Government loans.'[47] Keith-Roach, temporarily seconded to the Colonial Office, agreed: 'the total arrears are now 136,000 . . . and I doubt very much whether more than half will be recovered during the next five years. . . . I submit now that we should definitely inform the OAG that we can, in no circumstances, allow any additional loans of this nature.'[48] Despite the fact that a majority of the committee had in fact voted for its continuation, it was understood in London that 'the weight of the committee' (described as such because, while constituting a minority of committee members, it included key British officials like the treasurer)[49] called for their immediate cessation. The Colonial Office felt that there was enough in the report to confirm their deeply held belief that problems of overall control were inherent in any system of agricultural credit issued by the Palestine government.

Accordingly, the secretary of state informed high commissioner Samuel that

I have concluded with regret from the report of the committee appointed to investigate this question that the control of short term loans has proved quite ineffective and that the money borrowed has been, to a large extent, utilized for purposes other than those for which it was lent. In these circumstances I am quite unable to agree to the grant of any further loans of this nature and must again urge that every possible endeavour should be made to recover arrears and to discharge the Palestine Govt. liability to the Anglo-Egyptian Bank as soon as possible. Moreover, as at present advised, I am not disposed favourably to view any proposal for government participation in future in a scheme for agricultural loans in Palestine even after the present scheme is wound up.[50]

[46] 'Report on Agricultural Loans', Mar. 1924, CO 733/70, 399.
[47] Minute by Clauson, July 1923, CO 733/70, 388.
[48] Minute by Keith-Roach, July 1923, CO 733/70, 388.
[49] Minute sheets, 9 Nov. 1923, CO 733/51, 41.
[50] Thomas to Samuel, 7 Aug. 1924, CO 733/70, 431.

The agricultural bank was doomed—'dead as mutton', minuted one Colonial Office official.[51] Clearly though there was much greater support for a bank in Jerusalem than in London. Not privy to Colonial Office minute sheets, Samuel in particular was eager to form an official credit bank, particularly in the wake of cancelling the agricultural loans scheme. He supported the decision to discontinue the agricultural loan scheme, but was strongly in favour of an agricultural bank being established, and it is possible that he thought winding up the loans scheme would in fact provide the necessary impetus for the establishment of an official credit bank. At least, such was the idea planted by the minority report of the agricultural loans committee: 'if the Government once took the decisive step of discontinuing the issue of loans, the need for an Agricultural Bank would become so pressing that still further efforts would be concentrated on securing the speedy establishment of such a Bank.'[52] On the one hand, Samuel was anxious about 'what injury this withdrawal of capital must cause to the agriculture of the country, already in a state of severe depression'.[53] On the other hand, he was concerned about the political fallout from the decision to halt the issue of loans: 'it will be recognised also how serious a political effect is likely to follow when the villagers realize that one of the very few tangible benefits that have resulted from the British occupation is being withdrawn.'

Samuel placed a great deal of faith in the possibility of attaching the question of establishing an agricultural bank to the concurrent matter of raising a loan for the Palestine government.[54] In September 1924, Samuel went so far as to append the heading 'land bank' to the newly revised loan schedule,[55] but the Colonial Office was not receptive. Facing enough difficulty in trying to convince the British government of the merit of a loan for Palestine in the first place, the Colonial Office was not interested in muddying the waters by introducing Samuel's idea of a state-sponsored credit bank. Clauson dismissed the idea from the start: 'The claim has in my opinion an absolute posteriority after all other items in the loan schedule.'[56] Wariness over the extra funds involved was obviously a major factor in dismissing the idea, but even had the funds been found it is not

---

[51] Minute by Keith-Roach, 3 July 1923, CO 733/70, 388.
[52] 'Report on Agricultural Loans', Mar. 1924, CO 733/70, 399.
[53] Samuel to Colonial Office, 8 Feb. 1924, CO 733/64, 474.
[54] Samuel to Duke of Devonshire, 9 Nov. 1923, CO 733/51, 45.
[55] See 'Summary: Loan Statement at 30 Sept. 1924'. An amount of PP 146,250 was so attributed to the 'Land Bank'. See 'Estimates' in CO 733/87, 141.
[56] Minute sheets, 8 Feb. 1924, CO 733/64, 442.

likely that the Colonial Office would have approved. There was an over-riding fear that public officials would not be able to run a bank profitably due to the public pressure that would be exerted should the bank feel it needed to foreclose on people during a recession. As Keith-Roach observed, 'I do not see how Government can start one as it always looks bad for a Government to "sell up" people.'[57] There was little wavering from the view that the problems associated with the issuing of agricultural credit in any form could only be overcome by an official, private bank with a technically qualified staff operating on commercial lines.

Discussions over the agricultural loans issue left a reserve of antagon-ism in the Colonial Office. As one official summed up the situation, 'it is time that we got clear of this horrible entanglement, one of our last heritages from the bad old times'.[58] Their strong antipathy for any such scheme to be organized by public officials would plague such efforts for at least ten years. For example, when the establishment of an agricultural bank was again proposed at the end of the decade, the concern expressed in the Colonial Office was much the same. A committee appointed by high commissioner Chancellor to reconsider an agricultural bank sub-mitted a proposal in 1930 for its establishment on the basis of a minimum capital investment of PP 500,000, which they suggested might be raised by means of a loan.[59] After brief consideration in the Colonial Office, the high commissioner was immediately informed that the committee's recommendations were unacceptable. On the one hand, it was pointed out that there were problems associated with funding: the terms and character of the mandate (and also of the uncertainty due to the recent disturbances) made it difficult for Palestine to get the required capital on the London financial markets at a rate which would guarantee the success of the bank. Given the critical financial situation in Palestine at this time there was also mounting concern regarding the strict financial control of the Treasury. As there was absolutely no prospect of the Palestine government furnish-ing capital without recourse to a loan, the committee's recommendations were rejected.

On the other hand, funding concerns did not represent the whole picture in 1930 any more than they did in 1923. As one official elaborated, 'that is perhaps a temporary stumbling block but there are also the general economic objections' which surrounded the recommendation that the

[57] Minute by Keith-Roach, July 1924, CO 733/70, 388.
[58] Minute sheets, 9 Nov. 1923, CO 733/51, 41.
[59] See letter from Chancellor to Passfield, 11 Jan. 1930, CO 733/184/77067.

agricultural bank be financed, controlled, and administered by the government.[60] A memo that circulated in the Colonial Office at this time described these objections in the following terms:

> Experience elsewhere has shown that it is very difficult for a Government to recover sums so advanced. Political pressure on Government to increase advances and be lenient about security and repayment is always brought to bear eventually. At times of agricultural crisis when Government would be most in need of funds it might be impossible to recover principal or interest. Foreclosure on mortgages would lead to further slump in values. Colony would then be left to meet debt charges from general revenue.[61]

It was also pointed out that in the case of Palestine in particular government would always be exposed to charges of showing favour to the Arabs or to the Jews in its conduct of the bank's operations.

2. LOANS ISSUED AFTER 1927

In 1927, high commissioner Lord Plumer was able to obtain the sanction of the secretary of state to make some financial advances to cultivators. So severe was the drought in the Beersheba sub-district that the consequent failure of crops necessitated government help, particularly with regard to the purchase of seed for the next year's harvest and for the replacement of livestock. Continued economic problems from 1928 to 1936 made it 'urgently necessary'[62] for the Palestine government to issue loans annually, as it was feared that without such assistance Palestinian cultivators would be forced either to obtain the credit at usurious rates of interest charged by local moneylenders or, worse from the point of view of the Palestine Treasury, leave their land fallow. The loans thereby issued by government were lent at 5 per cent, and were characterized by two key features. First, very few exceeded PP 10: in fact, when Chancellor asked the secretary of state for approval in 1930 to make a sum of PP 35,000 available that year for short-term loans, he described it as a condition of their distribution that 'no individual advance [was] to exceed 15 [pounds]'.[63] Second, the

[60] Minute sheet, Jan. 1930, CO 733/184/77067, 4.

[61] Secretary of state Amery's telegram, 30 Nov. 1928. Quoted on Colonial Office minute sheets in CO 733/184/77067, 4–5.

[62] Chancellor to Passfield, 21 June 1930, CO 733/192/7/77292.

[63] Telegram from Chancellor to secretary of state for colonies, 10 Nov. 1930, CO 733/192/7/77292.

majority of the loans issued were recoverable in two equal annual instalments immediately following the harvests: in other words, loans were essentially issued to cultivators as short-term credit made necessary as a consequence of drought, locust, field mice, or other agricultural disasters, thus enabling cultivation in the coming season.[64] Chancellor's telegram, which related to the cultivation of the 1930 winter crops, was dated 10 November 1930 and concluded by urging: 'I request your approval and should be grateful for earliest possible reply since to be of full use, loans should be in hands of cultivators by 15th November.'[65]

In addition to government help, short-term credit to cultivators was supplied by this time by Barclays Bank (DC&O) in the northern district of Palestine, but it did not undertake the business of a mortgage bank and so did not make any long-term loans.[66] It appears that many of the loans were made to groups of villagers, enabling Barclays to take advantage of traditional methods of guarantee and repayment such as 'kefala mutasalsila', the method utilized in the payment of tithes to the Ottoman government.[67] In 1932, following the success of these arrangements, the Palestine government negotiated with the bank to extend their experiment with short-term loans throughout the whole of Palestine. In return, the bank required assistance in two ways. First, it was given a grant of PP 500 per annum for a period of three years in respect of each branch opened: under such arrangements, further branches were opened at Hebron and Gaza, while the imminent opening of a new branch at Ramle was put into abeyance by the 1936 disturbances. Secondly, government obliged by enacting an ordinance, based on similar legislation elsewhere in the empire,[68] entitled the short-term crop loans (security) ordinance, which strengthened the security offered by giving the bank a lien on crops. Under the provisions of the ordinance, the bank could take a charge on the crops of a borrower whether or not the crop was in existence at the time the charge was created. The ordinance also provided for close liaison between district officers and the bank in a number of actions: searching registers for other charges on a property; registering the bank's charge; and administering penalties against the fraudulent disposition of the crop

[64] Chancellor to Passfield, 28 June 1930, CO 733/192/7/77292.
[65] Telegram from Chancellor to secretary of state, 10 Nov. 1930, CO 733/192/7/77292, 30.
[66] Chancellor to Passfield, 11 June 1930, CO 733/184/77067.
[67] See Lowick, 'Cooperative Pamphlet No. 1: The Co-operative Organisation of the Arab Population of Palestine', issued by the Registrar of Co-operative Societies (Jerusalem, Apr. 1933), CO 733/233/17264, 22. Also ISA, Attorney General's Office, 12/21.
[68] See comparative tables in CO 733/184/77067.

so charged. By 1935, the year prior to widespread disturbance bringing to a halt most credit operations, the amount issued in loans by Barclays to Palestine cultivators approximated PP 230,000, repayable in instalments which fell due at dates varying according to harvest schedules.

The rate at which Barclays issued seasonal credit was a matter of some concern to the Palestine government. By the 1930s, British officials were placing a high priority on the success of cooperative credit societies. Officials wanted Barclays to make a formal undertaking to promote the cooperative movement in Palestine, and not compete with it. These concerns resulted in a number of practical measures: the bank could not give any short-term loans in any village where a cooperative credit society existed, or was about to be established; the bank charged individual borrowers interest at the same rate as that charged by cooperative societies to their members, that is 9 per cent; and, finally, the bank adopted a rate of 6 per cent for loans issued to the societies (who would utilize the difference to cover whatever expenses they incurred). Despite this, advocates of cooperatives remained concerned that the bank would find short-term lending a profitable business and be reluctant to substitute a society, which borrowed at a slightly lower rate and worked in a more independent manner, for village groups who paid a higher rate and were required to submit detailed explanations as to exactly how money would be spent.

3. COOPERATIVE CREDIT SOCIETIES

The question of agricultural credit was dramatically affected by the events of 1929. By attributing the causes of the riots to the growing displacement of cultivators from their holdings, the Shaw Commission focused attention on the political repercussions of landlessness. In elaborating on this, the commission observed that intensive cultivation required the sort of capital expenditure which no ordinary cultivator could afford:

It is, therefore, a matter of consideration whether the Government should not provide for the needs of the poorer people in this respect either by granting them loans or by reviving the Agricultural Bank or by some other means through which the peasant cultivator can be enabled to borrow money at a reasonable rate of interest for the development of his property. . . . The reconstitution of the Agricultural Bank would have the further advantage that it would in some measure remove a grievance which was put forward to us by the Arabs during our enquiry.[69]

[69] Great Britain, *Report of the Commission on the Palestine Disturbances of August, 1929* (London: HMSO, 1930), 122.

The report of the Shaw Commission reached the Colonial Office in March 1930, and was taken very seriously. The Colonial Office was understandably concerned about the process of peasant dispossession outlined in it. However, having just dismissed the recommendations of the committee appointed by high commissioner Chancellor to consider the question of establishing an agricultural bank, the Colonial Office was not interested in providing in this way for the needs of poorer cultivators who required credit facilities to improve methods of farming. Instead, it looked to the possibility of popularizing the idea of the cooperative society. Building a cooperative movement was first raised by the Johnson-Crosbie Commission, which warned that the economic situation of the farmer called for immediate relief.[70] The Johnson-Crosbie Report was cautious in its recommendations, particularly with regard to the provision of credit facilities, 'since it has been shown that the average farmer is hardly in a position to repay any loan from net profits'. The report continued, 'we recommend therefore that Government should provide credit facilities, but that loans should normally be given through the medium of a village group of a cooperative nature, which would be responsible for the issue, control and repayment of the loans'.[71] A further incentive for spreading the cooperative idea throughout Palestine was the success of its extension amongst the Jewish population. When the 1933 cooperative societies amendment ordinance was passed, it was based largely on the Palestine societies cooperative societies ordinance (which itself was based in many respects on the 1912 Indian cooperative societies Act) with one major difference: it called for an active and peripatetic registrar who would take a considerable part in the organization of societies, and subsequently in their guidance and inspection. While the Jewish societies were considered able enough to organize cooperative societies the Arabs 'require a trained Registrar as their leader, and in certain measure their controller, since they are unfamiliar with the movement and need education in it'.[72] In July 1930, Mr C. F. Strickland, formerly of the Indian Civil Service, was sent out to advise the Palestine government on the general subject of cooperative institutions, and in particular cooperative

---

[70] Report of Committee on the Economic Conditions of Agriculturalists and the Fiscal Measures of Government in Relation Thereto (Johnson-Crosbie Report) (Jerusalem, 1930), CO 733/185/77072.

[71] Ibid., para. 82.

[72] See Strickland, 'Memorandum on the Cooperative Societies Ordinance', CO 733/233/17264/1, 84.

credit societies.[73] His conclusions made a huge impact on the whole question of agricultural credit in Palestine.

Strickland's report was received in August. Its main feature—and one that probably more than anything endeared the report to officials in London—was the argument that the establishment of an agricultural bank in Palestine was undesirable. Strickland confirmed the fears of the Colonial Office that an agricultural bank supported by a government guarantee would be obstructed from taking such stringent measures as ordering a foreclosure. Borrowers throughout the country would believe that pressure or leniency by the bank was exercised at the will of British officials. Even if private capital was provided, Strickland contended that 'it was impossible that a board of commercial men could exercise that continuous supervision, or possess that detailed knowledge, which the temperament of the Arab borrower rendered desirable'.[74] The judgements Strickland arrived at about the 'character' of the Arab farmer, and in particular its 'instability', were central to his argument in favour of cooperative societies generally, an idea which came to include such things as societies for 'social and moral purposes' as well as rural credit societies.[75] 'The difficulty', wrote Strickland, 'will be the Arab character':

The first essential therefore for the organisation of the Arab fellah is to provide him with current resources through a cooperative credit society (leaving the clearance of his major debt to a later time), to form his character slowly in such a society during a term of years, and to train him to watch his expenditure and submit it to the criticism of his fellow members, to be punctual in payment, and to be loyal to his society rather than to those creditors who are the cause of his afflictions. It *must* be realised that it will not be possible to achieve this through an Agricultural Bank.[76]

And later,

Whatever weakness there may be in his character could be corrected if he were dealing in short term credit in a cooperative society under the supervision of his fellows, but long-term loans from a mortgage institution bring him under no such supervision, and it is not unlikely that he will be an unsatisfactory client.[77]

[73] 'Report by Mr. C. F. Strickland of the Indian Civil Service on the Possibility of Introducing a System of Agricultural Cooperation in Palestine' (Strickland Report) (Jerusalem, 1930).

[74] Ibid. 35.

[75] See 'Cooperative Pamphlet No. 1: The Co-operative Organisation of the Arab Population of Palestine', issued by the Registrar of Co-operative Societies (Jerusalem, Apr. 1933), CO 733/233/17264, 21.

[76] Strickland Report, 4–5.

[77] Ibid. 33.

In addition to all this, Strickland argued that an agricultural bank simply was not necessary. Although Strickland accepted that the one area where a bank would probably be preferable to a cooperative society was in the provision of long-term loans ('cooperative credit societies were not suitable agencies for this purpose'), he reasoned, in a somewhat tautological way, that 'long term credit is seldom justified'.[78]

Strickland was supported by Sir John Hope-Simpson who was at this same time continuing his investigations (as recommended by the Shaw Commission) into improving the methods of cultivation: 'The need is desperately urgent. The fellah population is so tightly bound in debt that no credit whatever is available to enable that development of agriculture which is so essential for progress . . . There is nothing but cooperation that will save him from his present depression.'[79] His conclusions included the admonition that 'The constitution of Co-operative Credit Societies among the fellahin is an essential preliminary to their advancement.'[80] Together, Hope-Simpson and Strickland presented an impressive case to officials in the Colonial Office who, by this point, were easily persuaded anyway. The Colonial Office was eager to be seen to be making some progress on the credit front, particularly as it began preparations for a White Paper.[81] What made the cooperative idea all the more attractive in London was that it did not need to be, in fact was not supposed to be, overly ambitious. Palestine's financial position at the time was increasingly seen as precarious. The necessity for a remission of tithes that year was one bad sign, and officials in London saw little margin for development work.[82] The timing was particularly awkward considering that the O'Donnell Commission, which was set the task of lowering expenditures through administrative down-sizing, was at that very time visiting Palestine. The Colonial Office knew that a great deal of resistance would be encountered from the Treasury for any extra expenditure, and that they needed to trim plans accordingly.

Developing a cooperative credit system was not expected to demand considerable funds. There was concern that some of Strickland's schemes were likely to be too expensive, for example his proposal for a government broadcasting station, but a step-by-step approach to the setting up of

---

[78] Strickland Report, 32.
[79] Sir John Hope-Simpson, *Palestine. Report on Immigration, Land Settlement and Development,* Cmd. 3686 (London: HMSO, 1930).
[80] Ibid. 150.
[81] See memorandum entitled 'Future Policy', CO 733/193/2/77336.
[82] Treasury to Williams, Colonial Office, 19 May 1932. CO 733/223/97253, 15.

cooperative institutions was palatable. In fact, as one Colonial Office official minuted, efforts to hurry the process with extra funds should properly be avoided:

> it is commonplace that cooperation is a plant of very slow growth. It is equally certain, as the result of experience in various countries, that attempts to hasten that growth usually fail; in the end, they do more harm than good. The end to aim at is steady—even if slow—organic growth. Only in that way can a solid foundation be laid. . . . Unless and until that is done, it is most improbable that advances on any considerable scale can be usefully or safely made . . . It seems to me that a good deal of rather humdrum organising work will have to be done before conditions are ripe for any large scheme.[83]

Lowick, appointed registrar for cooperative societies, underlined the need for caution in the initial formation of credit societies, and suggested that 'these societies will only be founded in such villages, where after instruction of the villagers by the Registrar and the staff and the making of careful enquiries regarding the position of the founders, there appears to be a fair prospect of the successful development of a society'.[84] Obviously some money would have to be available to start such societies, but since the amount required was not expected to be large, for a considerable time the feeling was that it could be found initially from the approximately PP 21,000 made available from the liquidation of the Ottoman Agricultural Bank.

Strickland's proposals for establishing cooperative societies dominated discussion around the provision of credit in the early 1930s. In addition to steps taken to ensure that the extension of Barclays credit facilities did not interfere or compete with the growth of cooperative societies, Strickland was also concerned about the impact of the newly instituted department of development. In October 1930 Sir John Hope-Simpson's report was published, as well as the White Paper (Cmd. 3692) which adopted Hope-Simpson's proposals for the government initiation of a large-scale development scheme aimed at increasing the amount of land available for new settlement. The plan proposed by Hope-Simpson envisioned that excess land occupied by Arabs would be expropriated by government with compensation and would then be developed for intensive cultivation. By this means, it was believed, land might be found in the first place for the Arabs who had been displaced by Jewish

---

[83] Minute by Hall, 25 Feb. 1930, CO 733/184/77067.
[84] Lowick, 'Cooperative Pamphlet No. 1: The Cooperative Organisation of the Arab Population of Palestine', CO 733/233/17264, 22.

settlement, and later for further Jewish settlement. In 1931, Lewis French was appointed director of development, for the purpose of working out the details of the proposed development scheme. Strickland reacted with alarm when he heard that the director of development was preparing to issue loans on long-term credit in regard to settlement schemes. Strickland had a personal meeting with the Colonial Office adviser on agricultural issues, J. A. Stockdale, in which he warned that 'if it did this before the cultivators had been trained in short term credit through co-operative societies, the government would run the risk of losing its money'. Strickland urged the priority of cooperative credit schemes in any policy of development, saying that his experience in the Punjab had convinced him that 'the best settlers under colonization schemes were those who had shown their worth in cooperative credit societies and had, through such societies, learned the meaning of credit and the necessity for the proper and economical use of money for development purposes'.[85]

So prominent and dominating a place had Strickland assured for the cooperative idea in general policy regarding credit that all other ideas were at risk. In this context, it is difficult to say whether Strickland's proposals were successful or not. For its part, the Peel Commission was uncharacteristically positive, noting in 1936 that 'between 1933 and 1935 more than 200 Arab villages had been initiated in co-operative practice'.[86] The government memorandum that had been submitted to it was even more glowing:

the manner in which co-operation has been taking root in Arab villages has justified the expectations formed. The villages have not been slow in realising its advantages and possibilities and the individual members have shown much loyalty and ample intelligence in the management of their societies ... Arab public opinion has welcomed Government initiative in this direction, and the Press has occasionally reported favourably on the efforts of the Registrar and his staff.[87]

What all this actually meant on the ground is less clear. But one can note that the 1937 report to the League of Nations reported only 120 societies that year, issuing PP 71,790 in loans made possible by advances from Barclays amounting to PP 62,272. Two analysts were led in 1938 to conclude, on the basis of information available to them, that 'it is clear ... that the Arab credit societies are still small'.[88]

    [85] Minute by Stockdale, 6 July 1931, CO 733/199/87064.

    [86] Great Britain. Palestine Royal Commission, *Report* (London: HMSO, 1937), 277.

    [87] Great Britain. Palestine Royal Commission, *Memoranda Prepared by the Government of Palestine*, 49.

    [88] George Hakim and M. Y. El-Hussayni, 'Monetary and Banking System', in Sa'id Himadeh (ed.), *Economic Organisation of Palestine* (Beirut: American Press, 1938).

4. AGRICULTURAL MORTGAGE COMPANY

The early 1930s was the formative period for the establishment finally, after all the abortive attempts in the 1920s, of an agricultural bank. However, a number of factors specific to this post-1930 period ensured that the bank, created in 1935 and known as the agricultural mortgage bank, ended up being a much more circumscribed and limited venture than one might expect after almost twenty years of colonial land policies in Palestine.

In 1933 proposals were on the table for a new government-guaranteed loan. The proposed loan was originally meant to be devoted to urgent public works of a renumerative nature but, given the evident level of disappointment which both the Jewish and Arab communities felt with the British administration at this point, it was deemed necessary to take political considerations into account. 'We must have capital,' acknowledged one Colonial Office official in 1933 who continued, 'and if you raise a loan for dull things like drains and water supplies and public works and duller things like married quarters, it seems to me you MUST, for political reasons, include in it something a little more positively developmental.'[89] In particular, concern was had for Jewish claims for parity in any guaranteed loan and also Jewish pressure for an agricultural bank to be established along their own lines. Various schemes previously presented had been rejected because they showed far too great a preference for the sole interests of the Jewish community.[90] One such scheme was described by a Colonial Office official in 1932 in the following terms:

As I understand the proposal, it is that the Government, hand in hand with the Jewish Agency, should compulsorily acquire all but the minimum homestead area of an Arab owner or occupancy tenant, paying him compensation, and at the same time telling him that, if he will use the compensation money for improving the homestead area which is left to him, he will be able to obtain an advance from a government controlled Agricultural Bank. This is surely unthinkable. It will no doubt be difficult enough to overcome Arab opposition to the measures of land expropriation involved in the Hope-Simpson/French Development Scheme, although such measures would be designed in the first place, at any rate, to provide land for 'displaced' Arabs. One can imagine the outcry that would be

---

[89] Minute sheets, CO 733/244/17464.
[90] See, in particular, Lewis French, 'Supplementary Report on Agricultural Development and Land Settlement in Palestine', paras. 54–60, 20 Apr. 1932, CO 733/214/97049.

aroused at the mere suggestion that the Government should combine with the Jewish Agency in a scheme for a redistribution of Arab holdings for the purpose of accommodating more Jewish settlers.[91]

What was decided in 1933 was that provision would be made in the loan schedule for government assistance with the formation of an agricultural mortgage company, then being discussed by a group of banking interests led by Sir Robert Waly Cohen.[92] Cohen's group had found it impossible to raise a sufficient amount of capital without a contribution from the Palestine government of PP 100,000 (later raised to PP 150,000) to constitute a guarantee fund as an additional security to bondholders.[93] In order for the scheme to be a financial success, the issue of bonds at no more than 4 per cent or 5 per cent was essential if the rate of interest to borrowers from the company was to be kept down to 8 per cent. After almost twenty years of dealing with credit problems in Palestine, British officials at last appreciated this reality. As one official put it, 'the choice then is between giving the guarantee and dropping the business'.[94] The future success of the bank had by now become too politically important in the context of the times for it to be dropped. The secretary of state had put his own personal support behind the scheme: without it, Treasury approval would not have been forthcoming, their objection to government participation in schemes being well known: 'My Lords do not wish to question the desirability of an agricultural credit institution in Palestine. As, however, the scheme now under consideration is expected to be a sound commercial proposition, they are not satisfied as to the necessity for Government subscription to the capital of the institution.'[95]

The political attractiveness of the agricultural mortgage bank lay in the fact that the Palestine government could conciliate the Jewish community through a scheme of financial support which appeared to be open equally to both Arabs and Jews.[96] In defending the allocation in the loan schedule, officials in the Colonial Office spoke of the 'political advantages' in supporting Jewish agricultural credit 'in a way which is not exclusively for Jewish benefit on the face of it'. Other officials agreed, one noting that 'on the "political" side, it would cover both Jews and

[91] Minute by Downie, 12 Dec. 1932, CO 733/223/97248.
[92] Roza El-Eini, 'The Agricultural Mortgage Bank in Palestine: The Controversy over its Establishment', *Middle Eastern Studies*, 33/4 (1997).
[93] Minute sheets, CO 733/242/17440.
[94] Minute by Campbell, 24 July 1933, CO 733/242/17448.
[95] Treasury to Colonial Office, 4 July 1933, CO 733/242/17448, 57.
[96] Minute sheets, CO 733/242/17448.

Arabs:—which would have obvious advantages'.[97] Despite it being widely accepted that the establishment of the agricultural mortgage company was a measure which overwhelmingly supported the Jewish community, and thus was not meant to deal with credit problems in Palestine generally, the potential for conflict between the operations of the bank and the newly enacted protection of cultivators ordinance, 1933, generated a great deal of discussion which also would be useful to explore.

The official policy that emerged in the wake of the 1929 riots leaned heavily towards attaching the cultivator (particularly the tenant) to the land. A new ordinance was passed in 1933 aimed at securing the tenant's subsistence upon the land, that is 'to enable the statutory tenant to maintain his customary means of livelihood'. To achieve this, it was legislated that 'no person lawfully occupying a subsistence area shall be ejected therefore save upon the recommendation of a Board with the approval of the High Commissioner'. Participants in the agricultural mortgage company (whose own interests in the Jewish national home were apparent) were highly critical of the ordinance. Their concern was with the creation of a new class of statutory tenants who were to be protected from eviction. For the bank, the chief problem that arose was that it was difficult to ascertain what tenancy rights existed at the time of the creation of a mortgage on a given property, as leases for three years or less were not subject to registration in Palestine. Since landlords might lease land for nominal annual cash rent (which would not meet payments of annual interest or loan instalments in event of landlord's default) in addition to other considerations (which might not be available to the bank), it was very difficult to assess the value of future tenancy rights for the purpose of estimating security for loans. Almost all tenancies for land cultivated with ground crops provided for payment of rent in cash and kind, or in services rendered, or in kind only. Either way, the proportion of cash was often small, and the rent thus a variable amount from year to year according to the yield and the percentage of the crop payable. Adding to the difficulty was that few tenancy agreements were thought to be put down in writing. The accumulated effect of all this was to diminish the security of the mortgage afforded by the property. As one lawyer who advised the company on this matter concluded, 'It seems to me clear that all these factors must considerably depreciate the value of the land, and it will become a problem whether land on which there are known to be a number of squatters

[97] Ibid.

is readily realisable at all.'[98] The concerns of the banking interests were similarly well expressed by Lord Lugard, at the 1934 Permanent Mandates Commission. Lugard asked if the Palestine government

did not fear that the negotiations for the Agricultural Mortgage Bank might be prejudiced by the new Protection of Cultivators Ordinance, which seemed to create statutory rights for squatters. Banks would be unwilling to advance money on the mortgage of land if they had continually to watch such rights were not being created.[99]

But British officials in Jerusalem and in London were unwilling to consider the possibility of weakening the ordinance, which had by then taken on great political, as well as practical, importance of its own, leading secretary of state Cunliffe-Lister, when hearing of the concerns of the bank, to note firmly, 'I am certainly not going to monkey around with the Cultivators Ordinance.'[100] It needs to be noted that, in many ways, the establishment of the agricultural mortgage company was considered as much a political problem as it was a solution. From the start, there was a great deal of suspicion (particularly in the context of previous banking proposals) of the company's motives in expressing the concern it did over the creation of statutory tenancy rights. When, for example, a representative of the company suggested in 1933 that, in the event of any rights not being registered, the tenant should not have the benefit of the protection of cultivators ordinance, the high commissioner was quick to dismiss any such alternative. In response, the high commissioner argued that, on the one hand, the machinery did not exist to make it possible to register leases of one year's duration, many of the leases being oral in nature with nothing written at all. On the other hand, even if the machinery did exist, the possibility, even likelihood, that many cultivators, for reasons of ignorance or inconvenience, would not make use of it would mean that they would lose their rights under the ordinance, and in the event of foreclosure on mortgage they could be evicted. But the problem of finding the machinery for the registration of such agreements was the least of the high commissioner's concerns: 'I am convinced that any further relaxation of Protection of Cultivators Ordinance would cause Company . . . to become an unwilling instrument for dispossession of Arabs.'[101] The high commissioner

[98] Letter from Horowitz, in CO 733/262/37448/Part 1.
[99] Minutes from Permanent Mandates Commission meeting, 1934. CO 733/257/37341.
[100] Minute sheets, CO 733/262/37448.
[101] ISA Attorney General's Office (RG 3)/3/5. See also CO 733/262/37448.

thought that prudence alone should dictate that loans be made on the assumption that property mortgaged might be subject to tenancy rights.[102]

If this meant far fewer mortgages, fine. The real fear of the Palestine government (which does not appear to have been revealed to the participants of the company) was that 'the Jewish interests in the Agricultural Bank will have, or will develop, sufficient influence over the policy of the Company to result in its being used as a weapon for disencumbering land of potential statutory tenants, thus defeating the objects of the Protection of Cultivators Ordinance'.[103] As the high commissioner pointed out, since Jewish land-purchasing agencies were alone in a position to pay the highest prices for unencumbered land so auctioned, it was probable that any land put up for auction by the agricultural mortgage bank would be acquired by them 'and the Company would thus in effect become an agency for transferring Arab lands to Jews, and for increasing the number of landless Arabs'.[104]

Meanwhile, steps were also being taken to allocate loan funds directly in support of the Arab community. In addition to the original PP 100,000 (later raised to PP 150,000) for the agricultural mortgage bank, provision was made in the loan schedule for PP 50,000 for the issue of loans for long-term development in the hills. The loans were to be issued directly by government officials (that is, by a local board consisting of the director of agriculture, the director of development, and an assistant treasurer), and it was decided not to demand only immovable property as security. The amount was, as high commissioner Sir Arthur Grenfell Wauchope himself admitted, 'derisory',[105] but it was necessitated, in the interest of parity, once an assessment was made of who would benefit from the bank. That is to say, the PP 100,000 allocated to the agricultural mortgage bank was considered as constituting PP 75,000 in support of the Jewish community, and PP 25,000 in support of the Arab community: the PP 50,000 for 'hill loans', as they became known, made up the difference to achieve the much sought after parity in the schedule of the government-guaranteed loan (i.e., in effect each group to receive PP 75,000).

In many ways, the 'hill loans' were a return to the system of credit provision introduced by the OETA, but on a much smaller scale. Anticipating British Treasury criticism, O. G. R. Williams noted that 'we may

---

[102] The government was, however, willing to establish a debenture guarantee fund from which losses on account of problems arising from the protection of cultivators ordinance might be recouped.

[103] Minute by Downie, 6 Mar. 1935, CO 733/282/75248.

[104] High Commissioner to Cunliffe-Lister, 9 June 1934, CO 733/262/37448.

[105] Wauchope to Sir William Ormsby Gore, 26 Jan. 1937, CO 733/330/75052.

have some difficulty in convincing them [the Treasury] about this one, the main point of which is that it should not be regarded as a purely business proposition, but to some extent as philanthropic'.[106] Stockdale agreed. In what amounts to a rather damning indictment of British attempts to provide credit since the beginning of their rule almost twenty years earlier, he wrote in 1935 that

[t]here is no doubt that the problem of the hill villages is one of the most acute agricultural problems in Palestine today. These villages really have a hard time to scratch a living on their present basis, and the High Commissioner is most anxious to do something to improve their lot. This cannot be done unless there is money available for capital improvements . . . The people will make the effort if they are encouraged and assisted to do so, and I do not think that the losses of the capital invested should be high.[107]

A particularly relevant point to raise in connection with the provision of credit during the mandate period concerns the steps taken in 1936 to prohibit the sale of what was called the subsistence area, or 'lot viable'.[108] The object of the 1933 protection of cultivators ordinance had been to protect tenants from eviction from their holdings; legislation to protect owners was not considered necessary or desirable at the time. However, increased Jewish immigration after 1933 caused Wauchope to change his mind and in 1935 he appointed a committee to consider possible remedies. The proposal arrived at was that legislation be introduced to make it a condition of every disposition of rural land that the person making it should retain ownership of the minimum area necessary for his subsistence. The eruption of the 1936 disturbances prevented the legislation from being passed, but the ordinance consented to by the secretary of state included mortgages, as well as sales, in the definition of disposition: 'we feel that if this [mortgage] were permitted', wrote Wauchope in a personal letter to the secretary of state, 'it would be almost impossible to avoid evasions of the law, and I know this to be your view.'[109] In fact, the clauses in the ordinance did not actually prohibit the mortgaging of a subsistence area, but such was the practical effect: the mortgaging of a subsistence area would be impossible, since the sale of the subsistence area in satisfaction of a mortgage was definitely prohibited.[110]

[106] Minute by O. G. R. Williams, 31 May 1935, CO 733/274/75092.
[107] Minute by Stockdale, 1 June 1935, CO 733/274/75092.
[108] The proposed legislation would not have applied to the Beersheba sub-district, to urban areas, nor to lands under citrus plantation.
[109] Wauchope to Thomas, 24 Feb. 1936, CO 733/290.
[110] Wauchope to Ormsby-Gore, 12 Aug. 1936. CO 733/290/Part 2.

One of the sharpest criticisms that this legislation confronted was that such legislation would lead to the cultivator abandoning his holding because, unable to mortgage his land, he would be prohibited from obtaining sufficient capital and thus from any substantial development. Wauchope responded with two observations which together serve as a useful epilogue to the eighteen-year history of the provision of credit facilities under British rule. On the one hand, Wauchope conceded that 'it is not believed that any harmful result will ensue as even at present it is impossible for a small holder to raise any appreciable sum on his holding'.[111] On the other hand, Wauchope responded with the remarkable (in the context of almost twenty years of British policy of individualizing title to land) proposition that 'I consider subsistence areas should be inalienable; but possibly after escheating to Government the holding might be returned to the village community as metrouke land, that is land held in common by the villagers.'[112]

5. CONCLUSION

Utilitarian approaches to property have long held that individual and secure rights to plots of land are the essential precondition to the expansion of credit facilities. The history of measures taken in mandate Palestine to provide agricultural credit facilities neither affirms this nor contests it. To maintain, for example, that Jewish cultivators were better served by credit facilities throughout the mandate on account of title to their land being duly registered ignores many specific attributes of Jewish landholding, including the prominence of larger political interests in the project of establishing a national home. Or to hypothesize that faster progress in the process of land settlement would have, ex post facto, made more funds available for agricultural investment is also difficult given the information available. But the opposite can be seen in Palestine: the sinking of wells, the planting of trees, and the breaking up of ground were as much an important part of the process of gaining legal recognition to land as a natural by-product.[113] Of the amounts of money injected into the local

---

[111] Wauchope to Ormsby-Gore, 12 Aug. 1936. CO 290/Part 2. Wauchope noted that the average advance on agricultural land was between PP 1 to PP 2 a dunam, 'which is too small for substantial development'.

[112] Wauchope to Thomas, 24 Feb. 1936. CO 733/290/Part 2.

[113] See Omar M. Razzaz, 'Examining Property Rights and Investment in Informal Settlements: The Case of Jordan', *Land Economics*, 69/4 (1993).

Arab economy through Jewish land purchases, whether these funds (much of which it seems paid off debts, or were reinvested in the land market, particularly urban property, or went into construction, or disappeared in 'conspicuous consumption') specifically privileged areas where title was secure and individual is difficult to determine. Moreover, so little is known about the 'unofficial' provision of short-term credit during the mandate, and about the rules that governed it, that it is also difficult to know how greater recourse to a land register would have affected it other than the likelihood of secure title lowering somewhat the rates charged.

What this chapter attempts to make clear though is that successive administrations in Palestine came to accept that banks providing long-term credit could be established only with government assistance.[114] But government measures towards this end were negligible, even though there was strong official acceptance of the necessity for credit facilities in Palestine. The role played by the Palestine government tended to develop only as one of providing short-term credit in desperate situations, due weight being given to the direct financial benefit to the government of improved taxation payments. The supply of short-term credit did not require land registers: short-term credit could safely and conveniently be provided for by new legislation which itself relied on traditional structures requiring repayment after the following harvest.

The reluctance to provide public sponsorship for long-term credit facilities was due to a number of considerations with which all colonial administrations had to grapple. The tension between individually defined title and long-term credit, on the one hand, and the desire to secure peasant agriculturalists to their land, on the other, was a puzzle for all imperial governments to sort out. Colonial parsimony was always a factor, as was the general disinclination (particularly amongst officials in London in the Colonial Office and the Treasury) for government officials to involve themselves in banking operations, which, it was believed, ought to be run as 'a strictly commercial enterprise'. 'In principal', minuted one Colonial Office official early in 1922, 'I deprecate government interference with private

---

[114] Two Arab institutions, the Arab Bank Ltd. and the Arab National Bank Ltd., made limited progress in the early 1930s, but benefited dramatically from the high agricultural prices prevailing during the Second World War which allowed cultivators not only to liquidate debts in unorganized financial markets but accumulate substantial savings. Dolf Michaelis, 'One Hundred Years of Banking and Currency in Palestine', in *Research in Economic History* (Greenwich: Jai Press Inc., 1986), 184–5, *A Survey of Palestine: Prepared in December 1945 and January 1946 for the Information of the Anglo-American Committee of Inquiry* (Washington: Institute for Palestine Studies, 1991), 559.

enterprise.' Most agreed: 'the government should interfere as little as possible in legitimate commercial enterprise,' wrote Clauson. 'At present it is much too prone to lay down elaborate regulations for everything.'[115]

The laissez-faire approach confronted significant stumbling blocks. In Palestine, the prominence of political considerations in the 1930s was such that by 1935 the need for some government involvement was finally accepted and assistance was given to an agricultural bank which aimed mainly to assist the Jewish farmer. As regards the larger Arab population, however, quite different factors were at play and efforts were instead directed towards taking the idea of private property right out of the credit equation altogether. Reasons for this include: the success Strickland had in pushing the need for cooperative societies in Palestine, with which (though they experienced very limited growth) nothing could be allowed to compete; the attempts to secure tenants to the land and thus knowingly jeopardize the security afforded to the property owner for a mortgage; and the further attempts to deal with the problems of dispossession and landlessness by legislating on the inalienability of the 'lot viable' and thus prohibiting outright the mortgage of subsistence land.

The importance in exposing the negligible role played by credit facilities in official thinking about property rights lies in recognizing the ad hoc character of colonial rule. The significance of defining property rights, while easily assumed in a philosophical sort of way, could not be translated into concrete action in a colonial context unless practices on the ground justified it. 'It is important to prevent the intrusion of this idea of property as the basis of credit,' insisted Strickland, knowing the thinking that he was up against.[116] For its part, despite the rhetoric, the supply of credit in Palestine at no point acted as a practical incentive to the process of individualizing rights to land. One can fairly conclude that the cumulated effect of the factors bearing on the provision of credit, as outlined in this chapter, rendered the whole issue more or less immaterial to the larger question of individualizing title to land.

[115] Minute sheet, 26 Jan. 1922, CO 733/18, 374.
[116] 'Report by Mr. C. F. Strickland of the Indian Civil Service on the Possibility of Introducing a System of Agricultural Cooperation in Palestine [Strickland Report]' (Jerusalem, 1930), 32.

4

Taxation

'The whole of this fiscal system has been swept away,' exclaimed a 1943 report by the naval intelligence division: 'Taxation of land and real property has been revolutionized.'[1] Given the fiscal demands on a colony, the potential for intervention in the patterns of revenue collection is dramatic. Frequently the main source of taxable wealth was the land, and usual colonial practice throughout the empire was to base a colony's revenue policy solidly upon an efficient and fair system of land registration. 'The land registry will, as in all countries be permanent,' wrote the acting high commissioner in 1922: 'It is essential for the collection of taxes that all land should be registered and that transactions therein should also be registered so that the correct owners, values, and areas are known.'[2] A registry was not just a record of rights to land but, as importantly, an assessment of revenue liabilities: until the completion of the survey, it was argued, an 'absolutely defensible' system of taxation was impossible.[3] Accordingly, official attempts to secure a stable source of revenue played a key role in the formation of policies defining property rights: 'I am inclined to think', minuted H. W. Young in the Colonial Office in 1921, 'that what is really required in Palestine is a comprehensive "settlement" in the Indian sense of the term, of the whole country.'[4]

However, the close relationship between revenue demands and secure, individual rights to property was never firmly established in the case of Palestine. 'What is wanted is a system of taxation based not on the crops but on the land,' agreed one Colonial Office official in 1923, warning also that 'this depends on the cadastral survey which is proceeding at present but very slowly'.[5] Despite the promises of the revolution expected upon the

[1] Great Britain. Naval Intelligence Division, *Palestine and Transjordan*, Geographical Handbook Series (Oxford: Oxford University Press, 1943).

[2] W. H. Deedes, for high commissioner, to Churchill, 10 Feb. 1922, CO 733/18, 580–1.

[3] 'Report of Tithes Commission', Mar. 1922, CO 733/20, 294.

[4] Minute sheets, H. W. Young, 14 Oct. 1921, CO 733/17, 716.

[5] Minute sheets, CO 733/45, 12.

completion of the cadastral survey of all cultivable land,[6] revenue policy and property were never directly related during the period of Britain's colonial rule in Palestine. The 1936 Peel Commission was not alone in protesting the fact that 'there is at present no connection between rural property taxation and land settlement'.[7] They explained their frustration in the following terms:

The object of 'survey and settlement' is the ascertainment of areas and boundaries, the preparation of maps to display them, and the compilation of a record of rights, which usually in the British Empire includes not merely a statement of the ownership of the land, but all the rights and easements connected with the use of the land, such as tenancies and sub-tenancies, grazing, fuel or irrigation rights. Often this record sets forth any fiscal obligations attaching to the land, whether revenue payable to the Government or rent payable to a landlord . . . Land settlement in Palestine differs materially from that in the British Empire, notably in India. It has nothing to do with the settlement of land revenue.[8]

The fiscal survey, conducted in preparation for the 1936 rural property tax, did map out 'registration blocks' which played a fundamental role in the process of settlement. But official recognition of individual rights to land did not otherwise achieve the key place in Palestine's taxation system one might expect from a colonial system. Rather, the challenges posed by Palestine's taxation regime forced the government to fall back on a variety of local practices, a pattern which affected official thinking about property rights in complex ways that are necessary to explore.

1. TAXES LEVIED ON RURAL PROPERTIES, 1917–1936

By a public notice dated 7 May 1918, all Ottoman taxes prior to the entry of the Ottoman Empire into the First World War were declared to have been reinstated ('and will be collected with effect from the 1st day of March, 1918').[9] The rush to completely re-establish the *status quo ante*

---

[6] 'Report of the Tithes Commission', Mar. 1922, CO 733/20, 260.

[7] Great Britain. Palestine Royal Commission, *Report* (London: HMSO, 1937), 228.

[8] Ibid. 208.

[9] M. F. Abcarius, 'The Fiscal System', in Sa'id Himadeh (ed.), *Economic Organization of Palestine* (Beirut: American Press, 1938), 509, Norman Bentwich (ed.), *Legislation of Palestine, 1918–1925: Including the Orders-in-Council, Ordinances, Public Notices, Proclamations, Regulations, Etc.*, 2 vols. (Alexandria: Whitehead Morris Ltd., 1926), Palestine, *Legislation of Palestine, 1918–1925 [Microform]: Including the Orders-in-Council, Ordinances, Public Notices, Proclamations, Regulations, Etc.*, Compiled by Norman Bentwich (Alexandria: Whitehead Morris Ltd., 1926), 369.

suggests that there was never really any question at the outset of replacing the Ottoman taxation system, as it was understood by British officials. The eagerness in restoring local taxes is reflected in the hasty and sometimes careless attempts of military administration to apply municipal taxes. The Ottoman municipal tax law of 26 February 1914, for example, was enforced by the British administration even though it had in fact come into effect after 1 November 1914 (and therefore never, in accordance with the provisions of the 1922 Palestine order-in-council, had the force of law).[10] Indeed, eagerness to secure revenue led one military governor to apply the *mussaqafat* law (roofed property tax) to the areas of Haifa, Acre, and Shefa Amr, another legally dubious venture that was not placed on solid ground until the passing of the 1933 *mussaqafat* tax validation ordinance.[11]

Faced with the need to defray the costs of the military occupation, the British army was forced immediately to set up some sort of revenue administration for rural areas. For reasons of expedience obviously, but also for diplomacy, the military officials were directed to retain the existing administrative machinery where possible and to keep interference with the local population to a minimum. Lord Allenby himself expounded the virtues of maintaining the status quo in the following terms:

By retaining these Kazas as administrative units, not only should we disturb as little as possible the methods of Government to which the inhabitants were accustomed, but we should also be enabled to make the fullest use of Turkish Governmental machinery . . . to carry on the administration with due regard to economy of staff . . . [and] as further advance was made, to bring automatically into the general scheme of administration any additional territory that might be occupied.[12]

As in other legal, administrative, and religious matters, the military administration of Palestine was guided in taxation policies by the prevailing doctrine of the status quo which found practical expression through adherence to the rules of international law as defined in the Hague Code of 1907. Another important factor involved was the fear expressed for the repercussions of French jealousy in regard to Britain's position in

[10] ISA, Attorney General's Office, RG 3, 19/92, box 716. See also, 'Civil Appeal No. 194 of 1935', Michael McDonnell and Henry E. Baker (eds.), *The Law Reports of Palestine . . . : [1920–1946]*, 14 vols. (London: Waterlow & Sons, 1933–47).

[11] Frederic M. Goadby and Moses J. Doukhan, *The Land Law of Palestine* (Tel Aviv: Shoshany's Printing Co. Ltd., 1935).

[12] Allenby to War Office, 2 Mar. 1918, FO 371/3389/2070[77141].

Palestine. Consider the position taken regarding application of the *temettu* tax, a matter discussed in earnest in September 1918. Provided the revenue was applied to military or administrative necessities, the application of the tax would have been justified, and it was generally recognized by British officials in London and Jerusalem that the tax was desirable primarily because 'unless enforced the burden of taxation would largely fall upon the agriculturalists in Palestine'. But, in the end, it was determined that the disadvantages outweighed the advantages since it 'would undoubtedly lead to representations from the French and Italian Governments who might see therein evidence of the determination of His Majesty's Government to establish a British Protectorate over Palestine'.[13]

As regards the levying of rural taxes, the decision was taken to keep intact the Ottoman system, and to do so in time for the winter tithe (that is, the grains which were planted in the winter months and harvested in June and July), but any arrears of tithes due the Ottoman government were cancelled 'in view of the hardship suffered by agriculturalists on account of the war'. It was reported that in 1917 the Turks had forcibly requisitioned as much as 37.5 per cent of the grain harvest in kind (in addition to the 12.63 per cent tithe), against payment in paper money. While all outstanding taxes were considered remitted, it was made clear that this would not prejudice the rights of the Ottoman Public Debt Administration.

In addition to the taxes directly affecting rural property under the *status quo ante*, a significant role was also played by the levying of various licences and fees. The most important of these, in terms of receipts gained for the Palestine Treasury, was the land registration fee, though survey fees and certain court fees were also charged. Adopting Ottoman practice, the 1920 land transfer ordinance varied the fee according to the nature of the transaction: for the registration of a sale, for example, 3 per cent on the market value of the property was charged, while 0.5 per cent was levied for partition, and 5 per cent for the registration of land hitherto unregistered. Fees payable during the land settlement process were dealt with separately in the 1928 land settlement ordinance, with 10 mils as a rule being charged per dunam registered (with a minimum charge set at 50 mils).[14] Property permanently registered in the name of corporate bodies and charitable institutions (for example, the Palestine Land Development Company, the Custodi di Terra Santa, etc.) was initially made

---

[13] Foreign Office to War Office, 9 Sept. 1918, FO 371/3410.
[14] Goadby and Doukhan, *The Land Law of Palestine*, 370–1.

subject to a special annual tax. When the Palestine government passed new laws early in the mandate enabling corporate bodies to register in their own name land hitherto held on behalf of nominees, it legislated that compensation be paid for the loss of such fees which presumably would have accrued had the land remained in individual ownership (and thus been subject to a normal number of transfers and successions). On the assumption that land was transferred once in every thirty years, an annual tax was levied so as to make up in thirty years the fee of 3 per cent upon the capital value.[15] The concern for revenue did not, however, extend everywhere: by the terms of the correction of land registers ordinance, Jewish land-purchasing agencies were released from the obligation of having to pay fees due on transactions made during the war period when the registers were closed.[16]

Figures collected by Dowson in 1930, for the specific purpose of determining how much of the revenues collected through fees and licences constituted net profit, revealed that the average payment demanded upon registration during the period 1920–7 was more than four times the cost rendered.[17] For the five years 1928–33, the sum collected in succession fees was PP 7,499, that is approximately 1,500 per annum. It was estimated that the fee could be reduced to one-third, and still cover the cost of the service provided.[18] By the mid-1930s, known as 'the era of speculation', the receipts of the land registry ballooned: in 1932 registration fees amounted to LP 97,876 and in 1935 receipts reached LP 455,146.[19] The considerable profits gained by the Palestine Treasury from these fees went straight into general revenue.

Though it always risked falling on deaf ears at the British Treasury, a certain amount of criticism was expressed by officials who considered that the fees charged were too dear and thus jeopardized the proper functioning of a reliable register of rights. High commissioner Samuel shared the general concern with the fallout of popular resentment: 'There is a disposition among the departments to *trop de zele* sometimes. I don't want this country to be a land flowing with licensed milk and registered honey.'[20]

---

[15] Samuel to Churchill, 12 Oct. 1922, CO 733/26, 174.
[16] 'Explanatory Note—Correction of Land Registers Ordinance, 1925', CO 733/94, 242–3.
[17] Dowson, 'Report on the Progress of Land Reforms in Palestine, 1923–1930', CO 733/221/97169, 40.
[18] Director of lands to chief secretary, 22 Feb. 1933.
[19] Great Britain. Palestine Royal Commission, *Report*, 227. See also appendix B.
[20] Quoted in Barbara J. Smith, *The Roots of Separatism in Palestine: British Economic Policy, 1920–1929* (Syracuse, NY: Syracuse University Press, 1993), 40.

Dowson was particularly critical of the fee schedule, viewing it 'virtually as a means of undeclared taxation',[21] and he drew the government's attention to 'the matter calling most imperatively for the reconsideration of the government in connexion with land registration . . . the scale of fees'.[22] Dowson worried that the enormous cost and effort being expended on the process of settling rights to land throughout Palestine was in danger of being squandered were adequate provisions not taken to ensure that registers be kept up to date. He argued that this would only happen if the public cooperated willingly and spontaneously 'into taking advantage of a measure that, properly presented and administered, is intrinsically beneficial and should be attractive in itself'.[23]

For Dowson, the key to securing such cooperation in land registration was to maintain as low a charge as possible. He argued that 'if the land holding public is to be brought to value, and to co-operate in, the maintenance of the new Register, the payments demanded upon registration should be strictly regarded as fees payable for the services rendered and be governed solely by the aggregate cost of those services'.[24] Dowson was not alone in recommending that the fees for the registration of property be reduced to a minimum sufficient to cover the cost of the service only. When Albert Abramson, Palestine's commissioner of lands, argued in 1932 that 'the maintenance of a record of title to immovable property is a public service'[25] he expressed the fear that unless fees were reduced 'half the good accomplished by Land Settlement will be undone in the course of a few years'.[26] Similarly, when reviewing the fees that were meant to be exacted from a *musha'* shareholder at the moment of partition, the 1930 committee on economic conditions commented that 'it is hardly surprising that the partition of mesha'a land has not progressed'.[27] Sir John Hope-Simpson concluded that 'the fees at present charged for the registration of dispositions of land, especially those on sale, mortgage and succession, are so high as to prevent the registration of changes in title

[21] Dowson, 'Survey and Land Settlement Estimates: Covering Memorandum', CO 733/92, 491.

[22] Dowson, 'Report on the Progress of Land Reforms in Palestine, 1923–1930', CO 733/221/97169, 38–9.

[23] Ibid. 39.   [24] Ibid. 40–1.

[25] Letter by A. Abramson, 26 Nov. 1932, ISA, Chief Secretary's Office, RG 2, L/126/34.

[26] Quoted in memo signed A.E.W., 14 Feb. 1933, ISA, Chief Secretary's Office, RG 2, L/126/34.

[27] Quoted in Lewis French, 'Supplementary Report on Agricultural Development and Land Settlement in Palestine', 20 Apr. 1932, CO 733/214/5/97040, para. 112.

consequent thereon. It is desirable, in the interests of the maintenance of an accurate record of rights, that these fees should be reduced.'[28] And, in 1932, Lewis French confirmed that 'the exaction of the excessive fees' remained the principal deterrent to partition, noting at the same time that by his own rudimentary estimations less than 1 per cent of land had been officially registered.[29]

When the Palestine administration in April 1935 finally bowed before the weight of such recommendations, it agreed only to waive particular fees ordinarily chargeable for land previously unregistered: fees for the registration of land sales and transactions were not written off. The 1935 transfer of land (fees) rules abolished the fees entirely when registration was applied for within six months from the date of the publication, and reduced them to 2 per cent when the application was lodged after the lapse of six months (that is, after October 1935). But the period of free registration was repeatedly extended, evidently to give *vakif* authorities the opportunity to complete registration of their property.

While the reason behind these moves to reduce some fees was stated to be 'to encourage registration', the difficulty in collecting fees was considered as well. The registration of unpartitioned *musha'* land was particularly cumbersome. Settlement procedures called for 'the entry of such land on the Schedule of Rights as customary tenure Masha' in the name of the Mukhtars for the time being of the village concerned'.[30] As no individual person in the village was actually concerned, fees could not practically be collected from anybody. It was left for the revenue office to work out the settlement fees for each village parcel and divide them amongst all co-owners. Achieving this was a clerical nightmare, especially when combined with the need to iron out similar difficulties involved in apportioning the *wirku* tax. In December 1932, the finance officer for the Jaffa area estimated that the labour involved in apportioning registration fees for the first twenty-seven villages settled amounted to 207 days.[31] The O'Donnell Commission confirmed the difficulties of collecting registration fees:

[28] Sir John Hope-Simpson, *Palestine. Report on Immigration, Land Settlement and Development*, Cmd. 3686 (London: HMSO, 1930).

[29] Lewis French, 'Supplementary Report on Agricultural Development and Land Settlement in Palestine', 20 Apr. 1932, CO 733/214/97040, para. 113.

[30] Commissioner of lands to chief secretary, 4 Jan. 1935, ISA, Chief Secretary's Office, RG 2 L/126/34.

[31] Naser, Jaffa district finance officer, to district commissioner, southern district, 19 Dec. 1932, ISA, Chief Secretary's Office, RG 2, L/126/34.

It will be seen that the sums due are very large . . . If fees continue to be assessed on this scale and are realised they will cover a large part of the combined cost of the Survey and Settlement Departments. So far, at any rate in the Jaffa sub-district, no attempt to collect them has been made. When we visited the Jaffa district offices we found that the clerks had been unable to cope with, had indeed abandoned, the task of compiling from the schedules of claims the sums due from each owner.[32]

Such revelations about the costs involved in actually collecting fees were obviously a key factor in the government decision to forgo the revenue. One should also note that the only service that was actually being rendered by the settlement procedure at this stage was the delineation of block boundaries, an invention that was only of practical significance to the tax collector. Considering the economic hardship of the early 1930s, it surely must have been feared that to force payment would provoke resentment and anger. All in all, steps taken in 1935 to write off certain registration fees should be viewed as little more than an attempt to bring the law in line with standard practice. The government's general unwillingness to forgo revenue was never seriously at issue.

The taxes directly affecting rural property under the *status quo ante* included the *wirku*, the *aghnam* (an animal tax), and the tithe. The *wirku*, also known as a 'house and land tax', was levied on immovable property of every description, *mülk, miri*, or *vakif*. Technically, the tax was supposed to be based on the capital valuation of the property and to vary according to the nature of the property: that is, on *mülk* land at the rate of 10 per mille of the capital value, on *miri* at the rate of 4 per mille (*mülk* land paid a higher rate of tax than *miri* presumably on account of tithe not being payable in respect of it).[33] The Ottoman government had promulgated a new law in 1910 which imposed a tax on buildings based not upon the capital value but upon a rental value of the property. The new tax was meant to cancel the *wirku* on buildings, but 'was never imposed in Palestine and has not therefore been enforced by the British Administration'.[34]

British officials complained bitterly about the difficulty in obtaining accurate statistics regarding the distribution of the *wirku* tax. Despite the fact that the incidence of *wirku* was technically supposed to vary according to different categories (that is, *miri* or *mülk*), no precise figures could

[32] Excerpts of the O'Donnell Commission, CO 733/208/5/87326, 59.

[33] Abcarius, 'The Fiscal System', 519.

[34] 'Report of the Palestine Administration, July 1920–December 1921', CO 733/22, 473.

in fact be obtained regarding its distribution. Had such statistics regarding *wirku* been available, perhaps the tithe could have been distributed individually in proportion to it. In the end, however, it was concluded that the existing assessment of *wirku* was so uneven that a distribution of tithe based on it would have been extremely unjust.[35] Moreover, British authorities could find few reassessments since the inception of the tax in 1886, although arbitrary all-round increases, in the order of an additional 56 per cent in the case of land, had been imposed by the Ottomans. As a result, *wirku* assessments of rural property, possibly incorrect in the first place, were unreliable or obsolete.[36] Finally, although the *wirku* tax was paid in the name of the registered person, the general pattern evidently was that such person or heirs would be responsible for seeing that it was collected from the actual possessor of the land, if the latter did not himself pay it in the name of the registered person.[37] Dowson concluded in 1925 that 'liability for payment is now commonly severed from traceable connection with the property on which it purports to have been originally levied'.[38]

From the outset, British authorities were hard pressed to bring the assessment and collection of the *wirku* tax on rural land into line with the Ottoman laws and regulations governing it, and the measures widely called for never came. It needs to be noted that, when the registers were reopened in 1920, *wirku* became payable on the basis of the transfer price or a valuation of the property made at that time, whereas properties not the subject of such transaction continued to be taxed on the old, usually undervalued (but not always), assessment. Although the additional 56 per cent surtax was abolished in respect of buildings registered at their post-occupation value, nonetheless the increase in the value of property after the war tended to result in unequal distributions: 'the registered werko value of one undivided half share of a property might be L.E.100, while that of the other undivided half share might be L.E.1,000. Why? Simply because a dealing has been registered in one and not in the other.'[39] Overall, little was done to modify the payment of *wirku* until it was

[35] 'Average Tithe Committee: Majority Report', 29 June 1926, CO 733/117, 9.

[36] 'Report of the Palestine Administration, July 1920–December 1921', CO 733/22, 459. Also Goadby and Doukhan, *The Land Law of Palestine*, 364.

[37] See letter from department of lands to Attorney General's Office, 21 Mar. 1923, ISA, Attorney General's Office, RG 3, 26/1.

[38] Dowson, 'Covering Memorandum to Report on the Land System in Palestine', CO 733/109, 241.

[39] Memo by A. Rizk, Mar. 1923, ISA, Attorney General's Office, RG 3, 26/1. See also CO 733/216, 14.

replaced completely with the 1936 rural property tax,[40] and the official attitude towards the payment of *wirku* is best captured by the 1926 average tithe commission which conceded that 'this assessment may be tolerated on the grounds that it is familiar, and that the amount to be paid is comparatively small'.[41]

Land which was left for the grazing of animals was not by law subject to tithe. Instead, the *aghnam* tax was assessed once annually on animals which grazed on such lands: during the months of February and March, sheep, goats, camels, buffaloes, and pigs were counted, although those animals used solely for ploughing (camels and buffaloes, for example) were exempt. Abcarius describes the *aghnam* as a 'droit de pasture rather than a tithe on the living produce of the soil'.[42]

Due above all to the poor functioning of the *wirku* tax regime, the revenue accruing from agricultural taxation at the outset of the mandate was disproportionately dependent upon the tithe. By the 1930s indirect taxation, particularly customs duties paid on imported commodities, increasingly consumed by the large influx of Jewish immigrants, became the most important source of government revenue.[43] But in the early years, revenue from the tithe was much more significant than the other land taxes put together, and was itself the largest single income earner for the state.[44]

Technically, the tithe was supposed to be equal to one-tenth of the gross yield of the land. The Ottoman government had however periodically inflated the rate, earmarking each increase for specific revenue purposes: 1 per cent for public education (1883 law); 0.5 per cent for an agricultural bank (1898 law); 0.5 per cent surtax for the Treasury (1897 law); and 0.63 per cent for military preparations (1900 law). Such measures brought the tithe to 12.63 per cent, a rate which the Palestine government continued to levy from 1918 until 1925, though with little interest in maintaining the related hypothecation of revenue. In 1925, looking for a popular reform with which to crown his period as high commissioner, Herbert Samuel asked the Colonial Office—or, more

---

[40] In urban areas, *wirku* was in fact replaced in 1928 by the urban property tax. In the Beersheba district, the inhabitants were exempted altogether from the payment of *wirku*.

[41] 'Average Tithe Committee: Majority Report', 29 June 1926, CO 733/117, 20.

[42] Abcarius, 'The Fiscal System', 525.

[43] Talal Asad, 'Class Transformation under the Mandate', *Middle East Report*, 53 (1976), Smith, *The Roots of Separatism in Palestine: British Economic Policy, 1920–1929*, 42.

[44] Smith, *The Roots of Separatism in Palestine: British Economic Policy, 1920–1929*, 40. Jacob Metzer, *The Divided Economy of Mandatory Palestine* (Cambridge: Cambridge University Press, 1998).

specifically, the British Treasury—for permission to reduce the tithe to its 'normal' 10 per cent: '[I]t would be a great gratification to me', wrote Samuel, 'if this boon to the cultivators could be conferred as one of the last acts of my own period in office.'[45] This was approved in London, but only subject to Palestine reducing government expenditure by the amount that would be sacrificed in the proposed reduction of tithes.[46] Pushing Palestine to 'cut its coat according to its cloth', the Colonial Office was ever conscious of 'snipping at the cloth' at the same time.[47] For their part, the cultivators' gratitude was not forthcoming: as the southern district governor noted, 'the general feeling is that it was only a concession of a long overdue right'.[48]

In the actual collection of the tithe, the instructions issued by the military administration in 1918 and 1919 differed from the previous Ottoman procedures in particulars, representing what has been referred to as 'part of the Europeanization of administration',[49] or alternatively as a 'tidying up'.[50] Specific measures included: the system of tax-farming, by which the task of assessing and collecting the tithe was auctioned off to the highest bidder, was eliminated (although there is no indication of how widespread this was); taxes were collected in cash instalments rather than in kind; the redemption price was fixed by the local British official, and estimated at slightly below the market price; and, finally, the tithe was assessed in kilos.[51] As a levy upon actual produce, and thus one which varied with the profits made by the cultivator, the tithe was fairer in theory than in practice.[52] The task of, first, equitably assessing the yield and marketable value of every cultivator throughout Palestine and, secondly, collecting fairly as well as economically from the rightful persons proved to be beyond the powers of the Palestine government. The operation of the tithe presented the government with a whole set of objectionable problems.

[45] Samuel to Amery, 27 Feb. 1925, CO 733/110, 233.

[46] In the end, it appears to have been accommodated by an increase in customs duties and the enacting of a new tobacco tax. See telegram from Samuel to Amery, 22 Apr. 1925, CO 733/93, 389.

[47] Minute sheets, CO 733/199/5a/87064.

[48] Abramson, 'Political Report', 25 May 1925, CO 733/93, 139.

[49] Nachum Gross, *The Economic Policy of the Mandatory Government in Palestine* (Jerusalem: Maurice Falk Institute for Economic Research in Israel, 1982), 9–10.

[50] Sarah Graham Brown, 'The Political Economy of Jabal Nablus: 1920–1948', in Roger Owen (ed.), *Studies in the Economic and Social History of Palestine in the Nineteenth and Twentieth Centuries* (Carbondale: Southern Illinois University Press, 1982), 96.

[51] 'Report of the Palestine Administration, July 1920–December 1921', CO 733/22, 475.

[52] 'Report of the Tithes Commission', Mar. 1922, CO 733/20, 213.

To start with, the system required that field crops be transported to a central village site (for example, the threshing floor).[53] They were then held up there until their bulk had been estimated by a government-appointed inspector who also fixed the redemption price, that is, the price supposedly securable by the cultivator on the market for his crop. As this assessment process could last up to a month, it interfered significantly with marketing arrangements, as well as subjecting the crops to possible theft, fire, insects, etc.[54] Adding to these problems was the fact that the estimated redemption price did not take into account such variable factors as the costs of production and transport (from the threshing floor to the market). Such costs proved to be doubly burdensome to the cultivator. Where labourers were employed to help with the harvesting or guarding of the crop, it was customary to pay them in kind. But by assessing the tithe on the threshing floor, and then fixing the redemption price at what was supposed to be the wholesale market price of the crop, the costs of production were thereby taxed along with the actual product.[55] It was also pointed out that seeds were being taxed twice because of this.[56]

The whole system, run as economically as possible by the department of revenue, relied to a great extent upon the cooperation of local officials, especially the village *mukhtars*. It was the *mukhtars* who personally undertook to collect the tithes from each individual taxpayer. Holding the *mukhtar* of the village responsible was much more economical than creating and funding a new clerical bureaucracy, but concern was expressed about the integrity and competence of certain local officials. In 1926, the district commissioner in Haifa related the following story:

I have frequently invited the village representatives, the paid estimator, the paid inspector, and the District Officer, and occasionally also the treasury expert, to estimate a given heap. In not a single instance have the quantities guessed at been identical, while the percentages varied from 10 per cent to 70 per cent. Not only is estimation merely guess-work, but an estimator's guesses are deliberately increased or decreased. An evening's entertainment by the village as a whole, by

[53] It was found to be impossible to institute assessment on the threshing floors in parts of the district of Beersheba, which was very large with perhaps hundreds of threshing floors, entirely unprotected as far as the government was concerned. So it was left to the discretion of the district governor as to whether the assessment was to be taken on the standing crops or the threshing floors. See advisory council minutes, 5 Apr. 1921, CO 733/2, 128.

[54] Advisory council minutes, 19 July 1921, CO 733/4, 558.

[55] Graham Brown, 'The Political Economy of Jabal Nablus: 1920–1948', 96.

[56] Executive committee, Palestine Arab Congress, to high commissioner, 26 Nov. 1924, CO 733/93, 213.

a particular family or by an individual, is sufficient inducement to the estimator or to the inspector to guess moderately in favour of his host.[57]

Of course, cultivators themselves were not without strategies deigned to foil the assessment process. For example, cultivators were believed to conceal crops outright,[58] or to press the lower layers of sheaves of wheat close together while laying the upper layers on loosely in order to make the heap of grain appear small.[59] Overall, though, official observations on the tithe's general defects allowed more for human error: 'it would be perfectly easy to demonstrate practically by actual experiment with the most reliable estimators and inspectors on a given threshing floor or grove that the whole system as means of physical measurement is worthless and as a basis of taxation grossly immoral.'[60] There was wide scope for corruption (*mukhtars* were, after all tithe-payers themselves), but more so for confusion, particularly considering the lack of standardized measurements. Lewis French, for example, complained that

the mukhtar is probably quite illiterate and can only answer inquiries with the vaguest replies . . . he is ignorant of areas based on measurements. He will describe fields by some such vague term as a 'fedan', which may be anything from 50 to 250 dunams according to the local method of reckoning.[61]

The redemption prices posted by the government were based on the standard kilogram, whereas local officials were dealing in measures that varied from district to district.

Not surprisingly, it was argued from an early stage that the country would be better off under a revamped system of land taxation. 'The tithe goose, if not killed outright, is being rapidly bled to death,' wrote the director of agriculture, E. W. Sawer: 'an insuperable obstacle to economic development has been set up and carefully maintained.'[62] On the one hand, the government would benefit from being relieved of the heavier than necessary cost of administration (entailed by the burdensome process

---

[57] 'Memorandum on the Average Tithe Committee', 25 Aug. 1926, CO 733/117, 37–8.

[58] 'Minutes of Twentieth Meeting of Advisory Council', CO 733/18, 228.

[59] J. E. F. Campbell, 'Notes on the Tithe Commission Report', CO 733/117, 33.

[60] Cited in Dowson, 'Notes on the Abolition of Tithe and the Establishment of Land Tax in Palestine', CO 733/152/1.

[61] Of course, such a representation may well be the result of an encounter with an astute and very clever *mukhtar*. Lewis French, 'First Report on Agricultural Development and Land Settlement in Palestine' (Jerusalem, 1931), CO 733/214/5/97040, para. 44.

[62] Sawer to chief secretary, 10 Aug. 1924, CO 733/85, 419.

of assessment), the worry of corruption and cheating, and the budgetary problems associated with having revenue dependent upon fluctuating harvest returns. 'I am much struck with the advantage of fixing the existing tithe for a period of five years in anticipation of the substitution of a land tax,' minuted a Colonial Office official in 1924: 'It would save the permanent cost of assessment (which Mr Dowson puts at 25,000 pounds or 8% of the revenue) and make staff available for work in the process of survey and land settlement.'[63] On the other hand, the cultivators for their part needed to be spared the difficulties of tithe assessment and collection and instead left to decide for themselves when to harvest, thrash, store, or realize their crops. In autumn 1925, Dowson summed up the widely felt frustrations:

there seems no room for doubt that the unceasing valuation of the whole agricultural production of a country with the degree of individual accuracy which the theoretical elasticity of the tithe demands, is an impracticable undertaking, making indefensible inroads upon the time and energies of all concerned.[64]

2. COMMUTATIONS AND REMISSIONS

Despite the many defects of the tithe, a decisive step in mitigating them was not taken until the promulgation of the 1927 commutation of tithes ordinance. Although the legislation followed closely upon the recommendations of the 1926 average tithe committee, set up especially to study the question, such a system had been advocated by concerned parties for a number of years. It had early on been recommended by nearly all district officers,[65] as well as by the Supreme Muslim Council, frustrated with the fluctuations in their revenue from year to year,[66] and steps had already been taken for commuting the taxation of land which was planted with tobacco.[67]

[63] Minute sheets, 23 May 1924, CO 733/68, 482.
[64] Dowson, 'The Land System in Palestine', CO 733/109, 262.
[65] Dowson, 'Report on the Progress of Land Reforms in Palestine, 1923–1930', CO 733/221, 17.
[66] The tithe was the main source of revenue for the Supreme Muslim Council, established in 1921 'for the control and management of the Moslem Awkaf and Sharia affairs'. The tithes on land dedicated for charitable purposes were assessed and collected by government collectors and then transferred to the SMC minus the collection charges fixed at 6 per cent of actual collections. See Palestine, *Legislation of Palestine, 1918–1925 [Microform]: Including the Orders-in-Council, Ordinances, Public Notices, Proclamations, Regulations, Etc., Compiled by Norman Bentwich*, 399.
[67] Minute sheets, CO 733/109, 81.

The recommendation of the 1926 average tithe committee was that commutation be effected by taking a four-years average of the value of tithes in money (as opposed to taking an average of the tithe in kind, separately from the average redemption price). The four-year period preceding 1927 was considered the most appropriate on which to strike an average (bearing in mind that the 12.63 per cent rate for the years 1922 to 1925 had to be adjusted to the 10 per cent rate). Two features commended this period as one on which to strike an average. On the one hand, it was important that the number of years be even, on account of the biennial olive cycle with a major and minor year. On the other hand, although complete financial returns were readily available from the revenue office for all six years since the establishment of a civil government in 1920, it was accepted that the price of crops in the early years of the Palestine government was abnormally high.

The reasoning that lay behind the committee's proposals was that a fixed assessment would eliminate inconveniences and losses arising from the annual procedures. It was believed that cultivators, knowing from the outset what taxes were due, would be better off without the interference of assessment operations. Moreover, commutation was expected to act as an incentive to adopt improved methods of cultivation, seeing that an increase in yield would no longer result in an increased tithe payment. As the 1922 tithe commission report had promised, 'nothing tends to encourage improvements and interest in land so much as a sense of security of tithe'.[68]

Initial responses to commutation were favourable. In June 1929, the commissioner of lands reported that it 'worked very well last year'.[69] Similarly, in a general report on the working of the commuted tithe, the high commissioner informed the Colonial Office of the ease with which the commuted tithe was applied, and proclaimed that the 'new system was generally welcomed'.[70] He continued by noting that the care with which the distribution of the commuted tithe had been carried out was evidenced by the fact that only ninety-one appeals were entered

[68] 'Report of the Tithe Commission', CO 733/20, 294.
[69] Abramson to Shuckburgh, 23 June 1929, CO 733/173/67332, 35.
[70] There were some exceptions. The Samaria sub-districts of Nablus, Jenin, and Tulkarem, where 'family feuds' rendered it difficult to secure equitable and orderly distribution, were initially excluded from the commutation process until 1929. Also, areas of the Beersheba district were excluded out of regard to 'the susceptibilities of nomads whose suspicions are liable to be excited by any form of census of individuals or property such as the procedure under the Ordinance entails'. Chancellor to Amery, 19 Apr. 1929, CO 733/171/12/67275.

by individuals against their distribution, of which less than twenty were upheld by the district commissioners. 'Generally', concluded the high commissioner in April 1929, 'there are grounds for believing that the agricultural community would strongly resent a return to the system of estimating crops . . . I would state that the system of commuted tithe has been found satisfactory and, unless unforeseen developments occur, it will be maintained.'[71]

Although commutation may have resolved some of the problems associated with assessment, it was soon enough evident that it exacerbated others, in particular those which arose from the arbitrary nature of the initial assessments. As one district commissioner pointed out, 'it must be admitted that the [commutation] proposal would perpetuate for an indefinite period the payment . . . of a tax which has been based mainly on guess-work'.[72] In light of the condemnation in which the previous system of annual assessments was held, there was little really to defend commutation from the charge of perpetuating these guessing games in the form of an average. While generally in agreement with the move to commute the tithe, Dowson warned in 1928, rather prophetically as it turned out, that it was 'an untrustworthy basis of village taxation' and that it would 'become more and more so as the population, the nature and quality of the crops, the means of transport and marketing, the prices of produce and other conditions affecting the gross value of the agricultural production of each village change'.[73]

And change they did. The 1929 world depression caused a huge fall in the prices of agricultural produce in Palestine. According to the Johnson-Crosbie Report, the value of agricultural produce in 1930 was half what it was the previous year. It attributed the fall in prices mainly to world overproduction and the dumping of foreign produce: 'The market is glutted, and the farmer is unable to sell his surplus produce.'[74] The report went on to blame the lack of demand for wheat and olive oil as chiefly responsible for Palestine's economic crisis, as these commodities were 'the principal means of barter, of transactions with money-lenders and of realising cash to pay tithes and taxes'. It was therefore essential that

[71] Chancellor to Amery, 19 Apr. 1929, CO 733/171/12/67275, 7.
[72] Cited by Dowson, in 'Notes on the Abolition of Tithe and the Establishment of Land Tax in Palestine', CO 733/152/1/57195, 35.
[73] Ibid.
[74] 'Report of Committee on the Economic Condition of Agriculturalists and the Fiscal Measures of Government in Relation thereto' (The Johnson-Crosbie Report), 3 July 1930, CO 733/185/77072, 184.

the Palestinian government devote greater energy in negotiating foreign markets for Palestine's agricultural produce and at the same time apply protective duties to the principal commodities. It was also the view of the committee that the Arab farmer was being buried under enormous debt, the bulk of which 'must have gone to pay for costs of production, cost of living, and part payment of capital and of interest on previous debts. Little of it appears to have been devoted to capital improvements.' The report drew particular attention to the burden of crippling tax rates, a problem greatly aggravated by the inelasticity of commutation. As the drop in prices in early 1930 represented a 50 per cent fall below the average prices on which the new commuted tax was based, it was calculated by the commissioner of lands that, if the commuted tithe continued to be demanded at the rate determined by the 1922–6 average, the cultivator would be forced in 1930 and 1931 to pay a tithe of 22 per cent on the amount which he was likely to obtain for his crops.[75] In arguing that immediate relief was necessary in the form of a reduction in the commuted tithe from 10 to 5 per cent (to parallel the fall in prices), the Johnson-Crosbie Report clarified that 'if the tithe had been collected on the old system, the loss resulting from the lower prices of cereals would have been approximately that sum'.[76]

The report also concluded that a major part of the problem of rural agriculture was that the Arab farmer was, in general, 'paying far more than his share of direct taxation'. Upon comparing the incidence of direct taxation on the rural farmer with that on the urban dweller, the report determined that the farmer paid taxes to an equivalent of 34 per cent of his rent, while the urban owner of immovable property paid less than 10 per cent, there existing no direct taxation in urban areas to counterbalance that paid by the cultivator in tithe and animal tax.[77] This argument found receptive ears in the Colonial Office where, years earlier, concern had been raised about the small tax liability of the urban professional and trading classes: 'it is these that the Palestine government want to get at.'[78] Dividing the total burden of taxation equally between the rural and urban sections of the population would have required in 1930 a rather

---

[75] Abramson, 'Memorandum on the Commuted Tithe for 1931', 11 May 1931, CO 733/207/6/87275, 29.

[76] 'Report of Committee on the Economic Condition of Agriculturalists and the Fiscal Measures of Government in Relation thereto' (The Johnson-Crosbie Report), 3 July 1930, CO 733/185/77072, 200.

[77] Ibid. 183.

[78] Minute sheets, 28 Nov. 1923, CO 733/51, 360.

prohibitive 100 per cent increase in the rate of urban property tax. So, as an interim measure, the committee recommended that, in addition to a short-term remission due to the 1930 fall in prices, the tithe be permanently reduced to 7.5 per cent, and that the rate of urban property taxes be increased such as was required to meet that deficit, the total revenue of the government remaining unaltered. The committee further recommended that an income tax be introduced in the long term.

Within months of receiving the proposals for tithe reduction, the Colonial Office was compelled to act upon the similar recommendations of Sir John Hope-Simpson. He had noted that

the Tithe should be entirely remitted if feasible. If it is found financially impossible to grant this measure of relief, as a temporary measure it might be possible to vary the Tithe in accordance with the variation of the market prices of agricultural produce.[79]

Variation of the commuted tithe in accordance with market prices was not possible, however. When commutation was discussed in 1926 and 1927, the Colonial Office had asked the Palestine government to consider the actual assessment to be subject to periodic revision. Officials were anxious about the potential for financial losses should the value of produce rise considerably during the period of tithe stabilization.[80] But Palestine's attorney general neglected to act on the Colonial Office's concerns and make any provision for reassessment in the commutation of tithes ordinance.[81] Consequently the Palestine administration was left with little recourse during the crises of the early 1930s, other than the ad hoc remission of tithes at rates which reflected the amount of relief needed by the cultivators.[82] As one official complained:

this illustrates one of the objections to fixing a commuted tithe instead of a tithe based on the actual crop. When the crop is a failure the grower demands remission of the bulk of the commuted rate. When the crop is a bumper crop, the Government does not benefit.[83]

---

[79] Hope-Simpson, *Palestine. Report on Immigration, Land Settlement and Development.* See also correspondence in CO 733/207/87275.

[80] Colonial Office to Palestine, 15 Nov. 1926, CO 733/117, 10.

[81] See minute sheets in CO 733/135/1.

[82] See 'Memorandum No. 16: Account of System of Land Taxation and of Effect of Recent Changes', in Great Britain. Palestine Royal Commission, *Memoranda Prepared by the Government of Palestine* (London: HMSO, 1937), 51–2.

[83] Minute sheets, CO 733/160/14/57534, 2.

The role played by the Treasury in London should also be considered in this context. In the early 1930s, the continual remission of tithes and the writing off of arrears, in addition to other measures that were taken of necessity in dealing with the crisis that afflicted rural agriculture, obliged the Palestine government to make decisions which, obviously, would adversely affect annual budgets. The Treasury rarely questioned the necessity of any of the reforms, but they nonetheless made their position on lost revenues very clear. Upon receiving the proposals for the remissions of the tithes in 1932, for example, the Treasury revealed that the decisions they took were based exclusively on fiscal considerations:

They cannot acquiesce in a budgetary deficit consequent thereon. Their authority for the proposal now submitted is therefore given on the understanding that should increases of revenue under other heads appear unlikely to cover the anticipated deficiency of the revenue, steps will be taken by means of reductions of expenditure to avoid a deficit on the year's working.[84]

No decision was ever made about changes to Palestine's taxation regime without first taking into account the effect such changes would have on government revenues. As it happened, the crisis that afflicted Arab agriculture in the early 1930s did in fact coincide with an abrupt rise in the revenues under 'other heads' (in particular, customs receipts and land transaction fees), giving the government some essential room to manoeuvre.

3. RURAL PROPERTY TAX

At the time of its adoption in 1928, the commuted tithe was widely justified as a stop-gap measure to lessen the hardships of the inherited system of tithes. Commutation had its share of critics, but most were won over at the time by the fact that it provided the quickest practicable escape from the existing tithe system. As Dowson noted in 1930, soon after its implementation, 'the advocates of immediate and general commutation of the tithe by villages have been fully justified by its success in removing the grosser evils of tithe collection'.[85] At the outset, commutation could also be commended, at least in a general way, for substituting taxation of

---

[84] Treasury to Colonial Office, 7 June 1932, CO 733/244.
[85] Dowson, 'Report on the Progress of Land Reforms in Palestine, 1923–1930', CO 733/221/97169, 17.

Table 1. Land classification

	Dominant use
A. Good-quality land	
1. High-class land, level or gently undulating with fertile soils and an adequate water supply	Intensive citrus, fodder, and vegetable cultivation
2. Good land, with loamy soils similar to (1), but with lower rainfall	Citrus, cereals, and vegetables
3. Good land, with deep alluvial soils, suitable for a wide range of ground crops and, where irrigation is available, for intensive farming	Cereals, fodders, and deciduous fruits
B. Medium-quality land	
4. Uplands of limestone, with steep and terraced slopes, much shallow soil and rock outcrop, with tracts of deeper soils in valleys	Cereals, olives, vines, and deciduous fruits
5. Uplands, similar to (4) but with more bare rock, steeper slopes, and less cultivable land	Cereals, olives, vines, and deciduous fruits
6. Semi-desert lowland, with good loess soils, but cultivation limited by low and very variable rainfall	Barley, wheat, and melons
C. Poor-quality land	
7. Lowlands, with limited seasonal crops and grazing; some broken land and some highly saline soil and extensive stretches of cultivable land if irrigated	Seasonal pasture with patches of irrigation on favourable sites
8. Dry eroded hills, (a) *Northern Belt*, with sufficient moisture for patches of cultivation where sufficient soil (b) *Wilderness*, with very arid conditions	Seasonal grazing and patches of cultivation Limited seasonal grazing
9. Coastal sand dunes	
10. Southern desert or negeb, deeply eroded uplands and southern rift valley	Desert with scanty patches of cultivation only when rainfall is sufficient

Note: As compiled by the research staff of the Anglo-American Committee of Inquiry in collaboration with the departments of agriculture, lands, irrigation, and statistics of the government of Palestine.

Source: A Survey of Palestine: Prepared in December 1945 and January 1946 for the Information of the Anglo-American Committee of Inquiry, vol. iv.

the possession of land for taxation of gross agricultural production.[86] Dowson himself was a key figure in the planning of amendments to commutation which came to fruition in 1936 with the promulgation of the rural property tax. The amendments suggested by Dowson tackled two major problems either ignored or aggravated by commutation: first, that it perpetuated a series of unreliable village assessments which were themselves derived from the very system which was being discredited and, it was thought, superseded; and, secondly, that it left untouched the parallel difficulties of the Ottoman house and land tax (*wirku*).

The solution proposed was to substitute for both the existing tithe and *wirku* a single 'sound—although necessarily incomplete' assessment achievable through what Dowson referred to as a 'block land tax'. In fact, a basic scheme for revising the tithe by classifying land according to its productivity was put forth as early as 1922,[87] and in 1925, Dowson argued that a more equitable and reliable tax assessment could be effected by dividing village lands into blocks of approximately uniform quality. By the terms of the 1936 rural property tax, these blocks would then be systematically valuated—that is, placed into predetermined categories of productivity. The blocks would be graded according to their relative economic values rather than be assigned a particular monetary value based on the income hitherto derived from a piece of land. It was felt to be easier to grade blocks on a continuous proportional scale which enabled differences of value to be expressed by degree. This avoided the more artificial creation of an absolute income value of land in terms of money. In other words, land of absolutely no economic value was graded at 0 while land of the highest economic value was graded at 100, while shades of difference between the two were expressed by intermediate numbers based on an index of 10. With the assistance of such standards it was thought possible to grade any block within a village with its appropriate index figure on the suggested scale and also to assure that the same standards were repeated throughout the country.

In a letter asking for Treasury approval of these categories of land, the Colonial Office explained that the rates of tax 'will have something like a definite relation to the amount which the agriculturalist is able to pay'. Accordingly, the rates aimed to represent a percentage (12.5 per cent on citrus, 10 per cent on ground crops) of 'net annual value'. The net annual

---

[86] See, for example, Dowson, 'Notes on the Abolition of the Tithe and the Establishment of Land Tax in Palestine', CO 733/152/1/57195.

[87] See, 'Report of the Tithes Commission', CO 733/20, 174.

value was calculated on a five-year average (1927–32) of market prices with an estimate of annual working costs (defined as two-thirds of the gross annual value). The Treasury, whose chief interest of course was its effect on revenue, pointed out that this process estimated the taxable capacity of the agriculturalist in light of only recent conditions which were, of course, bad, and asked that the changeover to a new system be postponed until conditions became more normal. The Colonial Office responded by asking 'what is normal?', arguing convincingly that the rates proposed should remain unaltered for at least five years on the basis that, even if agricultural conditions were to improve substantially before then, the agriculturalist ought to be allowed some time to recover from the cumulative effects of a succession of bad harvests.

Valuation of land in this way helped ensure that tax payments were governed by the ability to pay—that is, by the relative income-producing capacity of the land. Although, in principle, it was generally agreed that the assessment of the actual income-producing value of landed property was the main fiscal objective to be sought, it was thought that in practice such assessment would simply be too difficult. Neither the majority of landowners nor tenant cultivators were thought to keep any record of their income, and therefore no accurate estimate could be made of the quantity of produce derived from any particular plot of land. Discredited, the tithe registers could not be relied upon. Besides, the registers provided data for whole villages, not for individually owned parcels. The possibility of defining the value of blocks in terms of rental value was also considered, but as such a small proportion of rents was paid in money, the practical difficulties were thought to be too great. Rents payable in kind (a third of the gross produce, for example) were often complicated by other special considerations making their actual value difficult to determine. The rural taxation committee described this in the following terms: 'the actual rental value and net profits from cultivation of each individual holding in rural areas in Palestine cannot be ascertained as rents and wages are usually paid in kind and there are no crop records. Rural property is however easily divided into general categories representing degrees of fertility in respect of which the average net annual value can be estimated.'

It was hoped that the block land tax would operate as a sort of tax on incomes obtained from the ownership or use of the land. Early on, there was some discussion over whether it could be utilized as an 'economic weapon', with certain groups arguing in favour of making the unimproved value of the land, or market value, the basis of assessment. The advantage to be reaped in such a course, they argued, was that poorly developed land,

and poor husbandry, could be penalized fiscally. Moreover, there was precedent for such a course: the *wirku* tax, which would also be replaced by the new consolidated block land tax, was after all technically levied on the market value. However, this strategy was dismissed in the end as being both impractical and impolitic. On the one hand, to adopt the market value might cause a serious disparity of assessment between districts; on the other hand, so great was the desire for the early replacement of the commuted tithe, it was felt that the best course to pursue was that which was most familiar and available.

A key feature of the rural property tax that requires special consideration in this context is the extent to which it derived from well-known patterns and structures of local village life. British officials had long recognized, and regretted, the sub-division of village land according to its economic value that had long been used as an equitable basis for the apportionment of *musha'* and other shares. Yet, what commended the block land tax to officials was in fact the extent to which it relied precisely on this common knowledge held by the villagers themselves. The relative economic values of the blocks comprising a village could be readily determined because villagers were regularly accustomed to assessing the relative economic values of village land: such knowledge was put to practical use every day by villagers in their dealings with the land.[88] While exact figures for the amount of land subject to the *musha'* system are not available, the 1933 rural taxation committee noted that 'approximately half of the agricultural land is mesha'a and is held in common'.[89] By consulting in the field with village representatives, survey officers could easily complete the initial block surveys and valuations of *musha'* land.[90] Given that the values of these blocks had already been appraised locally by consideration of a combination of factors (fertility, location, access to water and transport facilities, security, and drainage), the constitution of a block land tax was the most expedient avenue for government to take. Moreover, the chances of a more equitable distribution of the incidence of rural taxation were also greater.

Financial provision was made for Dowson's proposals in the 1929 estimates by redistributing funds between the various branches involved: resources were siphoned off the normal procedures of land settlement and

---

[88] Government of Palestine, 'Explanatory Note in the Form of Questions and Answers on Survey, Land Settlement, and Registration of Title', *Palestine Bulletin*, 14–17 June 1928.

[89] 'Observations of Committee', CO 733/267/37560/Part 1, 89.

[90] Minute sheets, 16 Apr. 1928, CO 733/152/1/57195, 3–4.

redirected into a 'fiscal survey' to be undertaken by the survey department.[91] The basis of the new arrangements was that the 1/10,000 block mapping and valuation of villages for which the survey department was thereafter responsible would, in future land settlement procedures, form the primary unit of registration and settlement. As a corollary, surveyors hitherto attached to settlement officers were reassigned to survey. From 1930 on, each village and settlement was visited by official surveyors who, after consultation with those concerned, divided the village into blocks of land of similar crop productivity value. The survey was completed in 1934. The rural property tax ordinance was introduced thereafter and applied to all rural lands in Palestine, except Beersheba sub-district and the Huleh lands of Safad sub-district.

4. PUBLIC REVENUE AND PRIVATE PROPERTY

What impact did these changes to Palestine's taxation regime have on British thinking about the nature of property rights? On the fiscal front, colonial administrations were expected (assuming peace and order were secured) to 'pay their own way' and not be an imposition on the British taxpayer. As discussed, the raising of local taxes therefore demanded the immediate and constant attention of every colonial administration. As the main source of taxable wealth was in many cases the land, it followed that one of the chief responsibilities of all colonial governments was to construct a legal and administrative system by which landed property might be easily assessed and taxed.[92] Ideally, the procedure followed by a colonial government in linking landed property with public revenue was straightforward: first, identify the proprietor of a piece of land; second, define and demarcate the property; third, award title to it. On this basis, tax liability could be fairly and legally assessed. Taken together, these procedures constituted, at least on paper, a rather logical formula for the equitable assessment and collection of rural taxation. As Elizabeth

[91] Dispatch from officer administering the government to secretary of state, 18 Oct. 1928, CO 733/162/5/ 57589.

[92] See, for example, Robert Eric Frykenberg (ed.), *Land Control and Social Structure in Indian History* (Madison: University of Wisconsin Press, 1969), Thomas Metcalf, *Land, Landlords and the British Raj: Northern India in the Nineteenth Century* (Berkeley and Los Angeles: University of California Press, 1979), Richard Saumarez Smith, *Rule by Records: Land Registration and Village Custom in Early British Panjab* (Delhi: Oxford University Press, 1996), Elizabeth Whitcombe, 'The Benevolent Proprietor and the Property Law: A British-Indian Dilemma', *History and Anthropology*, 1/2 (1985).

Whitcombe notes in her study of rural taxation in colonial India, 'A law of property was fundamental to the business of government, a law which defined proprietary rights in land and, consistent with that right, the liability of the proprietor to meet the revenue demand levied by government: "there can be no public Revenue without private Property", as Sir Philip Francis succinctly expressed it.'[93]

Fiscal demands can therefore be said to have provided one of the main incentives behind the execution of a cadastral survey and the systematic settlement of title to land. The immediacy of these demands is clearly reflected in early reports out of Iraq which emphasized innovations in the post-war period that enhanced the accuracy of revenue collection, such as providing that 'the Land Titles Department shall communicate to the Land Revenue Department every transfer of land on its completion. This simple expedient for keeping their land revenue registers up to date had never occurred to the Turks.'[94] As the previous outline of rural taxation in Palestine reveals, however, the typically close colonial connection between rural taxation and the individualization of property eluded the colonial administrators there. The subject which merits special consideration is what this separation can tell us about changes to British thinking about property in mandate Palestine, the sort of rights the British were prepared to endorse, and the role this was meant to play in its administration.

It needs to be acknowledged at the outset that sentiments similar to those of Philip Francis in India were indeed routinely and succinctly expressed by British authorities in Palestine. The stated goal of almost all government officials throughout the mandate remained the replace-ment of the inherited land registry methods with a more comprehensive cadastral settlement of title to land on which to base revenue policy. The following examples reflect the respect with which, at least rhetorically, standard colonial revenue policy was treated by officials in Palestine. The report of the 1922 tithes commission concluded that

The need for a rapid and correct survey is urgent . . .

The Committee are unanimously of the opinion that a radical change in the system of taxation would be beneficial both to Agriculture and to Government. They suggest that the cadastral survey of Palestine be pressed forward with all speed with a view to the adoption of taxation on land instead of on the yearly produce.[95]

[93] Whitcombe, 'The Benevolent Proprietor and the Property Law: A British-Indian Dilemma', 374.

[94] *Iraq Administration Reports 1914–1932*, 10 vols., vol. i (Slough: Archive Editions, 1992), 40.

[95] 'Report of the Tithes Commission', CO 733/20, 294–5.

Upon receiving a copy of this report, the secretary of state for the colonies confirmed that 'it would be wise to substitute for the present arrangement with regard to tithes a system of land tax based upon survey',[96] and Dowson weighed into the discussion with the admonition that 'no unimpeachable system of taxing land directly or indirectly can be brought into operation until . . . the identification of particular holdings in villages and the registration of owners or cultivators'.[97] The 1926 average tithe committee confirmed that a '[satisfactory] land tax cannot easily be introduced until the Survey and Settlement of the whole country has been completed', and in 1928, Abramson, as commissioner of lands, described the features of this survey more fully:

Taxation of land however cannot be put on to a sound footing until the foundation exists for the completion of a trustworthy record of property. The record should comprise: a) taxable units of immovable property; b) taxable value of immovable property; [and] c) a tax roll of persons legally liable, in virtue of ownership and other rights, for the taxation levied thereon.[98]

This was again reiterated by the report of the 1935 rural taxation machinery committee which agreed that

The main defect in the machinery of assessment, is that the assessment operations were not preceded or accompanied by a survey whereby all parcels of land whether in separate or in common ownership were indicated on the ground and plotted on a map.[99]

It is clear then that the general colonial rule that the administration of taxation should be based on a comprehensive settlement of title to land was heavily endorsed by officials in Palestine. Given this level of support, why then was this close relationship between revenue and title never achieved in practice? There are two key features behind the way Palestine's revenue policy evolved until 1936 which help explain why settlement operations remained more or less extraneous to the functioning of the revenue administration.

[96] Churchill to Samuel, 22 Aug. 1922, CO 733/20, 170.
[97] Dowson, 'Notes on the Abolition of the Tithe and the Establishment of a Land Tax in Palestine', CO 733/152/1/57195, 28+40.
[98] Abramson, 'Proposal to Substitute a Land Tax for the Present Werko and Tithe', CO 733/152/1/57195, 99.
[99] 'Report of the Rural Taxation Machinery Committee' CO 733/267/37560/Part 1, 12.

5. FISCAL CONSIDERATIONS

First, it is helpful to recognize that every decision that was taken to modify rural taxation, or any other policy for that matter, was based almost exclusively on fiscal considerations. That is, they were designed either to limit the loss of revenue or minimize additional expenditure. As a Colonial Office minute made clear, 'revenue must be collected to the greatest possible amount, in other words, the country must be taxed up to the hilt and if there is anything left over beyond essential expenditure it must be decided on general principles whether the burden of taxation is to be lightened, or expenditure which is not essential, but which is desirable, should be incurred'.[100] Plans for increased settlement operations had always to deal with colonial parsimony and, in the words of the secretary of state for the colonies in 1924, 'the need of drastic economy in the cost of the administration of Palestine': 'if financial equilibrium is to be obtained, the "cromerian" policy of law taxation, strict economy in administration and caution in undertaking capital expenditure must be adopted.'[101] The role played by the British Treasury in London is particularly important. Their antagonism towards even momentary loss of revenue continuously impacted upon what reforms could be undertaken. As it happened, the Palestinian economy grew in ways that allowed for limited budgetary redistributions that could absorb the decreases in revenue incumbent upon some changes. But lack of funds certainly hampered efforts to achieve a comprehensive settlement of title to land in Palestine. There were many reasons behind the 'slow march of settlement'[102] but early on in the mandate it became clear to all that the funds required to expedite it so as to make it the basis of revenue collection were well beyond Palestine's means. Accordingly, officials continually had to redirect their attention to provisional measures that would facilitate revenue collection pending the comprehensive settlement of title to all of Palestine.

The 'bottom line' impacted upon rural taxation in indirect ways as well. For example, it resulted in a priority being placed on the need to increase urban taxation (particularly in the wake of the Johnson-Crosbie Report) and, as a consequence, scarce resources were redirected between

---

[100] Minute sheets, 15 Dec. 1921, CO 733/8, 341.

[101] Secretary of state to high commissioner, 1 Aug. 1924, CO 733/72, 18.

[102] Dowson, 'Notes on the Abolition of the Tithe and the Establishment of a Land Tax in Palestine', CO 733/152/1/57195, 22.

1928 and 1932 away from settlement operations of rural land and instead focused on achieving reforms in urban taxation. Surveys of rural land would otherwise have been completed much earlier had a special effort not been required to complete the survey needed for urban reassessments. The decision to concentrate on urban reassessments must primarily be seen as a fiscal one, the more lucrative avenue for the government to take at the time.

In addition to Treasury parsimony, the Colonial Office had its own concerns and priorities which seem to have detracted from efforts to produce a coherent fiscal strategy with regard to basing rural taxation on a comprehensive system of land settlement. In the Colonial Office, the levying of taxes was not only a revenue issue; it was also inherently linked to the expression of imperial power.[103] This factor dominated much of the official correspondence concerning rural taxation. This is not to say that the bottom line was less important to the Colonial Office than to the Treasury; rather that the importance of revenue collection to the position and reputation of district officers in particular was a political issue as well as an economic one. Changes to taxation had thus to pass a different kind of scrutiny than might be expected. Churchill lectured Samuel in 1922 on the vital role played by tax collection by warning that 'Any system which may result in the people of the country deriving the impression that this vital element in their social condition is not the immediate concern of the local representative of your administration would, in my opinion, tend very greatly to reduce his authority and influence.'[104] Accordingly the need to safeguard district officers' prestige remained a consistent theme of discussions on the subject of Palestine's administration: a detailed Colonial Office memo on the need for according them enough freedom of action put forth the following:

I would insist on the overwhelming importance of this, on the political and administrative side. The representatives of the Government in each administrative unit MUST be in the closest touch with the population if major troubles are to be foreseen, and avoided. And that knowledge must be, daily, at the disposal of the Government, under a routine system which works mechanically, as a matter of course.[105]

[103] For more, see F. D. Lugard, *The Dual Mandate in British Tropical Africa*, 5th edn. (London: Frank Cass, 1965).
[104] Churchill to Samuel, 22 Aug. 1922, CO 733/20, 170.
[105] Minute sheets, 4 Oct. 1930, CO 733/194/7/77399.

The actual operation of revenue collection in a colonial administration was generally recognized as the responsibility of district administration staffs, and the role this played in furthering their influence and authority in Palestine tended for a long time to outweigh the importance of many sought-after reforms, which aimed at greater centralization. The position which the Colonial Office tended towards on taxation reform is revealed in the following minute by Clauson, who elsewhere referred to the lands department as a 'potty little'[106] one:

It seems to me that Palestine has not grasped the good old rule of British administration common throughout India and the Colonies that one of the most important if not the most important duty of the administrative officer of the political service is to carry out the assessment and collection of the direct taxation of the country especially tithes. . . . In Palestine this important elementary duty has been overshadowed by the liability of the administrative officer in respect of such vital matters as the registration of children of school age, the shrouding of butcher's meat exposed for sale, etc.[107]

Sentiments such as these expressed by Colonial Office advisers resulted in a major decentralization of the whole taxation administration in Palestine in 1923. The responsibility for revenue assessment, collection, and accounting was thereafter divided between the three district commissioners, the commissioner of lands, and the treasurer, resulting in what a 1935 report referred to as

the absence of effective control and . . . the growth of different and often wrong practices in different parts of Palestine . . . The Committee have discovered a wide variety of internal regulations and practices between District and District and even between Sub-districts in the same District. They consider that there should be a standardized practice as regards assessment, collection and accounting for each tax throughout Palestine.[108]

Taken together, the numerous complex interests of the Colonial Office and the Treasury appear to have ensured that the priority of taxation remained throughout the mandate as it did under the period of military rule, that of 'tooling and screwing'. It is also clear that this hampered efforts to coherently restructure rural taxation on the basis of well-defined property rights. Instead of radically overhauling the inherited Ottoman

---

[106] Minute by Clauson, 16 May 1923, CO 733/45, 38.
[107] Minute sheet, 31 Mar. 1922, CO 733/20, 163.
[108] 'Report of the Rural Taxation Machinery Committee', CO 733/267/37560/Part 1, 42–3.

system of taxation, officials in London and Jerusalem tinkered with provisional moves aimed always at modifying current practice. The need for
frugality, and the concern for colonial power structures, consistently outweighed the need to produce a coherent fiscal strategy regarding taxation.
While lip-service continued to be paid to the ultimate goal of taxation
being based on settlement, changes and modifications were characterized
by their piecemeal approach. Consequently, the history of changes to
taxation during the mandate is best viewed as a history of ad hoc, provisional steps, the primary motivation behind every move being that of
expediency, as defined within the constraints set by the Treasury and the
Colonial Office. The provisional nature of changes in rural taxation is
perhaps best described by the 'terms of reference' which dictated the course
of action expected from the 1926 average tithe commission (and can be
said to be exemplary of most commissions): 'to consider and report upon
what measures can be advantageously taken in advance of Land Settlement to replace the existing system.'[109] Nobody ever doubted that the
best final solution was a tax based on a comprehensive survey, but the time
necessary to complete it was too long a period to tolerate. Accordingly,
the decisions that lay behind every change (from commutation to block
land tax) were based upon a comparison between the proposed solution
and the actual system of the day, not with an ideal system hypothesized.
High commissioner Plumer was clear on this:

it is obvious that the present tithe and werko taxes on land are unsatisfactory in
their incidence and effect; and the commuted tithe is admittedly only a palliative
measure which should be succeeded at an early date by a radical measure of
reform of land taxation. The gradual substitution for werko and commuted tithe
of a simple land tax to produce equivalent revenue and based on the village block
as the taxable unit, if practicable, would satisfactorily bridge the interim period
until an exact valuation of individual plots can be made.[110]

The slow march of settlement of rights ensured that the sort of individual
incidence so widely sought was not possible in the foreseeable future.
Officials embraced stop-gap palliatives which made the inherited system
of taxation as equitable and as economic as possible, in ways that were
not at all dependent upon the settlement of title to land. This was clearly
the context in which Dowson pitched his proposals, seeing 'no reason to
postpone, and it seems to me no justification for postponing, this readily

---

[109] 'Average Tithe Commission Report', CO 733/117/19560.
[110] Letter from Plumer to Amery, 23 Mar. 1928, CO 733/152/57195.

realizable portion of a greatly needed reform, until the complementary
determination and record of individual taxpayers can be simultaneously
effected in a proper and formal manner'.[111] The ideal of assessing and
collecting taxes directly from the owners of individual properties, a system which had proved its worth to colonial officials elsewhere, was too
inexpedient a course to follow in Palestine.

6. MEDIUM OF LOCAL KNOWLEDGE

While in principle the assessment of individually owned property units
remained the government's ultimate fiscal objective, its pursuit never presented itself as a practicable policy. Instead, the aim was to pursue a financial
policy that would secure a 'cumulative improvement' of systems.[112] The
search for provisional substitutes to deal on an immediate ad hoc basis
with the inherited problems of rural taxation, instead of waiting for the
ultimate land tax—'or, indeed a day longer than can be helped'[113]—led
British officials to a greater appreciation for the structures and patterns of
village life. The tendency to reinforce the structures of village administration can be explained partly by the tenet that provisional changes would
be introduced more efficiently and successfully the closer they conformed
to practices on the ground, and partly by the growing appreciation of
the fact that the absence of information in the hands of government
concerning the parcellation and the possession of land did not mean that
such information did not otherwise exist. As Dowson acknowledged in
1928, 'no reform is possible now or ever except through the medium of
. . . local knowledge'.[114] The role played by village leaders, *mukhtars,* and
the system of co-ownership known as *musha'* featured prominently in
modifications to taxation. It would be useful to consider each in turn.

[111] Dowson, 'Notes on the Abolition of Tithe and the Establishment of Land Tax
in Palestine', CO 733/152, 40. Elsewhere he argues, 'nor can it be admitted that human
knowledge and experience is so barren that no such provisional substitute for the ultimate
land tax can be devised, and that the perpetuation of the crying defects of the existing
tithe system for another ten or fifteen years is inevitable . . . There is no justification for
perpetuating two unrelated evils if one is immediately remediable, particularly as that one
is unquestionably the source of the greater hardship and inequality.' Dowson, 'Report on
the Progress of Land Reforms, 1923–1930', CO 733/221/97169.
[112] Dowson, 'Report on the Land System in Palestine', CO 733/109, 274.
[113] Dowson, 'Notes on the Abolition of Tithe and the Establishment of Land Tax in
Palestine', CO 733/152, 22.
[114] Ibid. 45.

The potential for a central role played by village leaders emerged early in the course of the military administration. Fortunately for the occupying forces, immediately pressed to ensure that local taxation offset their costs, many of the 'tax collectors' previously employed by the Ottoman government were available.[115] According to official sources, direct collection of taxes by the Ottoman government appears to have been the norm in Palestine from 1915 until the British occupation. These administrative measures were described in 1922 by a British-appointed commission of inquiry as follows

by this method an estimator was nominated by each group of four or five villages, control being exercised by agents appointed by the authorities of a kaza and a further supervision being provided by the vilayet authorities. . . . After a portion of the cereals had been assigned for the use of the troops, the remainder was sold by public auction against cash payments, or against drafts at short date guaranteed by reputable persons.[116]

The acknowledged tax collectors were forthwith commissioned to assess and collect the 1918 June and July harvest: 'these officials knew the aggregate amount of Werko payable by the inhabitants of a particular village. This sum was then distributed by the village elders, who provided lists of the persons liable and of the amounts payable by them.'[117] Although acceded to at the time as the most opportune way of collecting revenue, the central role played by the village elders long outlived the needs of military administration. Under the civil administration, the *mukhtar* continued to hold primary responsibility for the collection of the tithe in money. This was achieved by his registering a promissory note at the office of the notary public so that, in the case of a taxpayer who refused to accept his liability, the revenue department would, technically, lodge legal proceedings against the *mukhtar*. He in turn would take action against individual defaulters. In practice, however, pressure would usually be applied on behalf of the *mukhtar* by a British official whose 'prestige . . . is generally sufficient to ensure payment'.[118]

When commutation was implemented in 1927 as part of an effort to ameliorate the problems associated with the tithe assessment process,

[115] Great Britain. Palestine Royal Commission, *Memoranda Prepared by the Government of Palestine*.

[116] 'Report of the Tithes Commission, 1922', CO 733/20, 193.

[117] Great Britain. Palestine Royal Commission, *Memoranda Prepared by the Government of Palestine*.

[118] 'Report of the Tithes Commission, 1922', CO 733/20, 212.

the question of distribution of liability had of course to be addressed. In dealing with this issue, the Palestine government again found that they were dependent on local knowledge to give practical effect to the official proposals. The only annual tithe payments hitherto recorded by the revenue authorities were for village units: as the collection of the tithe was, in the first instance, by *mukhtars* on behalf of their respective villages, no general provision was ever made for the maintenance of tithe accounts for individual cultivators or property owners. When the tithe was estimated annually, the official estimator compiled a tithe-payers book which was kept by the *mukhtar* of the village who was responsible for the collection of the tithe. The government revenue officer (for all sub-districts, except six) merely compiled village tithe registers in which were entered only the name of the village and the aggregate amount of tithe due on each crop from the village. So, if the proposals for commutation were to be accepted, the question remained of how to distribute among the individual tithe-payers the average amount commuted for the village as a whole.

Since only the village communities themselves possessed the knowledge that would enable the distribution of the aggregate commuted tithe fairly among the actual holders of cultivated village land, it was decided that the villagers should be allowed to effect the distribution among themselves: 'the process is familiar to them for the ordinary purposes of village life', noted the average tithe committee, adding that the same solution had been adopted in Syria.[119] Accordingly, the government continued to rely on the *mukhtars* and, it should be noted, in fact grew increasingly appreciative and respectful of their knowledge of the relative productivity of every portion of village land. For their part, it was evidently rather straight-forward for the *mukhtars* to distribute the tax liability: in *musha'* villages, in proportion to individual shares; in non-*musha'* villages, the productiv-ity of the land was measured in terms of wheat. According to the average tithe committee: 'all land of the classes now under consideration is sown in the ordinary course of crop rotation with wheat; the local cultivators habitually describe the area of any plot of land in terms of the wheat seed required to sow it and are familiar with the average yield from that amount of seed (five-fold, ten-fold, etc.).'[120] As for orchards, both oranges and olives, it was believed that ownership changed rarely enough that sufficient data could be acquired by the government directly for deter-mining the commuted assessments of individual owners. The structure of

[119] 'Average Tithe Commission Report' (1926), CO 733/117/19560, para. 11.
[120] Ibid., para. 12.

Jewish colonies provided further justification for the institution of a block land tax: Jewish officials kept their own land records for the colonies as a whole, and had long asserted that their own registers (transferred in 1925, with the records of the German colonies, to the official land registry) were far more reliable than government registers anyway.[121]

So, while stated policy was for the progress of land settlement to assure a direct link between cultivator and government, practice on the ground throughout the 1920s and early 1930s was to reinforce the medium of local institutions. The 1933 report on the machinery of tax collection confirmed the central position of the *mukhtar*, noting first that many

have had long periods of service under the Ottoman Government. Several of these are already well over the retiring age but in some cases their services have been retained because of their intimate knowledge of the Ottoman House and Land Tax procedure and of persons from whom the tax is rightly due.[122]

The continued remission of tithes in the early 1930s led to a brief reconsideration of the role played by *mukhtars*, and in particular the remuneration that was granted them for their administrative duties.[123] On account of the reduction in tithe payments, the amount of remuneration paid to *mukhtars*, which was generally calculated as a percentage of the amount collected, was significantly reduced. The concerns expressed by the Palestine administration were twofold. On the one hand, as we have seen, the arrangements for the assessment and collection of the tithe as laid down by the 1927 commutation of tithes ordinance devolved the greater part of the work and responsibility upon the *mukhtars*. But increasing alarm was expressed during the early 1930s about the capacity of *mukhtars*, not only to manage collection but also to account for the increasing build-up of arrears. The results were increasingly apparent in respect of dilatory collection and the absence of essential records, leading one Colonial Office official to the rather extreme conclusion that the machinery for tax assessment and collection 'in recent years has broken down completely'.[124]

However, closer attention was at the same time drawn to the larger role played by *mukhtars*, in maintaining everything from village records

---

[121] 'Correction of Land Ordinance, 1924', CO 733/76, 203.
[122] 'Report of the Rural Taxation Machinery Committee', CO 733/267/37560/Part 1, 113.
[123] 'Report of Committee on Arrears of Werko, Tithes and Agricultural Loans', CO 733/227/97401.
[124] Minute sheet, CO 733/227/97401. See also CO 733/247/17570.

to public security. In 1930, Strickland called for an increased role to be played by *mukhtars* and for their remuneration to be raised.[125] And in August 1933, Wauchope agreed that

Mukhtars should receive an adequate remuneration for the multifarious public duties which they are called upon to perform. These duties extend far beyond the scope of tax collection and delivery. Mukhtars play their small but necessary part in almost every activity of district administration. They are the essential link between Government and the villagers and the channel of information and communication between the District Officer and the fellahin. For these many services almost their sole remuneration is a percentage of the tithe, and if owing to the effects of tax remissions even this exiguous reward is to be further reduced, then the Mukhtars will inevitably become disheartened and discontented at a time when owing to the prevailing unrest, their steadying influence in the villages is most needed to counteract the instigation and incitement of the politician from the towns.[126]

The report on the machinery of tax collection repeated Wauchope's concerns, cautioning against the replacement of *mukhtars* by official tax collectors and against the abandonment of the system by which they were paid a percentage of the tithes collected:

If this be done it will be necessary for Government to consider well in advance what alternative methods are available for remunerating Mukhtars for the considerable amount of other administration work which they perform for Government. If no such steps are taken, it will not be possible to retain the services of the Mukhtars who are a valuable link between Government and the population.[127]

Accordingly, the high commissioner asked not only that the rebate owed to *mukhtars* be increased to 5 per cent of the taxes collected, but also for the continuation of the *mukhtar* system in respect of the collection of the rural property tax. Even the 1935 rural property tax eventually took the form of a tax estimated for, and payable by, a village, to be distributed, and collected, by the *mukhtars* on behalf of government. As described in 1940, the tax 'calls for the posting of Rural Property Tax Rolls in the village to which the land liable to tax is adjacent and for the allocation of tax through the agency of the village'.[128]

---

[125] Strickland Report.

[126] Wauchope to Cunliffe-Lister, 7 Dec. 1933, CO 733/244/17470.

[127] 'Report of the Rural Taxation Machinery Committee', CO 733/267/37560/Part 1. In 1932, the following numbers of *mukhtars* were responsible for the collection of the commuted tithe: Jerusalem, 337; southern district, 369; northern district, 638.

[128] See ISA, Attorney General's Office, RG 3 19/106, box 717.

Like the role played by *mukhtars*, the system of co-ownership of land widely practised in Palestine, known as *musha'*, featured prominently from the outset in all plans to modify the tax regime. This requires some taking in: whereas the idea of securing the position of certain local leaders is a well known feature of indirect colonial rule, particularly as practised by Britain, it is equally well understood by students of mandate Palestine that *musha'* was widely condemned as an age-old tribal practice and an obstacle to agricultural progress. One would expect, therefore, that the only possible agenda for *musha'* in official plans to reform taxation would be its obsolescence. Such would certainly be expected in any plan to base rural taxation on a comprehensive settlement of title to land. In fact, quite the opposite happened in Palestine. As has been noted, revenue officials always lacked the most necessary figures on which to base reforms. Because of this, the assessment and collection of taxation, especially until 1936, was based on the village unit, whether it be the tithe as collected in haste by the military administration, or the 1927 commuted average assessed on the village as a whole. So, the difficulty remained of how to distribute among the individual tithe-payers the amount expected from the village. In this regard, a certain amount of gratitude was expressed for the prevalence of *musha'*, making it relatively straightforward to distribute the village's assessed amount of tax in proportion to individual shares:

Owing to the 'musha' system, which prevails or has at some time prevailed throughout most of the country, agricultural practice has divided cultivable land into blocks of approximately equal fertility (known in the north as 'mawaqis' and in the south as 'qitaat'). Under the 'musha' system, not only had each owner holdings in various blocks, but also at each periodical repartition he had to exchange those holdings for others in the same blocks respectively. Each owner was therefore vitally interested in securing that the classification of the land was as accurate as possible, and in addition he had a very accurate idea of the relative values of the land in the different blocks. Thus the experience of many past generations has provided material of unsurpassed reliability which may conveniently be used for purposes of valuation.[129]

In non-*musha'* villages, it was proposed that the villages themselves be allowed to effect the distribution, the feeling being that, as much non-*musha'* village land was only recently divided, the system was still often familiar to them. As Abramson explained,

[129] 'Report of the Rural Taxation Committee', Oct. 1932, CO 733/216/97060.

where official or unofficial partition of musha land has already been made, the divisions are still known and named by the villagers, who also know the productivity and the relative value of the land in them. These divisions having been made after many years experience of the productivity of the soil, are based on so accurate a knowledge of the soil that there are not only main divisions but sub-divisions of those and minor divisions of the sub-divisions.[130]

It was nonetheless recommended that some criteria be established for judging complaints that might be lodged against such a distribution, and wheat was agreed upon as the measure of productivity.

The 1936 rural property tax was the strongest confirmation yet of the important place which the system of *musha'* had quietly secured in Palestine's taxation regime, not only in distribution but now assessment as well. As we have seen, the idea behind a block land tax, first suggested in 1925, was that the assessment of land for fiscal purposes could best be effected if, irrespective of actual property boundaries, surveys were drawn up which defined blocks of contiguous land of closely equal value. Each block could then be assessed in turn, and all land follow the assessment of the block in which it is situated. The scheme of course had the great virtue of being expedient: the constitution of blocks of land of approximately equal value, Dowson explained, was 'familiar to the people and [had] long been used by them as an equitable basis for the apportionment of mesha' and other shares. Its adoption also as an equitable basis for assessment of land tax is therefore an obvious move, which will be readily understood; and it is one that cannot easily be bettered for simplicity of operation.'[131] Accordingly, the blocks on which the new rural property tax were based (and which later also became the blocks used for registration purposes) were fixed in consultation with village elders and were invariably the same as the divisions of land which a great many villagers had always used for their periodical partition of land for cultivation purposes.

Having condemned the practice of *musha'* for so long, few officials ever openly acknowledged the increasing reliance on it. The courts were not overly troubled: when asked in September 1926 to rule that *musha'* was legally inadmissible, the supreme court sitting as a court of appeal held that

---

[130] Abramson, 'Proposal to Substitute a Land Tax for the Present Werko and Tithe', CO 733/152/1/57195, 98.

[131] Dowson, 'Report on the Land System in Palestine, December 1925', CO 733/109, 235.

this court has already given effect to similar village customs . . . and no authority has been quoted in either of those cases or in the present Appeal for the view that a village custom governing the distribution of the common cultivable land of the village is contrary to law; though the intention of Article 8 of the Land Code may well have been to put an end to Mesha' holdings by inducing the co-owners to partition and register their separate titles.[132]

In his discussion of the ambiguity shown towards *musha'* in the context of land sales, Roger Owen observes that 'a policy of benign neglect may well have seemed the more prudent course', and notes further the significance of the two-volume, 1,120-page *Survey of Palestine*, prepared by the government for the Anglo-American Committee of Inquiry in 1946, not mentioning *musha'* once.[133] One colonial officer who did acknowledge the government's growing dependence on such institutions was Abramson:

while the musha system must be condemned because it has delayed the agricultural improvement of the country, it has one virtue which is of considerable benefit at this stage. As has already been explained, because of it villagers have elaborated and perpetuated the gradation of productivity values by blocks of land which will provide many of the elements for the valuation of land for a land tax, and those divisions, adapted as registration blocks, demarcated and mapped by the Department of Surveys, can be adopted with few modifications as fiscal blocks for a land tax.[134]

Ideological predispositions aside, there was no escaping the fact that the official recognition and mapping out of *musha'* practice on the ground, in terms of a block valuation, would provide the most concrete instrument for the taxation of property, in the shortest possible time.

7. CONCLUSION

Entrenched from the beginning of the mandate, the position of the *mukhtar*, and of *musha'*, as well as other structures of daily village life, played increasingly crucial roles in the practical administration of rural taxation, particularly as mechanisms for its assessment and distribution.

---

[132] 'Land Appeal no. 121 of 1926', in Sir M. McDonnell (et al.) (eds.), *The Law Reports of Palestine . . . : [1920–1946]*, 14 vols. (London: Waterlow and Sons, 1933–47), i. 236.

[133] Roger Owen, 'Defining Traditional: Some Implications of the Use of Ottoman Law in Mandatory Palestine', *Harvard Middle Eastern and Islamic Review*, 1/2 (1994).

[134] Abramson, 'Proposal to Substitute a Land Tax for the Present Werko and Tithe', CO 733/152/1/57195, 98.

The corollary of this desire for expedience and convenience at every turn is that the untiring rhetoric of individualizing property rights so as to bring about a direct relationship between government and individual in the collection of taxes became less and less pertinent or appropriate. All in all there seem to have been many sound administrative reasons for consolidating such village structures as the practice of *musha'* and the *mukhtar* system, just as there were understandably expedient reasons for keeping intact a taxation system that continued to tax the produce rather than the land.

The important place attributed to the process of individualizing property rights, while commanding space in the intellectual musings of official reports, pronouncements, correspondence, commissions, etc., paled when put up against the expediencies of colonial administration. In 1924, the secretary of state for the colonies weighed the various pressures in the following terms:

The establishment of a satisfactory system of land tenure and land tax in Palestine with as little further delay as possible is of outstanding economic importance to the country, while its financial position demands that the necessary reforms shall be introduced as inexpensively as possible. The successful accomplishment of these ends presents many difficulties.[135]

The desired expediency in the collection of as much tax as possible, in such a way moreover that did not unduly disrupt the stability of social structures on which colonial control relied, outweighed the stated ideals regarding property rights. In view of these considerations in the formation of taxation policy, the weighing of priorities is perhaps best achieved by the terms employed in one Colonial Office minute: 'the fundamental principle if things are to work smoothly should be to keep as close as possible to definitely ascertainable fact.'[136]

[135] Colonial Office to Foreign Office, Sept. 1924, CO 733/72, 622.
[136] Minute sheet, Oct. 1932, CO 733/216/97060. This sentiment had first been expressed by the 'Report of the Rural Taxation Machinery Committee', CO 733/267/37560/Part 1.

5

Development

Up until the 1920s, the rocky coastline just south of Haifa was broken by strips of sand which, extending a few miles inland, impeded spring-fed streams as well as run-off water from Mount Carmel. Among the marshes which formed around these dunes, two large areas were inhabited by the indigenous Arab population: the Zor el Zerka, home to a group of about eighty families, known collectively as the Ghawarneh Arabs, as well as a group of thirteen families referred to as the Kabbara Arabs; and the Barrat Caesarea, home to approximately forty-one Arab families.[1] Estimated at approximately 800 persons, the two groups earned their livelihood chiefly from the marshes. Upon the establishment of British mandatory rule in Palestine, British officers quickly focused their attention on what they perceived to be the economic potential of this region and marshalled their resources to pave the way for development initiatives.

This chapter raises questions about the relationship between the construction of property laws in the British colonial administration of Palestine and the discourse of development. It draws specific attention to the impact of attempts by the local inhabitants of the Zor el Zerka and the Barrat Caesarea to assert rights to their land in the face of official attempts at 'improvement', and to engage the Palestine government in a complicated legal battle over compensation. Aspects of the dispute would drag on for many years: after failed attempts to reach a negotiated settlement on certain issues, court proceedings began in 1928. Drawing conclusions from a single case study can of course be problematic. However, this approach will allow us to examine certain essential, and sometimes technical, features of colonial rule, particularly about how the rule of law was observed and strategized by colonial governments. Peasant cultivators were far from passive in the legal encounter, and the way that relations between them and the major agencies of the state unfolded in the legal arena affected the

---

[1] In the documentary record, the lands of the Zor el Zerka are also known as Kabbara: for the sake of consistency and clarity, I refer throughout to the Zor el Zerka.

contested process by which land policies were formulated and implemented. Constituting one of the government's very first attempts to dispose of what it thought of as government property, the bruising political and legal battle over rights to the Zor el Zerka and Caesarea lands ensured that officials thereafter were very wary of the legal position of the government in land cases.[2]

1. THE COLONIAL CONTEXT OF DEVELOPMENT

Taking advantage of the land's diversity, the inhabitants of the Zor el Zerka and the Barrat Caesarea drew their livelihood from a variety of means, chiefly herding cattle which could be watered in the marshes, manufacturing mats and baskets from reeds growing in the marshes, selling tamarisk wood cut from the marshes, and cultivating plots of land, the location of which might shift each year. British officials were initially highly critical of this way of life, seeing only untapped economic potential. That criticism reveals much about how British officials believed the land of Palestine ought to be developed, and how they believed rights to that land should properly be defined and regulated.

First, there was the desire for the enhanced tax base and more efficient revenue system that would flow from market-oriented development and investment.[3] As stressed by high commissioner Samuel in a letter to the Colonial Office, 'it is perhaps hardly necessary for me to point out that [the Zor el Zerka/Caesarea lands] can not be left as they are . . . The benefit to be derived from the point of view of Public Revenue is considerable.'[4] There was a widely held belief that large areas of Palestine were 'imperfectly cultivated' and that fuller use ought to be made of the natural resources to produce marketable commodities to increase both production and consumption, thus providing a greater tax yield. As the local district commissioner summed up, 'the provision of thorn bushes

---

[2] 'It is to be remembered', wrote the acting high commissioner in 1928, 'that the Government cannot afford to take action in land which might lead to difficulties similar to those which were consequent upon the grant of the Athlit-Kabbara-Caesarea lands.' H. C. Luke to L. S. Amery, secretary of state for the colonies, 11 Oct. 1928, CO 733/156, 18. See also discussion of the disposal of *jiftlik* lands of the coastal plain in CO 733/116/17199, and discussion of a concession for reclamation of lands around lake Huleh in: CO 733/46, 334; CO 733/49, 69; and CO 733/51, 101.

[3] See D. K. Fieldhouse, *The West and the Third World: Trade, Colonialism, Dependence and Development* (Oxford: Blackwell, 1999).

[4] Samuel to Colonial Office, 13 July 1922, CO 733/23, 145.

for goats to feed upon (I speak figuratively) seems hardly consistent with a policy of land development and intensive cultivation'.[5] The lands of Zor el Zerka and Barrat Caesarea also acquired added economic value to British administrators who feared the prospect of 'creeping dunes' rendering sections of the nearby railway, and other infrastructure, useless.[6]

Second, like similar initiatives elsewhere in the empire, the development plans of the Palestine government were rooted in ideas about the need to transform the nature of indigenous property rights to stimulate individual enterprise. Colonial officials frequently expressed their faith in the evolutionary superiority of settled cultivation over extensive agriculture, individualized property rights over communal holdings. Both the attorney general and the local district commissioner, for example, likened the government's position on the future of the Zor el Zerka and Barrat Caesarea to a defence of 'progress' and 'civilisation': a chaotic pre-colonial land regime being made orderly and productive by British rule: '[t]here are concentrated in this Kabbara Concession all the difficulties that arise out of the conflict of a progressive civilisation and a deep-rooted tradition.'[7] Because there was no immediately obvious way for British administrators to define or classify the inhabitants' presence in or proprietorship over this property, officials quickly presumed they were dealing with a juridical vacuum, even though, as will be described, hard evidence of the inhabitants' rights to the land was available. After his three-day visit to the region, the chair of a newly formed land commission was unwilling to concern himself in any serious way with what he saw as 'a few bedu families' who 'only just managed to eke out a livelihood': '[t]he only persons at present on the lands are a very small number of negroes who . . . merely use part of the swamps as grazing ground for a small number of bufalloes which they own. *They have no rights to any of the lands.*'[8] To colonial officials, the supposed failure of the indigenous population to improve the land was not only a reflection of economic waste, but justified the view that they were dealing with a legal vacuum.

Beyond sharing these broad features of imperial practice, there were some unique features to British efforts to develop the Zor el Zerka and the

[5] Symes, district commissioner, to chief secretary, 21 Feb. 1923, ISA, RG 2, Chief Secretary's Office, no. 231.

[6] Sawer to Bentwich, 18 Mar. 1923, ISA RG 2, Chief Secretary's Office, no. 231.

[7] Norman Bentwich, 'Note on the Kabbara Concession', 18 June 1924, ISA, RG 2 Chief Secretary's Office, no. 231.

[8] Quoted in 'Confidential Letter', members of Luke Commission to high commissioner, 27 Jan. 1923, CO 733/62, 124. Italics added.

Barrat Caesarea. The stress on development in Palestine owed much to the promise of facilitating the establishment of a Jewish national home. Clearly, development in Palestine can in part be understood in terms of the prevailing assumption that increased prosperity for all of Palestine's population was the most promising and benign way to square the disruptive effects of Jewish immigration from Europe. 'If Arabs and others', explained the 1920 land commission,

Sell their excess land to new settlers they admit strangers by that fact in their areas and their exclusiveness and shyness to the stranger will gradually be overcome. They will slowly but surely realise the benefit of settled habits and of economic and agricultural intercourse with experienced farmers. New settlers will build hospitals, schools, and other institutions of public security. Exclusiveness by new settlers should be avoided and the fellah and Arab will be quick to realise the benefit of the stranger in his neighbourhood.[9]

The settlement of Jewish immigrants as would-be colonists, notes Barbara Smith, could be framed in a typically colonial mode of thought: 'the European settlers, with their superior education, technological know how, and capital, would bring material benefits to the "natives" and provide the "backward" Arabs with an example to which to aspire: the injection of Zionist "yeast" would produce a "cake" to be shared with the Palestinian Arabs.'[10]

The apparent enthusiasm in the 1920s for development in Palestine had nonetheless to be exercised within the constraints thrown up by the framework of the colonial state. The first set of constraints was financial in nature. Budgetary concerns seriously constrained the willingness of colonial officials to engage in expensive development projects and from this frugality emerged a growing dependence on private and corporate European capital. 'Every encouragement should be given to these pioneers,' exclaimed the land commission.[11] A second source of tension that confronted the proponents of intrusive development projects was politico-economic in nature and was fuelled by the desire for political stability. Whereas colonial assessments of development needs often required state interventions aimed at radically redefining agrarian structures, political stability was usually sought by securing rural populations to the land for fear that a growing transient population constituted a greater political

---

[9] 'Report of Land Commission', CO 733/18, 635.
[10] Barbara J. Smith, *The Roots of Separatism in Palestine: British Economic Policy, 1920–1929* (Syracuse, NY: Syracuse University Press, 1993), 7.
[11] 'Report of Land Commission', CO 733/18.

threat. A third source of tension was legal in nature and emerged from the pressure to respect the status quo. British officials, as noted, eagerly assumed a juridical vacuum wherever they could, yet their authority in Palestine was meant to be exercised in conformity with existing laws.

2. THE 1921 CONCESSIONARY AGREEMENT

All these pressures interacted in interesting ways in the government's elaboration of plans for the Zor el Zerka marshes and the Caesarea sand dunes. Prior to the war, the Palestine Jewish Colonization Association (PJCA)—an agency of Baron de Rothschild—had engaged in negotiations with Ottoman officials to acquire a concession to drain the Kabbara marshes, but nothing became operative or received government ratification.[12] When the request was again made in July 1920 by the PJCA to drain, afforest, and settle these lands, the government officials responded enthusiastically. A land commission was deputed to ascertain the general characteristics of the area and to formulate proposals 'to secure the profitable use of land which is now left waste'.[13] On the basis of the commission's cursory evaluation, the Palestine government hurried into an agreement with the PJCA, granting it a 100-year lease over an area of about 40,000 unsurveyed dunams and the right to 'improve and develop' the marshes and dunes.[14]

The sense of urgency in the commission's recognition of the land's economic potential stands in sharp contrast to the neglect shown towards the land's inhabitants. After its tour of the area, the commission concluded that these areas were waste and thus at government's full disposal. As far as the commission was concerned, the responsibility for satisfying what were considered at the outset to be the unwarranted claims of an insignificant resident population ought best to be placed on the shoulders of the concessionaire, the PJCA.[15] But the PJCA failed in this case to

[12] 'Report of Commission of Enquiry', Jan. 1923, CO 733/42, 204.
[13] 'Note for the Press on the Land Commission', 18 Aug. 1920, ISA RG 2, Chief Secretary's Office, nos. 80 and 81.
[14] For terms of agreement, see 'Administrative Report for Dec. 1921', CO 733/18, 116.
[15] Other than positing that local Arabs might be employed as wage labourers in the drainage works, there was no mention in the concession document itself of the inhabitants. As explained by Albert Hyamson, the PJCA was known for its attempts to provide for the Arab inhabitants of the land it acquired for settlement schemes: 'As a rule they bought land for development, so land which had previously supported a hundred families could in future support a thousand. The thousand families after development were, however,

engender local support for the concession. The inhabitants appointed a lawyer, Wadi Boustany, to defend their rights and Boustany immediately wrote off to the Colonial Office, arguing that

[The] plain fact is that the interests of the 850 bona fide citizens permanently settled are not at all taken into account in this concession, the benefits of which are exclusively limited to this JCA . . . [T]his concession amounts to nothing short of handing over a portion of the lands held by bona fide fellow countrymen to a foreign company, registered in London, and its terms, as brought to our cognizance, do not bind such company to the necessity of keeping those legal bona fide citizens on their lands.[16]

Boustany's letter revealed to advisers in the Colonial Office that despite the inhabitants' invisibility to the official land commission, evidence of their rights to the land existed: it could be found in the records of Ottoman law cases and the reports of Ottoman administrative officials, as well as in personal histories. These records indicated that approximately 800 inhabitants and their ancestors had permanently lived on the land for over 100 years, enjoying officially recognized rights in respect to their use of the land. Upon receiving this letter, the Colonial Office—worried about the potential for political disturbance—immediately demanded certain guarantees from Palestine's high commissioner: 'I should be glad to receive an assurance that the properties of Arabs who have a legal title to their land would be excluded from the operation of the lease, as there would appear to be no power by which they could be included in a lease granted to other parties.'[17] But the wariness expressed by the Colonial Office did not deter the Palestine government in its development plans. Though the 1921 concessionary agreement appeared flawed to the Colonial Office, officials in Palestine did not waver in their endeavour to secure the

not all Jewish. Provision on the developed land—not by payment of compensation or the endeavour to find land elsewhere—was always made for the original residents, who were as a rule better after the development work had been completed than before.' Albert M. Hyamson, *Palestine under the Mandate: 1920–1948* (Westport, Conn.: Greenwood Press, 1950), 83. It has been suggested that Baron Rothschild wanted to clear the land with Arab labour out of concern for the safety of Jewish immigrants, but one Jewish labourer is quoted as protesting: 'Ours is the privilege of dying for Kabbara because we claim for ourselves the privilege of living on it.' See ESCO Foundation for Palestine, *Palestine: A Study of Jewish, Arab and British Policies* (New Haven: Yale University Press, 1947). The offer of employment to the Arab inhabitants of the Zor el Zerka and Caesarea concessionary areas was ambiguous: local Arabs were to be given preference over other Arab labourers for work of drainage, canalization, and subsequent clearing of the lands.

[16] Letter to colonial secretary, 23 May 1922, CO 733/23, 168.
[17] Churchill to Samuel, 10 Aug. 1922, CO 733/23, 177.

execution of the project (without, that is, having to incur the financial burden). In a confidential memo, the district governor, George Symes, captured the sense of frustration that was growing in Jerusalem: 'the public interest and civilisation as represented by the [PJCA] concession are in sharp and irremediable conflict with the sentiments and selfish interests of the Arab populations.'[18] If the project was to be executed, the inhabitants had to be removed. How to do this, in such a way as would accommodate at some basic level the legal concerns upheld by the Colonial Office, engaged the Palestine government, and especially the attorney general, in two related projects: determining legal measures for expropriation but, first, ensuring that the rights of the inhabitants were defined in a way that would most expeditiously facilitate that expropriation. It is useful at this point to consider the two holdings separately.

3. THE ZOR EL ZERKA, THE ATTORNEY GENERAL, AND THE COLONIAL CONSTRUCTION OF LAWS

The claims on behalf of the inhabitants of the Zor el Zerka were made in regard to cultivation, pasturage, woodcutting, and other long exercised uses of the land. In support of their claims, Wadi Boustany, their lawyer, made reference to an official Ottoman demarcation commission of 1875 which specifically granted certain rights to the local population for the grazing of cattle. The commission presumably had based its decisions on the fact that occupation had at that time already been long-standing. Although Palestine's attorney general, Norman Bentwich, accepted the official recognition of those rights, he was careful to dispute the precise nature of the legal right to graze. Boustany argued that the entry in the demarcation report describing the land as grazing land indicated that, according to Ottoman land law, the land was of the *matruke* category. By the terms of article 91 of the Ottoman land code, *matruke* land is land left for the use of the public. It could take two forms: land which was left for the general use of the public, such as public highways, and land left for the use of a particular village (or group of villages), such as pastures. However, Bentwich disagreed that the reference to the Zor el Zerka in the official demarcation report was evidence of an assignation of *matruke* within the

---

[18] Symes, 'Strictly Confidential: Athlit-Kabbara Concession', 13 June 1922, ISA RG 22 Land Registration and Land Settlement, 'Athlit', G 39/1, box 3525.

meaning of Ottoman law, and he chose his words carefully when describing the sorts of rights he was prepared to consider: 'It should be made clear to the Arabs that the Government does not recognize them as having any legal title in the land of Zor el Zerka but simply as having rights of common which it is proposed to treat as having a legal basis.'[19] Bentwich specifically renounced the claim that the entry in the demarcation commission report constituted the land as *matruke*. He was prepared to grant that, by the terms of the report's entry, the inhabitants enjoyed rights corresponding to the English right in common but he was at pains to deny that this necessarily constituted rights corresponding to Ottoman legal categories:

The rights in common in matrukeeh land are expressed throughout to be relative or appendant to the inhabitants of a town or village. Article 91 of the Land Code provides that the trees of woods or forests assigned *for the use of a town or village* shall be cut by the inhabitants of such town or village only. Article 97 commences 'in a pasture ground assigned to a village, the inhabitants of such village only can pasture their animals.' And Article 271 of the Civil Code, the Mejelle, on which the section of the Land Code is based, provides that 'the lands near *inhabited places* belong to the inhabitants, in order that they may make use of them as pasturage, threshing floors, and places for timber.'[20]

Given this interpretation, Bentwich urged the significance of there being no 'village' of the resident Arab population (official reference to 'camps' and 'tents' conveniently precluded official recognition of a 'village') to which the rights of grazing and cutting wood mentioned in the report of the 1875 Ottoman demarcation commission could be appendant in accordance with Ottoman law. Bentwich was thus able to satisfy himself that 'the true interpretation'[21] was that there was no legal constitution of the lands inhabited by the Arabs of the Zor el Zerka as *matruke*: 'so far as can be ascertained, they have for all time lived in the camps in the Zor el Zerka lands . . . [B]ecause they are not, properly speaking, the inhabitants of a village, . . . therefore the lands may not, according to the provisions of the land law, become legally Matrukeh.'[22]

It is important to realize that the prevalence of the development ethos necessitated that the attorney general reason his conclusion the way he

---

[19] Minutes by Bentwich, undated, ISA RG 2, Chief Secretary's Office, no. 231.

[20] Bentwich, 'Opinion on the Arab Claims to the Lands Comprised in the Kabbara-Athlit Concession', CO 733/48, 361–2. Emphasis in original.

[21] Ibid. 367.

[22] Ibid. 365.

did. While he reluctantly admitted to recognizing that the Arab inhabitants of the Zor el Zerka held something equivalent to the English rights in common, he had at the same time to determine what steps were necessary for the expropriation of those very rights. The process of expropriation would have been complicated greatly had the land been recognized as *matruke*. Within the prevailing understandings of articles 91 to 100 of the Ottoman land code, it was considered doubtful whether *matruke* land could be converted to any other purpose. If, therefore, the Palestine government was to confirm the claimants' assertion that the land over which they exercised rights was *matruke*, the land would not be ready for the development and improvement envisaged for it.

Bentwich faced a number of obstacles in his endeavour to negotiate Ottoman law in these ways. In addition to the contrary interpretations put forth by Arab lawyers, obstacles were raised by Palestine's own solicitor general, Robert Drayton. Drayton questioned in particular the assumption that the government had any power to expropriate the Zor el Zerka. He observed that the administration's own regulations declared that where it was necessary to expropriate land for public purposes the Ottoman law of expropriation of 21 January 1913 would be applied:

the Municipalities of the vilayets shall have power to expropriate any places whether or not containing buildings for any public purposes such as the opening of a new street or enlargement of an existing street, the institution of a public garden, the foundation of hospitals, asylums for disabled persons or orphanages, the construction or enlargement of market places, ports, promenades, water courses, or reservoirs for extinguishing fires or other purposes and such other works or construction as may be necessary for the sanitation of the town.[23]

Drayton was not convinced that these terms covered the purposes of the expropriation of the Zor el Zerka: 'the Attorney General no doubt had good reasons for holding that these purposes are public purposes within the meaning of Article 1 of the law referred to above,' he wrote to the high commissioner, 'but I must confess that those reasons are not apparent to me.'[24]

---

[23] Minutes by Drayton, acting attorney general, 2 May 1923, ISA RG 2, Chief Secretary's Office, no. 231.

[24] Ibid. Two years later, Dowson shared the same concerns regarding the powers vested in government and the procedures to be followed: 'there appears to be some ambiguity here,' he wrote, complaining of 'not being able to get hold of the text of some of the relevant documents and to ambiguous citation of dates'. See Dowson, 'Preliminary Study of Land Tenure in Palestine', CO 733/109, 173.

Bentwich's response is telling. Though he did not actually have a copy of the law, he accepts that the administration declared the Ottoman law of 1913 to be applied for the expropriation of land where necessary. He explained to Samuel, however, that 'the intention and the effect' of the notices was only to 'determine the machinery by which expropriation is to be conducted': 'it is submitted that it would be a most unreasonable interpretation of the Public Notice to hold that it restricted the Government's powers of expropriation to those which are required for municipal purposes.'[25] Moreover, Bentwich contended there was another Ottoman law still in force in Palestine: the law of 6 December 1879, as amended by the law of 30 April 1914. This enactment provided for expropriation by the government of land for any public purpose such as 'the opening or extension of a street . . . the improvement of water courses or rivers . . . the establishment of all sanitary works or institutions, and, generally, all other works or institutions for the benefit of the public'.[26] As to the question whether the purposes for which the concession of the Zor el Zerka lands had been made were in fact public purposes within the scope of the stated law, Bentwich was satisfied that the expropriation of such land was indeed covered: 'it is submitted on this point that the drainage of the marshes, afforestation for the purpose of protecting the cultivated lands and the railway from invasion of sand drifts . . . are clearly works or institutions for the benefit of the public, similar in nature to the works specifically mentioned in Section I of the Ottoman law.'[27] The Colonial Office, noticeably uncomfortable with the circuitous interpretations adopted by the attorney general, did not welcome the idea of expropriation. Immediately upon hearing of the sorts of rights recognized for the Zor el Zerka, the Colonial Office demanded clarification: 'the guiding principle should be . . . that legal claims, *i.e.* area to which individuals are decided by you to have legal claims, should be excluded from the scope of the lease and the [PJCA] should be informed that any such areas were wrongly included.'[28] But the Palestine government was determined to expropriate and develop. Rather than take steps to exclude the claims to the Zor el Zerka from the scope of the lease to the PJCA, as advised, it set out to convince the Colonial Office that the Zor el Zerka simply

[25] Samuel to Devonshire, 19 Oct. 1923, CO 733/50, 243. Compare with the narrow restrictions imposed in his definition of *matruke*, as outlined above.

[26] Cited in Bentwich, 'Athlit-Kabbara Concession', 24 May 1923, ISA RG 2, Chief Secretary's Office, no. 231.

[27] Ibid.

[28] Colonial Office to Samuel, 24 May 1923, CO 733/44, 509.

could not be excluded from the lease without nullifying the whole scheme of development.

Efforts to this end were accompanied by the noticeable identification of the region in official circles as one of mosquito-breeding swamps. The reclaiming of them for intense cultivation, insisted high commissioner Samuel, was 'a sanitary work' for the benefit of the public.[29] It is worth considering with some care this attempt to frame the government's development project in terms of public sanitation. Perhaps encouraged by the positive response received from the League of Nations' permanent mandates commission (PMC) in Geneva, Samuel himself made something of a personal campaign out of the fight against malaria. Upon the completion of a tour of the country in October 1923, Samuel concluded that 'apart from politics, one of the improvements from which I have derived most satisfaction is the great progress that has been made in many places combatting malaria'.[30] Only days earlier, he had emphasized this point in a letter to the Colonial Office that pressed for sanction of the development plans for Zor el Zerka: 'it is not the case of another's gain being their loss, but of a common gain being secured by the carrying out of a sanitary measure which, quite apart from the reclaiming of the land, is required for the purposes of public health.'[31]

In understanding the official position on public health, several factors ought to be borne in mind. First, it should be recalled that in the 1920s malaria had become a prominent issue in the League of Nations, a concern which in fact led to the creation of a malaria commission in 1924. Colonial officials, and Samuel especially, were no doubt very conscious of just how much could be justified before the PMC if it could be said to have been done in the name of combating malaria. Secondly, one must consider the actual approach taken by the government to combat malaria. The campaign consisted almost entirely of measures that suited the government agenda. Samuel's reference to sanitary measures required for public health does not in itself demonstrate an interest in the well-being of the local population. Boustany insisted in a telegram to the Colonial Office that 'alleged raison d'etre public utility health proved unfounded'.[32] Certainly for some Colonial Office officials, there was an uncomfortable whiff of special pleading about Samuel's recourse to arguments about the

[29] Samuel to Devonshire, 24 Aug. 1923, CO 733/48, 354.

[30] 'Notes on the High Commissioner's Tour', CO 733/50, 517.

[31] Samuel to Devonshire, 19 Oct. 1923, CO 733/50, 243.

[32] Telegram from Boustany to secretary of state for the colonies, 23 June 1922, CO 733/40, 199.

benefits bestowed upon public health generally: as one official minuted, 'public utility is a term which should include the Arabs in its scope. They therefore should be found room on the improved lands.'[33]

Much doubt was expressed in the Colonial Office as to whether the development of the Zor el Zerka could in fact be defined as a work for the benefit of the public. Which public? To many, the draining of the marshes appeared not to benefit the general public so much as a comparatively small portion of that public. Sir John Risley expressed these concerns when he noted that

so far as the local public consists of immigrant Jews or other non-indigenous persons, the old-established Arab villagers might well contend that they and their ancestors have always lived near these marshes and have taken no scathe there-from, and consequently that as they form (probably) by far the largest section of 'the public' immediately interested, the draining of the marshes could not be held to be a 'work . . . for the benefit of the public'.[34]

Despite the Colonial Office's persistent questioning of legal positions arrived at by the Palestine government, the attorney general exercised a fair degree of autonomy in proceeding with his justifications and plans for developing and improving the Zor el Zerka and Caesarea lands. To be sure, legislation for Palestine was subject to the approval or disapproval of London, but officials there did not have in their possession, nor could they find in relevant libraries, reliable texts of the Ottoman legislation cryptically referred to by the Palestine government. 'I do not pretend to have formed any clear picture of this,' admitted R. V. Vernon at one point.[35] More specifically, Sir John Risley complained that

it is difficult and I think it would be dangerous for me to attempt to advise upon an Ottoman law which is presented to me in the form of a French translation which is 'not guaranteed'! Apart from that I am quite unable to identify the English words quoted . . . with any provision contained in . . . the Ottoman law as translated in the volume and I must assume that the original of these words is to be found in the amending law of 1330 (1914) which is mentioned in para 3 of the despatch and which is not before us.[36]

---

[33] Minute by Moody, 24 Aug. 1923, CO 733/48, 349.

[34] Minute by Sir John Risley, Aug. 1923, CO 733/48, 349. A big part of the Colonial Office agenda that lies behind the criticism of the Palestine government's expropriation plans is evidently the concern for the consequences. As noted on the same minute sheet, monetary compensation for expropriation 'will finally leave them stranded and landless. They will then become a danger to public security.'

[35] Minute sheets, 11 Feb. 1925, CO 733/89, 32.

[36] Minute sheets, 24 Aug. 1923, CO 733/48, 349.

The responsibility for determining which Ottoman laws could be utilized, and how, was largely left to the Palestine attorney general's own discretion.

Despite all this legal groundwork, or perhaps *because* of it, the Palestine government did not in the end expropriate the rights of the inhabitants of the Zor el Zerka. In July 1924, it was reported that the municipality of Haifa had in fact nominated persons to assess the value of the rights to be expropriated. With the ball rolling, it was also decided officially that the PJCA need not wait for the completion of expropriation proceedings and should be at liberty to enter onto the land of the Zor el Zerka and commence engineering operations. Bentwich justified, 'it is desirable that the Arabs should understand that the Concession is to be carried out'.[37] In fact, shortly after this news was released—and very likely as an intended consequence of its release—the PJCA announced it had reached a definite agreement with the Arab inhabitants. In return for cash and some land elsewhere, the Arabs agreed to formally renounce all legal rights to the Zor el Zerka. That the expropriation announcement intimidated the Arabs into accepting a negotiated compromise cannot be discounted, and in fact as much was admitted later by the acting high commissioner, when he made reference to the Zor el Zerka, 'the common rights and easements of which have been disposed of under threat of expropriation'.[38]

4. THE BARRAT CAESAREA AND THE ROLE OF THE COURTS

In contrast to the difficulties he encountered with the legal case presented on behalf of the Zor el Zerka, Bentwich more readily dismissed the documentation brought in support of the rights of the Arabs of the Barrat Caesarea. Here, Bentwich argued for a rather complicated differentiation between claims of the inhabitants that had a 'moral' basis and those that had a 'legal' basis. Investing the inhabitants with 'moral' or equitable rights by virtue of their long-standing presence in the area achieved two ends. On the one hand, it implied that the colonial government was indeed taking steps to respect and protect the status quo. On the other, it still fulfilled the government's plan to improve and develop: recognition of moral rights simply satisfied the administration that removal of the inhabitants was

---

[37] Bentwich to chief secretary, 18 July 1924, ISA RG 2, Chief Secretary's Office, no. 231.
[38] Clayton to colonial office, 19 Aug. 1924, CO 733/72, 195. Also see Smith, *The Roots of Separatism in Palestine: British Economic Policy, 1920–1929*, 102.

morally justifiable so long as their settlement elsewhere was made. The creation of what one official categorized as 'merely moral' rights was to be the first step towards facilitating the government's acquisition of legal rights to the land in question. As Symes explained, 'I maintain that the Government has towards these people precisely the same responsibilities as a private owner who sold—or leased—his property would have towards the tenants already established on the land. The latter, if they are to be evicted, must be provided for.'[39] In practical terms, therefore, by endowing the inhabitants with moral rights to the Barrat Caesarea, British officials effectively subsumed for the state the legal rights of ownership.

Ideally, as far as the government was concerned, the moral or equitable grazing rights of the Arab inhabitants of the Barrat Caesarea would have been satisfied in much the same way as ultimately were those of the Zor el Zerka Arabs, that is through a negotiated settlement with the concessionaire. The difficulty here, however, was that the terms of the concession in this neighbourhood—namely, the fixing and afforestation of sand dunes—were of a more costly and less remunerative nature than was the development plan for the Zor el Zerka. Indeed, because of the difficulties to be encountered in this region generous terms appear to have been granted in respect to the more profitable areas included in the concession. Government officials became worried. They knew that the PJCA was not as anxious to include the Barrat Caesarea in the lease and they also knew that the Arab inhabitants knew. The PJCA had the upper hand, and in the summer of 1924 it declared that, if no satisfactory solution could be reached, the government should relieve it from the obligations of afforesting the dunes and reserved for itself the right to give up the lease of that portion of the region.[40] Finally, in 1928, the attorney general brought an action in the district court of Haifa against the Barrat Caesarea Arabs claiming the land in question was waste land. But the judges were unable to agree, and during the 1930s the situation became ever more complicated with the Arab inhabitants building more houses, sinking more wells, and changing or extending the cultivation and grazing areas in the disputed territory. One frustrated official with the lands department concluded in 1946 that 'nobody has admitted understanding exactly what was the effect of the judgement'.[41]

[39] Symes to Abramson, chair of land commission, 1 May 1922, ISA RG 22, Land Registration and Land Settlement, G39/1, box 3525.

[40] Clayton to Colonial Office, 19 Aug. 1924, CO 733/72, 195.

[41] Memo entitled 'Caesarea Lands Case', by crown counsel, 7 Nov. 1946, ISA, Attorney General's Office, RG 3, 7/10, box 703.

Before discussing some of the more significant points arising from the legal proceedings, consideration should be given as to why it took until 1928 for the government to turn to the courts. It is clear that the attorney general was reluctant to take the case of the Barrat Caesarea to court: 'there is at present', Bentwich declared in 1924, 'no question of legal proceedings.'[42] Many British officials, for whom the whole matter was never meant to be more than an administrative one, were eager to put the onus for the satisfaction of such claims as were held by the inhabitants on the shoulders of the concessionaire. Not all officials, however, agreed with this approach. From very early on, anxious voices from within the Colonial Office pressed for a definitive legal decision,[43] and there was significant disagreement as well from within the Palestine administration:

I am of opinion that the Palestine Government would be well advised to receive an opinion on the legal titles involved in the concessionary area from a Committee composed in the manner suggested by the Secretary of State . . . [I]ts weight and its prestige, derived from the judicial characters of its members, would invest in it an authority, which would be a source of strength for the Government . . . and which, moreover, would command the respect, not only of the public of Palestine, but also of those in England who find a puerile amusement in attributing constantly to the Palestine Government motives of not impartial a character . . . It is because of that, that I have constantly advanced the view that a judicial pronouncement on title by the competent court might be absolutely necessary.[44]

The director of agriculture brought the following pressure to bear:

we are struck by the inability . . . to express an opinion on the legality of claims of grazing and other prescription rights . . . There are no authoritative directions of general application for a determination of prescriptive rights . . . We are being driven by experience to the conclusion that neither our legal advisers nor our district officials are conversant with Forest Law, which is, after all, a very technical branch of legislation.[45]

Despite these criticisms, there was general agreement that going to court was best avoided. For one, a legal battle had the potential of becoming a public relations nightmare. The courtroom in general constituted an area where government felt more vulnerable and officials did not look forward to the political ramifications of being put in the position of having to

[42] Bentwich to chief secretary, 4 Mar. 1924, ISA RG 2, Chief Secretary's Office, no. 231.
[43] See, for example, colonial office minutes, Feb. 1923, CO 733/42, 686.
[44] Mills to chief secretary, 15 June 1923. ISA RG 2, Chief Secretary's Office, no. 231.
[45] Sawer to attorney general, 18 Mar. 1923, ISA RG 2, Chief Secretary's Office, no. 231.

defend the PJCA in legal proceedings against the local population.[46] As Sir Henry Bushe, assistant legal adviser in the Colonial Office, observed: 'it does not seem to make for peace or concord to tell a number of nomadic Arabs that they can sue the Government if they are not satisfied.'[47] It was to avoid a legal confrontation pitting the government of Palestine against its Arab inhabitants that many government officials favoured an administrative settlement. Symes put forth the government position clearly:

after careful and anxious study of the matter in all its aspects, I make the following recommendation . . . There might be given—I suggest liberal—compensation in money or in land . . . for the suspension of their weaving and grazing operations; . . . knowledge that monetary compensation will be forthcoming may cause a gradual dispersion of Arabs to other neighbourhoods. This dispersal might be quietly and tactfully accelerated . . . I fully recognise that this is no counsel of perfection . . . but I conceive this to be a lesser evil as contrasted with the propaganda and scandal (from the narrow Arab standpoint) that would be caused by the immediate expulsion of 150 families with their flocks and herds and their tales of distress and hopelessness for the future.[48]

As one Colonial Office official pleaded, on a minute sheet which was otherwise full of harsh criticisms of the Palestine government's attempts to avoid legal recognition of legal rights, 'if the solution offered is actually tending to peace it is better to leave it alone. Everybody in Palestine prefers administrative to legal action in such matters.'[49]

Closely related to this fear of the poor publicity from a legal battle was the growing uncertainty regarding the government's position. The Colonial Office questioned in particular the thoroughness of the attorney general's categorization of moral and legal claims. 'I am not sure at all', observed H. W. Young, 'that "steps taken which contemplate generous satisfaction of moral claims" will meet the case.'[50] The uncertain legal position of the Palestine government suggests other problems associated with recourse to the courts. For example, it is clear that the question as to who was to bring the action to the courts weighed heavily. The question of who was to be regarded as plaintiff and who was to be regarded as defendant was crucial because the position of defendant was considered from the outset to be the stronger one: it was the plaintiffs who had to prove their case.

[46] Devonshire to Samuel, 24 May 1923, CO 733/44, 509.

[47] Minute by Bushe, Feb. 1923, CO 733/42, 686.

[48] Symes, 'Strictly Confidential: Athlit Kabbara Concession', 13 June 1922, ISA RG 22, Land Registration and Land Settlement, G39/1, box 3525.

[49] Minute by Moody, Feb. 1923, CO 733/42, 686.

[50] Minute by Young, Feb. 1923, CO 733/42, 686.

In the event, when the case ultimately did go before the courts in 1928, the decision pretty much realized the government's fears. The two judges were divided in their judgements as to whether there was enough evidence in the proceedings to prove that all the lands were waste and so the government, as plaintiff, did not succeed in proving its claim.

5. CONCLUSIONS

Though one is cautious about what conclusions can fairly be drawn from a case study approach (there is always another case), this examination of the Palestine government's plans to develop the Zor el Zerka and Barrat Caesarea lands draws attention to a number of important features that characterized the way a development agenda inscribed itself in the early years of British rule in Palestine.

First, one should take note that the context in which development projects were explored was one generally dominated by the assumption that all such changes undertaken by the government would be within the framework of the law. Despite the obvious authoritarian characteristics of the colonial state, its strategies for development nonetheless observed the rule of law (or, at least, aimed to appear to do so). The main rationale here was the search for legitimacy. This can be said to have been all the more true to the imperial enterprise in the post-First World War Wilsonian international order. It was most useful to defend, before critics in Geneva and London, any unpopular action as within the scope the law. 'It seems to me', minuted one Colonial Office official, 'that the first thing to do is to get the rights and wrongs of the case from a legal point of view thrashed out.'[51] Thereafter, officials in Palestine were somewhat constrained in their action by the need to convince themselves and London that 'all tenant cultivators' interests are most strictly maintained'.[52] However, by according a moral validity to certain traditions and customs of Palestine's land regime, rather than obdurately ignoring them, the colonial authorities expected to bolster their legitimacy without unduly constraining their freedom of action. The need to legitimize their rule was also revealed in the emphasis on ideas of progress and improvement (the draining of malaria-breeding swamps, the afforestation of invasive dunes, the transition

[51] Minute sheets, CO 733/42, 202.
[52] Minute by Mills, 23 June 1922, CO 733/40, 198. Note that Mills, an official of the Palestine administration, was seconded to the Colonial Office at this time.

to intensive agriculture). The representation of colonial land policy as enlightened and modern underpinned the whole development endeavour. But, as has been noted about colonialism generally and as is revealed in the steps taken by the Palestine government in the case presented here, the common good which the colonial state claimed to represent was determined by the needs of empire, more than by the needs of the socio-political structure that it administered.[53]

A second set of questions can be raised regarding how law was actually constructed in a colonial context. Adherence to the rule of law offered not only to legitimize colonial power, it could also disguise it.[54] Although adherence to the rule of law in mandate Palestine was professed in a rather straightforward way by the official declaration that existing Ottoman laws would be conformed to, this chapter demonstrates that British legal officers were in fact very busy attempting to transform laws. The attorney general's preference might have been to discover law rather than construct it, but given the ambiguities of the process there were options.[55] Conforming to Ottoman law is best seen as an ad hoc exercise: Ottoman laws and practices regarding property rights were studied, reformulated, and institutionalized only when the relevant situation imposed itself. It is instructive in this context to recall that the Colonial Office in London, which approved all legislation, did not even have copies of the relevant Ottoman laws regarding something as important as expropriation until appended to a dispatch on the subject of the concession studied here. Any understanding of the process by which Palestine's legal officers arrived at their final definition of Ottoman law must rest on a detailed appreciation of the particular circumstances in which laws were considered and of the particular ends for which they were intended. This is to say, the process of conforming to Ottoman law was frequently a means to an end, not an end in itself. Laws (such as the law of expropriation, or the law defining the

[53] See Jurgen Osterhammel, *Colonialism: A Theoretical Overview*, trans. S. L. Frisch (Princeton: Markus Wiener, 1997), 58.

[54] See Janet Abu Lughod, *Rabat: Urban Apartheid in Morocco* (Princeton: Princeton University Press, 1980).

[55] See Martin Bunton, 'Inventing the Status Quo: Ottoman Land-Law during the Palestine Mandate, 1917–1936', *International History Review*, 21/1 (1999). Legal historians have written much about this process: as Martin Chanock has observed, 'common law jurisprudence . . . no longer pretends that common law courts simply "find" law. It knows that they "make" it by choosing among a range of possibilities [of] what to "find".' Martin Chanock, 'Paradigms, Policies, and Property: A Review of the Customary Law of Land Tenure', in Kristin Mann and Richard Roberts (eds.), *Law in Colonial Africa* (Portsmouth, NH: Heinemann Educational Books, 1991), 71.

nature of *matruke* land, or the nuanced separation of legal and equitable rights) were defined and redefined in ways that reflected specific colonial priorities (development) and that expedited specific colonial projects (marsh drainage).

A last set of questions can be raised about the problems faced by British officers in their attempts to align Ottoman laws with the administrative necessities of the colonial state. The case study presented here suggests that the use of law as a developmental tool—to enforce local cooperation and ensure international legitimacy—was not without its challenges. Lawyers and legal advisers within and outside of Palestine could contest legal definitions. As has been noted for colonial Africa, legal proceedings became an important arena for opposing imperial measures,[56] law being an arena where the colonial state was less monolithic and omnipotent an entity than is often presumed and was forced to confront unwelcome opposition to its self-perception as an objective authority neutrally exercising the rule of law.[57] So although law played a central role in the colonial designs for Palestine, it has to be seen as an ambiguous one given that rule of law also provided a way of resistance. The role played by Wadi Boustany, legal adviser to the Arab inhabitants, in this process merits a great deal more consideration than is given here, but nonetheless illustrates the agency of local actors and suggests limits on the colonial state's capacity. When confronted with Boustany's interpretation of the inhabitants' rights in Ottoman law, the attorney general fought hard to assert and defend his own interpretation. Much more appears to have been at stake here than an economic development project. We are provided with a sense of how nervously colonial officials reacted to the exposure of limits to their authority and rule. As Jurgen Osterhammel has observed, the colonial state's 'guiding principle' was 'never to let the initiative be snatched away and never to lose face. The state always had to have the last word.'[58]

The case study presented here allowed for a closer examination of the widely circulated proposition that British officials sought to secure the title of Palestinian cultivators in their land so as to encourage their development of it: 'One of the greatest hindrances to the development of Palestine', minuted one Colonial Office official, 'is the uncertainty of titles to land.'[59] In fact, early on, there emerged in official circles a

[56] Richard Roberts and Kristin Mann, 'Law in Colonial Africa', in Mann and Roberts (eds.), *Law in Colonial Africa*, 3.
[57] Osterhammel, *Colonialism: A Theoretical Overview*, 58.   [58] Ibid. 59.
[59] Minute sheets, CO 733/193/2/77336.

development ethos which favoured certain rights in land over others and, above all, one that endeavoured to see that landholders' rights were subservient to the state's interests. Rather than seek to confirm and secure the rights which the inhabitants of the Zor el Zerka and Caesarea lands held to the land, the Palestine administration became increasingly impatient with any sorts of rights that might interfere with the increasing priority given to the administrative goals of the state.

Conclusion

Throughout the mandate period, numerous problems were confronted by the land settlement process. Chief among these were limited funds, lack of staff, poor equipment, the demands of training, mis-coordination between various procedures, sickness, the distractions of sporadic and special projects, the increase in the amount of litigation which paralleled the increases in land values, and repeated political disturbances. All of these factors undoubtedly took their toll on the progress of survey and settlement,[1] as no doubt did the amount of time spent attending meetings about land issues and in preparing minutes of reports about them.[2] Nonetheless, authorities consistently attached a great deal of significance to the land registers themselves. This concern was evident at the end of the Second World War when an already overextended state apparatus took great measures to ensure the safe custody of the government's land records. The prevailing sense of public insecurity, and, more specifically, the actual damage done to the Jerusalem registry in 1944, convinced the acting director of land registration, J. F. Spry, of the need to photograph the records: the intention was that the images would be developed and stored in England until such time as they could be transferred to a successor authority in the region, should the original records not survive the chaos of impending civil war. In December 1947, cameras were flown in and set up in Jerusalem. Official procedures were clear: 'No photographing was ever to take place unless at least one member of the permanent staff of the Department was present, and unless a British officer was present, there was to be at least one Arab and one Jew.'[3] Given the disorder

---

[1] Dov Gavish, *A Survey of Palestine under the British Mandate, 1920–1948* (London: Routledge Curzon, 2005).

[2] I. N. Camp, 'Annual Report of Baisan Demarcation Commission for 1927', 23 Dec. 1927, ISA RG 22, Land Registration and Land Settlement, G/41/5, box 3599. Camp reports spending half his time meeting with Dowson.

[3] J. F. Spry, 'Appendix III: Note on the Photographing of the Land Registers', Spry Papers, Private Papers Collection, Oxford, St Antony's College, Middle East Centre.

surrounding the work and the hurry with which it was carried out, it was clearly impossible to photograph all records of value, since their volume was too great. It was decided, therefore, to photograph only 'the Ottoman registers, the register of deeds, the registers of title and the registers of writs and orders'.[4] In the summer of 1948, over 1,700 spools of film, each of a hundred feet, were sent to England for safe keeping. Prior to their return to the region, microfilm copies of registers were acquired by the United Nations Conciliation Commission for Palestine and, subsequently, copies of those were supplied to other authorities.[5]

The huge effort expended by the Palestine government in 1947 to photograph the land records is testament to the significance attached to the registers as an instrument of government rule. But it is also an indication of the importance that would continue to be attached to the land registers by those who British government officials left behind. Land records, explained J. F. Spry in his reports detailing the whole endeavour, were '*doubly important*, both to any future government and to the hundreds of thousands of individuals whose title to land depended on them'.[6] On the one hand, the importance of the land registers to the British colonial administration of Palestine required that a specific categorization of useful knowledge be represented in them; on the other hand, a key feature of this usefulness is the social recognition and legitimacy it earned by its close association to what was already considered important by the landholders themselves. Ottoman registries continued to constitute the basis of a large number of claims to real rights in Palestine and reference to Ottoman registers was necessary throughout.

Nonetheless, colonial manipulation and bias were to some extent inherent in the process: local idioms, relevant on the ground for the definition of property relations, were converted into government categorizations and classifications. However, if the colonial period witnessed a process of registration filtered through the fiscal and cultural preconceptions of the British government officers who recorded and adjudicated the information, the idea of a systematic programme of transformation is difficult to

---

[4] J. F. Spry, 'Appendix III: Note on the Photographing of the Land Registers'. Also photographed were the deeds books of Jerusalem (to supplement incomplete registers) and ledgers relating to mortgages.

[5] Michael Fischbach, 'Documenting Land Ownership in the Palestinian Authority', *Middle East Report* (Winter 1997), 45, Sami Hadawi, *Land Ownership in Palestine: Arab Rights and Interests* (Amman: Publishing Committee, 1981), 62–3.

[6] J. F. Spry, 'Note on the Custody of the Records on the Termination of the Mandate'. Emphasis added.

sustain. This book has sought to shed light on the overall impact of British rule on property rights in mandate Palestine in two ways: first, by challenging the assumption of a monolithic and consistent policy towards landed property; and, second, by challenging the assumption that the impact of British policies necessarily resulted in a radical change in how property relations were actually defined and constructed.

Land registration clearly gained its importance to colonial officials because of the uses to which it could be put—particularly those of a fiscal and economic nature. Land registration was able to achieve these utilitarian goals largely through the sorts of processes of standardization and schematization by which governments come to understand the societies over which they rule, through centralized administrative grids imposed upon diverse regions.[7] In the case of a colonial census, for example, the effect of the grid was to reduce populations to 'replicable plurals'.[8] As for the cadastral map, it has been described by Roger Kain and Elizabeth Baigent as a 'partisan' and 'active' instrument of control 'which both reflects and consolidates the power of those who commission it': 'where knowledge is power, it provides comprehensive information to be used to the advantage of some and the detriment of others . . . in portraying one reality as in the settlement of the New World or in India, it helps obliterate the old.'[9] In Palestine the 1928 land (settlement of title) ordinance sought to provide comprehensive information through a multifold process. Individual parcels of land were first mapped, measured, and precisely positioned on a cadastral map and linked to a system of triangulation. Once this was achieved, 'verbal' descriptions of an actual parcel of property, such as reference to physical boundaries, were omitted from the register and replaced by a reference number. Settled rights to particular parcels were recorded on separate folios all of standard size and bound in registers, which, officials were proud to declare, 'conforms to the best modern practice'.[10] Efforts by British officers to make land registration as efficient as possible meant that officials insisted on certain mechanisms by which individuals had to

   [7] James Scott, *Seeing Like a State: How Certain Schemes to Improve the Human Condition Have Failed* (New Haven: Yale University Press, 1998).

   [8] Benedict Anderson, *Imagined Communities: Reflections on the Origin and Spread of Nationalism*, rev. edn. (London: Verso, 1991), 184. See also Roger Owen, 'The Population Census of 1917 and its Relationship to Egypt's Three 19th Century Statistical Regimes', *Journal of Historical Sociology*, 4/9 (1996).

   [9] Roger J. P. Kain and Elizabeth Baigent, *The Cadastral Map in the Service of the State: A History of Property Mapping* (Chicago: University of Chicago Press, 1992), 344.

   [10] Frederic M. Goadby and Moses J. Doukhan, *The Land Law of Palestine* (Tel Aviv: Shoshany's Printing Co. Ltd., 1935), 282.

present their knowledge of landholdings. Information, for example, was to be documented and recorded on pieces of paper of a particular quality and of a particular size:

> to leave the public free to continue to present heterogeneous documents customary in the past, is to impede the efficient working of the Land Registry gratuitously . . . It is upon details of this sort that rapidity, efficiency and economy of working largely depend.[11]

Emphasis on standardized, 'nationally accurate' details was further impressed upon the local population through the precision with which parcels of land were located: that the technical schemes of the survey department to precisely locate parcels of land represented a new mould—into which distinctions between indigenous idioms of boundaries had somehow to be fitted (or not)—is underlined by the department's report on training local candidates: 'the art of [survey] drawing and the conception of accurate measurements are conspicuously absent from candidates, and it was found necessary to limit a four month course to drawing, use of instruments, traverse, and simple survey with chain and offset.'[12]

Older 'realities' certainly appeared at risk. In Palestine, topographical diversity and variations in climate had ensured wide regional variations in actual areas of land defined by variable units of measurement. Attempts at the outset of the mandate by British officers to determine measurements resulted in exposing a range of calculations that were geographically, sometimes temporally, bound, not subject to any abstract, standardized, centralized formula.[13] Local measures had tended to be human in scale and therefore relational and contextual, revealing much about the factors that posed the need for a calculation in the first place.[14] *Jiftlik*, for example, was a term that referred in places to a unit of land defined by the notion 'such as needs one yoke of oxen to work it'. *Musha'* land—land collectively owned by members in a village—was subject to redistributions among cultivators according to a variety of calculations and measurements all of which were necessarily derived from localized conceptions of units of land. The categorization of land as *mevat*—vacant land, not in the use

---

[11] Dowson, 'Report on the Progress of Land Reforms in Palestine, 1923–1930', CO 733/221/97169, 35–6.

[12] 'Annual Report of Director of Surveys, 1921', 8. See also Gavish, *A Survey of Palestine under the British Mandate, 1920–1948*.

[13] Goadby and Doukhan, *The Land Law of Palestine*, 295 n. 1.

[14] Martha Mundy, 'Village Land and Individual Title: *Musha'* and Ottoman Land Registration in the 'Ajlun District', in Eugene L. Rogan and Tariq Tell (eds.), *Village, Steppe and State: The Social Origins of Modern Jordan* (London: British Academic Press, 1994).

of the inhabitants of a town or village, which can be cultivated with the leave of an official—was conditional on 'lying at such a distance from towns and villages that a human voice cannot be heard at the nearest inhabited place'.

The process of schematization inherent to the land registration process simplified local practices in order to be 'legible' to the colonial state.[15] Local definitions tended to be most problematic to British officers when revenue was at stake. A committee established in 1922 to consider the estimation and collection of tithes noted the following:

The Government standard is a kilogram. Estimators are acquainted with this weight, but more often than not the cultivator calculates the tithe due by him not in kilos but in a local measure. These measures vary from district to district and even from village to village so that the commissions must be capable of converting the equivalent weight or measure into kilogrammes, when discussing the yield of produce with the representatives of the village. Again, an estimator or cultivator who is used to hill measures may have no knowledge of those in use in villages of the plains. Weights or measures though of the same nomenclature often bear no relation to each other, thus a keleh in Beersheba is different from a Keleh in Galilee, a mid in Jenin differs from a mid in Acre and so forth. A jarrah of oil in Southern Palestine is not used as a measure in Northern Palestine. Olives are measured in Galilee by capacity measure, elsewhere by weight. There are no Government sets of weights and measures for tithe commissions to use on the threshing floor.[16]

The average tithe commission ran up against the same situation in 1926. It observed that 'local cultivators habitually describe the area of any plot of land in terms of the wheat seed required to sow it and are familiar with the average yield from that amount of seed (five-fold, ten-fold, etc.)'[17] and concluded that an approximate relative valuation to parcels of land could best be arranged by calculating their potential productivity in terms of the wheat harvest. The 'Report of the Committee on the Economic Condition of Agriculturalists and the Fiscal Measures of Government in Relation thereto' had a very difficult time expressing figures in dunams:

it was impossible to obtain the size of holdings in dunams since the dunam is not a unit in common village use. The area of the feddan varies from twenty four dunams at Rameh in the Acre Sub-District to the feddan 'rumi', or double

---

[15] Scott, *Seeing Like a State: How Certain Schemes to Improve the Human Condition Have Failed.*

[16] 'Report of the Tithes Commission', CO 733/20, 210–11.

[17] 'Average Tithe Committee Majority Report', CO 733/117, 20.

feddan of three hundred dunams in Burka in the Nablus District, but the feddan most used is between 100 and 160 dunams, and 120 dunams may be regarded as a middle figure. A feddan (mashi) originally represented the area that one man could plough himself with one yoke of oxen during the course of the year. It now tends rather to represent an average holding in the locality concerned.[18]

Almost ten years later, Lewis French unleashed his frustration with the lack of abstract, uniform measurements:

the only local agency between the land and the headquarters is the village representative known as the *mukhtar,* assisted more or less by a body of elders. . . . [The *mukhtar*] is ignorant of areas based on measurements. He will describe fields by some such vague term as a 'fedan', which may be anything from 50 to 250 dunams according to the local method of reckoning the year's work of the plough animals; or he may reply by letting you know how many pounds of seed are required to sew his dunams, all of which conveys more to himself than to his interlocutor.[19]

In the early years of the mandate, the British colonial administration perpetuated in its transactions local uses of the dunam, providing it with the different values accorded to it by the most relevant local custom. For the purpose of the assessment of the tobacco land tax, for example, the dunam was calculated as the equivalent of 900 square metres; by the Beisan demarcation committee as the equivalent of 919.0324 square metres. By 1925, however, there was wide agreement in favour of standardizing the dunam at 1,000 square metres, an action which first required that a weights and measures ordinance be enacted to declare that HMG's standard metre was to be the standard in Palestine (an act which itself presumed that the government was actually provided with a reproduction of this standard).[20] Dowson advised that the new unit of measurement be distinguished from other varieties of the term in use by naming it 'the standard *dunam*' or, more significantly, 'the national *dunam*'. In defending the use of the term 'national *dunam*', he explained that 'this would further help to explain to the people . . . whose land areas would be different in the new unit, how the change had come about'.[21] Pressing for a national dunam rather than endorsing whatever units of measurement were found to exist within villages suggests similarities with what Richard Saumarez

---

[18] 'Report of Committee on Economic Condition of Agriculturalists and the Fiscal Measures of Government in Relation Thereto (The Johnson–Crosbie Report) 3 July 1930, CO 733/185/77072, 151.

[19] Lewis French, 'First Report on Agricultural Development and Land Settlement in Palestine', CO 733/214/5, 74.

[20] Amery to Plumer, 10 Nov. 1925, CO 733/97, 540.

[21] Dowson, 'Standardisation of the Dunam', 20 Nov. 1924, Co 733/97, 539.

Smith has referred to as 'active social engineering': fitting people and their definitions of agricultural relations into a preordained, uniform—and colonial—mould. In this context, one can usefully draw attention, as Martha Mundy does, to the transformative nature of land registration particularly in regard to the reduction in the autonomy of rural communities vis-à-vis central authority.[22] In the case of mandate Palestine, some British officials worried about possible disturbances arising from opposition to processes of standardization and centralization, particularly on the part of village leaders. Early on, high commissioner Samuel worried about how so radical a change as standardizing a system of weights and measures would be accepted: 'When a new Government was established in a country, it was perhaps a mistake to make many new changes at once.'[23] For other British officials, depriving village leaders of 'licit or illicit powers and prerequisites' through uniform methods of registration was hardly considered a draw-back: when confronting opposition, Dowson's suggestion was, again, to stress 'the interest of the nation at large'.[24] Indeed, transformation and change were themes that colonial officials themselves frequently stressed: rational and objective categorization, stressing Western scientific methods and knowledge, was viewed as justification for the colonial enterprise (and simultaneously as a useful display of its authority).

However, attempts to discern the full extent of the colonial impact on localized definitions of property rights must also recognize the limits of colonial power to enact such change. Moreover, the extent to which such policies even necessitated a radical transformation needs to be properly assessed. An important check on the transformative effect of colonial land registration processes is provided by Dowson himself: 'A caution should be given', warned Dowson, 'against allowing the use of labels such as "cadastral survey", "settlement," "demarcation" and the like, to hypnotize the mind and block intelligent consideration of the actual processes so labelled . . . A dispassionate consideration of the actual value, *as measured by the use made,* of the . . . operations made . . . will show that [these warnings] are not superfluous.'[25] Otherwise, official plans would be entirely set aside by the people: 'it was of course', wrote Dowson in 1936, 'as impossible to prevent disposition of land by the mass of Palestinian landholders, large

[22] Mundy, 'Village Land and Individual Title: *Musha'* and Ottoman Land Registration in the 'Ajlun District', 63.

[23] 'Advisory Council Minutes', 5 Jan. 1921, CO 733/1, 437.

[24] Dowson, 'Covering Memorandum to the Report on the Land System in Palestine', CO 733/109, 244–5.

[25] Dowson, 'The Land System in Palestine', 19. Emphasis added.

and small, as it was to halt Canute's sea.'[26] Dowson's stress on the use made
of the colonial registries when making these dispositions is clearly important. As part of their larger project of defending and justifying the British
presence in Palestine, officials frequently prefaced their approach to land
questions by juxtaposing a romanticized liberal self versus an archaic,
backward other. However, to be useful (whether establishing taxation
liabilities, settling disputes, or acting as collateral) records of land had to
be 'kept consonant with fact and become authoritative in reality as well as
in theory',[27] and, as Dowson himself emphasized, 'no system can incorpor-
ate fairy tales with its facts and yet be a dependable or for long even a
comprehensible record'.[28] And this meant aiming for the understanding
and cooperation on the part of the public through an equitable settlement
of claims, not simply a legal imposition. Dowson, and evidently Torrens
himself, were not unaware of the problems of representation, once arguing the point that the register, like the map, 'was a good servant but bad
master', an instrument that could be made to conform to actual requirements: 'we should not let it fall short of these requirements, because we
are afraid that it may not be kept in its place.'[29] Either way, the political
and administrative success of land registration would be measured in the
end by its stability, which itself could only be obtained by an approach
nearest 'to what the people themselves will consider a just settlement'.[30]

To achieve this, Dowson pushed 'the necessity of securing the cooperation of the population in the execution of reform',[31] which itself was
directed towards simplifying laws and regulations, and reconciling their
statutory expression with extant practices and needs.[32] '[T]he settlement
of ninety per cent of the property parcels would present little difficulty,
if investigations were carried out on the spot in the presence of villagers

[26] Dowson, 'Memorandum II. Reviewing the History of Cadastral Survey Settlement of Title and Associated Measures in Palestine between 1913 and 1936', CO 733/
361/12, 21.

[27] Dowson, 'Preliminary Study of Land Tenure in Palestine', CO 733/109, 194–5.

[28] Ibid. 192–3.

[29] At the 1931 conference of empire survey officers, Sir J. S. Stewart Wallace, chief land
registrar of HM Land Registry, presented a talk, chaired by Sir H. G. Lyons, calling for
elasticity and flexibility 'in a world of practical expedients and compromises'. Discussion
between Dowson and Wallace can be found in Sir J. S. Stewart Wallace, 'Land Registration
in England in Relation to Maps and Surveying', in *Conference of Empire Survey Officers
1931: Report of Proceedings* (London: HMSO, 1931).

[30] Dowson, 'Preliminary Study of Land Tenure in Palestine', CO 733/109, 147.

[31] Dowson, 'Covering Memorandum to Report on the Land System in Palestine',
CO 733/109, 244.

[32] Dowson, 'Preliminary Study of Land Tenure in Palestine', CO 733/109, 203.

and other interested parties, by officers who knew the language and were in touch with local customs and feeling.'[33] In securing cooperation, emphasis was continually placed as we have seen on local knowledge.[34] The ideal settlement officer was described by Dowson as one who 'knows Arabic well and can really deal with villagers without an interpreter . . . he is courteous and sympathetic to the people and is liked by them; he is patient at arriving at a solution and knows that it is necessary to be so.'[35] Village structures also took on a key role, such as the role of the *mukhtar*[36] and, rather remarkably, even *musha'*: survey blocks (constituted by a number of parcels in land of approximately equal value) were drawn up on the basis of village distributions. In the field, emphasis was placed squarely on achieving a system which was 'substantially equitable and accepted by the mass of the people as such'.[37] 'And so,' writes Mundy of land registration in Transjordan in the 1930s, 'when British Mandate authority, armed with an ideological hostility to the regime that preceded it and with a century of dogmatic and practical commitment to fixed individual private property in land proceeded to effect cadastral registration its officers turned to village authority in the definition of legal right.'[38]

As Mundy reminds us, it is important to keep in mind the extent to which the administrative grid previously established by the Ottoman Empire was available to the British rulers. The process of translation and schematization was embodied in the Ottoman registers; 'the "application" of Ottoman law required that the official charged with registering title establish a relation between the unitary categories of the law and the terms used previously by villagers'. [39] The British had available to them Ottoman legislation which already anticipated the compulsory registration of rights over immovable property. Dowson explained how the 1913 law for the survey and registration of immovable property provided comprehensively for: the fixing of village boundaries, the definition of plots of land by a

[33] Dowson, 'Report on the Progress of Land Reforms, 1923–1930', 23.

[34] Also Plumer to Shuckburgh, 22 Apr. 1926, CO 733/114, 101.

[35] Dowson, 'Note III: Staff Notes', CO 733/92, 517.

[36] Described as 'the natural channel' by Lewis French.

[37] Dowson, 'Report on the Progress of Land Reforms in Palestine, 1923–1930', CO 733/221/97169, 23–4. See also Michael Fischbach, *State, Society, and Land in Jordan* (Leiden: Brill, 2000).

[38] Martha Mundy, 'The State of Property: Late Ottoman Southern Syria, the *Kaza* of Ajlun (1875–1918)', in Huri Islamoglu (ed.), *Constituting Modernity: Private Property in the East and West* (London: I. B. Tauris, 2004), 238.

[39] Mundy, 'Village Land and Individual Title: *Musha'* and Ottoman Land Registration in the 'Ajlun District', 63. See also Eugene L. Rogan, *Frontiers of the State in the Late Ottoman Empire: Transjordan, 1850–1921* (Cambridge: Cambridge University Press, 1999).

cadastral survey; the settlement and registration of title thereto; and the valuation of land and buildings to put in place a property tax. To be sure, British authorities no doubt shared ulterior motives in stressing continuities with administrative structures *ante bellum* (say, before audiences to whom they had to defend their 'tutelage' of mandate Palestine), but Dowson's explanation of Ottoman precedent is revealing of other factors involved:

It will thus be seen that this law sought the same objectives that have been sought by British administration in the same field since the war and substantially in the same way; but it was too loose and doctrinaire an instrument to be successfully implemented textually under British administration, although the Turks, who would probably have interpreted it with greater elasticity, might have obtained useful results from it, if the war had not intervened.[40]

When forced, the commissioner of lands had recognized as much in the 1930s: 'the objects of Land Settlement are in fact the same as the fundamental objects of the Ottoman Land Code and of the laws of Registration . . . in reality no change has been introduced into the substantive laws of the country by the Land Settlement Ordinances.'[41] British officials in Iraq were clearly somewhat impressed by Ottoman precedents: 'The Tapu Department or the Department of the Registration of Land Title is perhaps in theory the most admirable part of the Turkish organization . . . Though the procedure in obtaining title deeds may be long, those title-deeds, when obtained, are clear of doubt, and thus in the end the credit of the landowner is better secured.'[42] While the interpretation of Ottoman laws by the British administration in Palestine was, as already noted, not unproblematic, the fact such material was available to British officers in the development of their land policies certainly dulls their transformative impact and suggests the overall importance of continuities. Registration of title to land was not invented by the British, its attributes not previously unrecognized.[43] The colonial land registration process,

---

[40] Dowson, 'Memorandum II. Reviewing the History of Cadastral Survey Settlement of Title and Associated Measures in Palestine between 1913 and 1936', CO 733/361/12, 16.

[41] Abramson, 'Observations on the Recommendations on Land Settlement in the Report of the O'Donnell Commission', CO 733/208/5/87326.

[42] 'Adminstrative Report, January–March 1915', *Iraq Administration Reports 1914–1932: [Sources Established by Robert L. Jarman]*, 10 vols., vol. i (Slough: Archive Editions, 1992), 99.

[43] See also Peter Robb, 'Landed Property, Agrarian Categories, and the Agricultural Frontier: Some Reflections on Colonial India', in Gregory Blue, Martin Bunton, and Ralph Croizier (eds.), *Colonialism and the Modern World: Selected Studies* (Armonk, NY: M. E. Sharpe, 2002), David Washbrook, 'Orients and Occidents: Colonial Discourse Theory and the Historiography of the British Empire', in R. Winks (ed.), *Oxford History of the British Empire*, v: *Historiography* (Oxford: Oxford University Press, 1999).

though different and particular, nonetheless forms part of a longer process of change in the landholding patterns of the region known as Palestine. Mechanisms aimed at registering land were part of a strategy of governance which the British shared with the Ottomans. As Michael Fischbach has noted about Transjordan, the fact that cultivators were 'familiar with a bureaucratic state intervening in its land matters certainly facilitated British goals', and the willing cooperation on the part of villagers was key to the steady progress of land settlement there.[44]

The colonial period, with its technological and bureaucratic advances, may have seen the intensification of a central authority at the expense of local autonomies, but still it must be recognized that there were countervailing tendencies. There was a prevailing tension between, on the one hand, land settlement aiming at uniformity across Palestine and, on the other hand, the necessary efforts at employing and securing local village structures. For example, despite the emphasis on precision and uniformity, ambiguity does not disappear in mandate Palestine nor was its complete elimination necessarily desirable. 'Leniency and sympathy in applying a minimum of rules are not wasted,' wrote Lewis French: 'Cases have come to my knowledge where villagers have been persuaded to plan reasonably good partitions; but refused eventually to carry them out on their lands when pressed to abide by too precise official instructions.'[45] Indeed, at the end of the day, standard dunams and national dunams stood beside 'customary dunams', 'Beisan dunams', and 'the old Turkish dunam'. One Colonial Office official minuted that 'if a standard is legally and officially adopted, its use will become general in the ordinary course of things and it is unnecessary and may lead to trouble to exclude other systems or modes of measuring'.[46] There appears to have been great scope for a village to articulate and satisfy its own needs in the land registration process. While one does not wish to erase the power differential between the colonial settlement officers and the colonized property owner, it is nonetheless important to fully recognize the extent to which, in securing cooperation, colonial officers placed an emphasis on local knowledge and on village structures, such as the *mukhtar*, and on how cultivators themselves defined their rights to the land and its resources. Richard Saumerez Smith observed similar features in the land registration processes in India:

---

[44] Fischbach, *State, Society, and Land in Jordan*, 123.

[45] Lewis French, 'First Report on Agricultural Development and Land Settlement in Palestine', CO 733/214/5, 69.

[46] Minute sheets, 21 Sept. 1925, CO 733/97, 533.

the settlement of rights in the field was, after all, 'a judicial affair that operated through people, requiring public attestation of registers at each stage of the preparation and the hearing of disputes; it was not a matter of simply fitting the official grid of classification over whatever historical facts could be established.'[47] Smith points to the 'contractual nature of the record at the time': the registers acted as 'a primary interface between ruler and ruled: an instrument of rule that required the formal acceptance of those whom it was to govern; an agenda of negotiation between the will of the sovereign and the practice of the sovereign's subjects'.[48]

The recorded representations of the land settlement officers (more so than the regular courtroom system) are better viewed as the result of contested negotiations among officials and landholders than the result of externally imposed British transformations. To paraphrase David Washbrook, if colonial land registers were products of an imagination, 'it was of an imagination shared between colonizers and certain groups, at least, among the colonized'.[49] Of course, it is one thing to say that registers were both an instrument of colonial rule and a representation of local agency but, as John Comaroff has observed of colonial law generally, "quite another to explain when it was the former, when the latter, and in what proportions'.[50] Again, we are pushed to acknowledge the specific elements in a given situation. Where necessary, land registration policies in mandate Palestine transformed local realities, but colonial constructs also clearly overlapped at times with patterns and structures among the colonized, themselves of course neither static nor rooted in antiquity but constantly responsive to changing circumstances. A certain amount of overlap was required: as with any thinly stretched administration, colonial structures required a degree of collaboration. Moreover, the mandatory land registration process, though different and particular in the inter-war period, formed part of a longer process of change in the landholding patterns of the region known as Palestine. One only needs to recall the large number of Ottoman records that were microfilmed alongside British ones in 1948 to appreciate that mechanisms aimed at the registering of land were part of a strategy of governance that the British to some extent shared with the Ottomans.

---

[47] Richard Saumarez Smith, *Rule by Records: Land Registration and Village Custom in Early British Panjab* (Delhi: Oxford University Press, 1996), 30.

[48] Ibid. 66.

[49] Washbrook, 'Orients and Occidents: Colonial Discourse Theory and the Historiography of the British Empire'.

[50] Quoted in Forman and Kedar, 'Colonialism, Colonization and Land Law in Mandate Palestine: The Zor Al-Zarqa and Barrat Qisarya Land Disputes in Historical Perspective'.

In addition to challenging assumptions of the transformative impact of colonial policies on local definitions of property rights, this book has also challenged ahistorical and essentialist assumptions of a consistent 'British way of thinking' towards landed property in the first place. Guided by their experience in colonial rule elsewhere in the empire, as well as by their participation in intellectual debates at home, British officials came to Palestine with general notions of how a 'civilized' people should be ordered, chief among them being the right to property as a necessary, even natural, human right. From a utilitarian approach, certain assumptions in particular emerged as most pertinent to their strategies for ruling Palestine: the notion that institutionalizing individual and secure title to land would facilitate the transfer of land to the most enterprising entrepreneurs (while at the same time fulfilling obligations connected to the establishment of a Jewish national home); that authoritatively defined title to property was essential for the provision of credit; that a reliable and comprehensive record of individual title to individual plots was the fairest and most efficient way to raise taxes from agricultural resources; and that firm title endowed the individual with the security necessary to develop and invest in the land.

But the role property plays in any society is always contested, never absolute, and colonial assumptions constructed around the ideal definition of property could be expected to change. Of necessity, the British approach to property in mandate Palestine was ad hoc: 'Palestine was, as a matter of fact, organized during the war, under great pressure of events . . . it was all rather haphazard.'[51] The 1936 Peel Report expressed some concern with the fact that 'the government of the country has, in fact, from the very start been driven to work at high pressure and has never had an opportunity for calm reflection'.[52] The inherent inconsistency of the British administration of Palestine was recognized early on. 'Our work in Palestine', argued a memorandum drawn up by the Middle East department of the Colonial Office in 1924, 'has been severely hampered by continued uncertainty': 'The plant has been continually dug up to see how it is growing. It could not be expected to thrive under such conditions. What we want now, if only we could get it, is a period of settled policy and settled administration.'[53] But this was not to be: 'the march of events

---

[51] Minute sheets, 2 Oct. 1930, CO 733/194/7/7739.
[52] Great Britain. Palestine Royal Commission, *Report* (London: HMSO, 1937), 160.
[53] 'Memorandum by Middle East Department, Colonial Office', CO 733/78, 106.

tends everywhere to outstrip legislation', reflected one settlement officer in 1935, 'and particularly is this the case in this country.'[54] The definition of property rights in mandate Palestine was never simply an intellectual exercise, and at no time was colonial land policy informed by a single coherent set of expectations. British land experts, advisers, and officials generally looked fondly upon the writings of J. S. Mill and Sir Henry Maine, and to the apparent successes of colonial policies elsewhere, but the makeshift nature of British rule in Palestine demanded that local rights in property be defined and institutionalized only in ways which satisfied specific problems. The object of this book has been to chart the shifts in the way British officials viewed private property in Palestine by locating them in historical transformations, and by doing so to show how private property came to be regarded as just as much a problem as it was a solution. Increasing anxiety over the creation of a politically active land-less class, especially after the 1929 riots, made the idea of individual rights in land less and less attractive, with state officials becoming noticeably apprehensive of securing the rights of the inhabitants to the land if it meant they might then dispose of it, become landless, and more prone to political disturbance. As an incentive for the settlement of title to land, the provision of agricultural credit was, for all practical purposes, irrelevant in mandate Palestine and the idea of individualizing property rights so as to bring about a direct relationship between government and individual in the collection of taxes simply inexpedient. Finally, though government proposed to secure the title of Palestinian cultivators in their land in order to encourage their development of it, in fact there emerged early on in official circles a development ethos which impatiently favoured certain rights in land over others and, above all, endeavoured to see that landholders' rights were subservient to the state's interests.

To be sure, the typically colonial desire to herald the individualization of property rights was untiring throughout the mandate. But the historical record needs to be read carefully. Official expressions of support for land settlement tended, as the mandate progressed, to be more and more of a philosophical and ideological nature. Despite the rhetoric, private property would probably have fared better had the Ottomans still ruled.

[54] Letter from land settlement officer, 31 Dec. 1935, ISA RG 22, Land Settlement and Land Registration, LS 13/6, box 3560.

Select Bibliography

ARCHIVAL SOURCES

Public Record Office, Kew (PRO)
  Colonial Office, Record Group CO 733.
  Colonial Office, Record Group CO 814.
  Foreign Office, Record Group FO 371.
Israel State Archives, Jerusalem (ISA)
  Palestine Government, Attorney General, Record Group 3.
  Palestine Government, Chief Secretary's Office, Record Group 2.
  Palestine Government, Land Registration and Land Settlement, Record Group 22.
Private papers collection, the Middle East Centre, St Antony's College, Oxford
  Sir E. Dowson, S. G. Kermack, H. G. Le Ray, Middle East Development Division, Sir J. F. Spry.
Private papers collection, Rhodes House Library, Oxford
  Sir J. R. Chancellor.

PUBLISHED SOURCES

Abcarius, M. F. 'The Fiscal System.' In Sa'id Himadeh (ed.), *Economic Organization of Palestine*, 507–56. Beirut: American Press, 1938.
—— *Palestine: Through the Fog of Propaganda*. London: Hutchinson, 1946.
Abramson, Albert. 'An Aspect of Village Life in Palestine.' *Jerusalem Post*, 6 July 1937.
Abu-Lughod, Ibrahim. 'The Pitfalls of Palestiniology.' *Arab Studies Quarterly*, 3/4 (1981), 403–11.
Abu Lughod, Janet. *Rabat: Urban Apartheid in Morocco*. Princeton: Princeton University Press, 1980.
Adler, Raya. 'The Tenants of Wadi Hawarith: Another View of the Land Question in Palestine.' *International Journal of Middle East Studies*, 20/2 (1988), 197–220.
Anderson, Benedict. *Imagined Communities: Reflections on the Origin and Spread of Nationalism*. Rev. edn. London: Verso, 1991.
Asad, Talal. 'Class Transformation under the Mandate.' *Middle East Report*, 53 (1976), 3–8+23.
Bentwich, Norman. 'The Legislation of Palestine, 1918–1925.' *Journal of Comparative Legislation and International Law*, 8 (1926), 9–20.

Bentwich, Norman (ed.). *Legislation of Palestine, 1918–1925: Including the Orders-in-Council, Ordinances, Public Notices, Proclamations, Regulations, Etc.* 2 vols. Alexandria: Whitehead Morris Ltd., 1926.

—— *England in Palestine.* London: Kegan Paul, Trench, Trubner & Co. Ltd., 1932.

—— and Bentwich, Helen. *Mandate Memories, 1918–1948.* London: Hogarth Press, 1965.

Benvenisti, Meron. *Sacred Landscape: The Buried History of the Holy Land since 1948.* Trans. Maxine Kaufman-Lacusta. Berkeley and Los Angeles: University of California Press, 2000.

Blue, Gregory, Bunton, Martin P., and Croizier, Ralph C. *Colonialism and the Modern World: Selected Studies.* Armonk, NY: M. E. Sharpe, 2002.

Boyle, Susan Silsby. *Betrayal of Palestine: The Story of George Antonius.* Boulder, Colo.: Westview, 2001.

Bromley, Daniel W. *Environment and Economy: Property Rights and Public Policy.* Oxford: Blackwell, 1991.

Bunton, Martin. 'Inventing the Status Quo: Ottoman Land-Law during the Palestine Mandate, 1917–1936.' *International History Review*, 21/1 (1999), 28–56.

—— 'Dowson, Sir Ernest Macleod (1876–1950).' In H. C. G. Matthew and Brian Harrison (eds.), *Oxford Dictionary of National Biography.* Oxford: Oxford University Press, 2004.

Burke III, Edmund. 'Orientalism and World History: Representing Middle Eastern Nationalism and Islamism in the Twentieth Century.' *Theory and Society*, 27/4, Special Issue on Interpreting Historical Change at the End of the Twentieth Century (1998), 489–507.

Chanock, Martin. 'Paradigms, Policies, and Property: A Review of the Customary Law of Land Tenure.' In Kristin Mann and Richard Roberts (eds.), *Law in Colonial Africa*, 61–84. Portsmouth, NH: Heinemann Educational Books, 1991.

Christelow, Alan. *Muslim Law Courts and the French Colonial State in Algeria.* Princeton: Princeton University Press, 1985.

Colson, Elizabeth. 'The Impact of the Colonial Period on the Definition of Land Rights.' In Victor Turner (ed.), *Colonialism in Africa, 1870–1960*, 193–215. Cambridge: Cambridge University Press, 1971.

Cox, Susan. 'No Tragedy on the Commons.' *Environmental Ethics*, 7 (1985), 49–61.

Cronon, William. *Changes in the Land: Indians, Colonists, and the Ecology of New England.* New York: Hill and Wang, 1983.

Cuno, Kenneth M. 'Joint Family Households and Rural Notables in 19th-Century Egypt.' *International Journal of Middle East Studies*, 27/4 (1995), 485–502.

De Soto, Hernando. *The Mystery of Capital: Why Capitalism Triumphs in the West and Fails Everywhere Else.* New York: Basic Books, 2000.

Dodge, Toby. *Inventing Iraq: The Failure of Nation Building and a History Denied.* New York: Columbia University Press, 2003.

Doukhan-Landau, Leah. *Equitable Rights to Land and the Remedy of Specific Performance of Contracts for the Sale of Land.* Jerusalem: Institute for Legislative Research and Comparative Law, 1968.

Doumani, Beshara. 'Rediscovering Ottoman Palestine: Writing Palestinians into History.' *Journal of Palestine Studies,* 21/2 (1992), 5–28.

—— *Rediscovering Palestine: Merchants and Peasants in Jabal Nablus, 1700–1900.* Berkeley and Los Angeles: University of California Press, 1995.

Dowson, Sir Ernest, and Sheppard, V. L. O. *An Introductory Note on Registration of Title to Land.* London: Moore's Modern Methods, Ltd., 1929.

—— —— *Land Registration.* London: HMSO, 1956.

Drayton, Robert Harry. *The Laws of Palestine: In Force on the 31st Day of December 1933.* Rev. edn. 3 vols. London: Waterlow and Sons Ltd., 1934.

Dumper, Michael. *Islam and Israel: Muslim Religious Endowments and the Jewish State.* Washington: Institute for Palestine Studies, 1994.

Edney, Matthew. *Mapping an Empire: The Geographical Construction of British India, 1765–1843.* Chicago: Chicago University Press, 1997.

Eisenman, Robert H. *Islamic Law in Palestine and Israel: A History of the Survival of Tanzimat and Shari'a in the British Mandate and the Jewish State.* Leiden: Brill, 1978.

El-Eini, Roza. 'The Agricultural Mortgage Bank in Palestine: The Controversy over its Establishment.' *Middle Eastern Studies,* 33/4 (1997), 751–76.

—— 'British Forestry Policy in Mandate Palestine, 1929–1948: Aims and Realities.' *Middle Eastern Studies,* 35/3 (1999), 323–4.

ESCO Foundation for Palestine. *Palestine: A Study of Jewish, Arab and British Policies.* New Haven: Yale University Press, 1947.

Falah, Ghazi. 'Pre-State Jewish Colonization in Northern Palestine and its Impact on Local Bedouin Sedentarization, 1914–1948.' *Journal of Historical Geography,* 17/3 (1991), 289–309.

Farouk-Sluglett, Marion, and Sluglett, Peter. 'The Transformation of Land Tenure and Rural Social Structure in Central and Southern Iraq, 1870–1958.' *International Journal of Middle East Studies,* 15/4 (1983), 491–505.

Fieldhouse, D. K. *The West and the Third World: Trade, Colonialism, Dependence and Development.* Oxford: Blackwell, 1999.

Firestone, Ya'acov. 'The Land-Equalizing Musha' Village: A Reassessment.' In Gad G. Gilbar (ed.), *Ottoman Palestine, 1800–1914: Studies in Economic and Social History.* Leiden: E. J. Brill, 1990.

Fischbach, Michael. 'Documenting Land Ownership in the Palestinian Authority.' *Middle East Report* (Winter 1996), 45+48.

—— *State, Society, and Land in Jordan.* Leiden: Brill, 2000.

Fisher, Stanley. *Ottoman Land Laws: Containing the Ottoman Land Code and Later Legislation Affecting Land with Notes and an Appendix of Cyprus Laws and Rules Relating to Land.* London: Oxford University Press, 1919.

Fitzgerald, Sir William. 'A Review of the Development of Law in Israel.' In International Lawyers Convention in Israel (ed.), *International Lawyers Convention in Israel, 1958*. Jerusalem: Jerusalem Post, 1959.

Forman, Geremy, and Kedar, Alexandre. 'Colonialism, Colonization and Land Law in Mandate Palestine: The Zor Al-Zarqa and Barrat Qisarya Land Disputes in Historical Perspective.' *Theoretical Inquiries in Law*, 4/2 (2003), 491–539.

Frykenberg, Robert Eric (ed.). *Land Control and Social Structure in Indian History*. Madison: University of Wisconsin Press, 1969.

Gavish, Dov. *A Survey of Palestine under the British Mandate, 1920–1948*. London: Routledge Curzon, 2005.

—— and Kark, Ruth. 'The Cadastral Mapping of Palestine, 1858–1928.' *Geographical Journal*, 159 (1993), 70–80.

Gerber, Haim. *The Social Origins of the Modern Middle East*. London: Mansell, 1987.

Goadby, Frederic M., and Doukhan, Moses J. *The Land Law of Palestine*. Tel Aviv: Shoshany's Printing Co. Ltd., 1935.

Graham Brown, Sarah. 'The Political Economy of Jabal Nablus: 1920–1948.' In Roger Owen (ed.), *Studies in the Economic and Social History of Palestine in the Nineteenth and Twentieth Centuries*, 88–176. Carbondale: Southern Illinois University Press, 1982.

Granovsky, Abraham (Avraham Granott). *Land Taxation in Palestine*. Jerusalem: 'Mischar w'Taasia Publishing Co., 1927.

—— *Land Policy in Palestine*. New York: Bloch Publishing Company, 1940.

—— *The Land System in Palestine: History and Structure*. London: Eyre and Spottiswoode, 1952.

Great Britain. *Palestine Royal Commission Report* (Peel Report). London: HMSO, 1937.

Great Britain. Naval Intelligence Division. *Palestine and Transjordan*, Geographical Handbook Series. Oxford: Oxford University Press, 1943.

Great Britain. Palestine Royal Commission. *Minutes of Evidence Heard at Public Sessions (with Index)*. London: HMSO, 1937.

—— *Memoranda Prepared by the Government of Palestine*. London: HMSO, 1937.

Gross, Nachum. *The Economic Policy of the Mandatory Government in Palestine*. Jerusalem: Maurice Falk Institute for Economic Research in Israel, 1982.

Hadawi, Sami. *Land Ownership in Palestine: Arab Rights and Interests*. Amman: Publishing Committee, 1981.

Hakim, George, and El-Hussayni, M. Y. 'Monetary and Banking System.' In Sa'id Himadeh (ed.), *Economic Organisation of Palestine*, 455–504. Beirut: American Press, 1938.

Hanna, Abdallah. 'The Attitude of the French Mandatory Authorities towards Land Ownership in Syria.' In Nadine Méouchy and Peter Sluglett (eds.), *The British and French Mandates in Comparative Perspectives*, 457–75. Leiden: Brill, 2004.

Hanna, Susan S., Folke, Carl, and Maler, Karl-Goran (eds.). *Rights to Nature: Ecological, Economic, Cultural, and Political Principles of Institutions for the Environment.* Washington: Island Press, 1996.

Harris, R. Cole. *Making Native Space: Colonialism, Resistance, and Reserves in British Columbia.* Vancouver: UBC Press, 2002.

Haycraft, Sir Thomas W. 'Palestine under the Mandate.' *Journal of the Central Asian Society,* 15 (1928), 167–86.

Himadeh, Sa'id (ed.). *Economic Organisation of Palestine.* Beirut: American Press, 1938.

Holling, C. S., Berkes, Fikret, and Folke, Carl. 'Science, Sustainability, and Resource Management.' In Fikret Berkes and Carl Folke (eds.), *Linking Social and Ecological Systems: Management Practices and Social Mechanisms for Building Resilience,* 342–62. Cambridge: Cambridge University Press, 1998.

Hope-Simpson, Sir John. *Palestine. Report on Immigration, Land Settlement and Development,* Cmd. 3686. London: HMSO, 1930.

Hopkins, Anthony. *An Economic History of West Africa.* London: Longman Group Ltd., 1973.

Humphreys, Sally. 'Law as Discourse.' *History and Anthropology,* 1 (1985), 241–64.

Hyamson, Albert M. *Palestine under the Mandate: 1920–1948.* Westport, Conn.: Greenwood Press, 1950.

Ionides, M. G. 'Irrigation in Palestine.' *World Today* (1947), 188–98.

Iraq Administration Reports 1914–1932, 10 vols. (Slough: Archive Editions, 1992).

Islamoglu, Huri. 'Property as a Contested Domain: A Reevaluation of the Ottoman Land Code of 1858.' In Roger Owen (ed.), *New Perspectives on Property and Land in the Middle East,* 3–61. Cambridge, Mass.: Distributed for the Center for Middle Eastern Studies of Harvard University by Harvard University Press, 2000.

—— 'Politics of Administering Property: Law and Statistics in the Nineteenth-Century Ottoman Empire.' In Huri Islamoglu (ed.), *Constituting Modernity: Private Property in the East and West,* 276–319. London: I. B. Tauris, 2004.

Jones, A. Philip. *Britain and Palestine, 1914–1948: Archival Sources for the History of the British Mandate.* Oxford: Oxford University Press for the British Academy, 1979.

Kain, Roger J. P., and Baigent, Elizabeth. *The Cadastral Map in the Service of the State: A History of Property Mapping.* Chicago: University of Chicago Press, 1992.

Kallner, D. H., and Rosenau, E. 'The Geographical Regions of Palestine.' *Geographical Review,* 24/1 (1939), 61–80.

Kamen, Charles. *Little Common Ground: Arab Agriculture and Jewish Settlement in Palestine, 1920–1948.* Pittsburgh: University of Pittsburgh Press, 1991.

Kanya-Forstner, A. S. 'French Expansion in Africa: The Mythical Theory.' In Roger Owen and Bob Sutcliffe (eds.), *Studies in the Theory of Imperialism,* 277–94. London: Longman, 1972.

Kedar, Alexandre (Sandy). 'The Legal Transformation of Ethnic Geography: Israeli Law and the Palestinian Landholder, 1948–1967.' *New York University Journal of International Law and Politics,* 33/4 (2001), 923–1000.

Khalidi, Rashid. *Palestinian Identity: The Construction of Modern National Consciousness.* New York: Columbia University Press, 1997.

Kirk-Greene, Anthony. *On Crown Service: A History of HM Colonial and Overseas Civil Services, 1837–1997.* London: I. B. Tauris, 1999.

Levine, Mark. 'Land, Law and the Planning of Empire: Jaffa and Tel Aviv during the Late Ottoman and Mandate Periods.' In Huri Islamoglu (ed.), *Constituting Modernity: Private Property in the East and West,* 100–46. London: I. B. Tauris, 2004.

Ley, Cuthbert H. *The Structure and Procedure of Cadastral Survey in Palestine.* Jerusalem: Greek Convent Press, 1931.

Lockman, Zachary. 'Railway Workers and Relational History: Arabs and Jews in British-Ruled Palestine.' *Journal of Comparative Society and History,* 35/3 (1993), 601–27.

Lowdermilk, Walter Clay. *Palestine, Land of Promise.* London: Harper & Brothers, 1944.

Lugard, F. D. *The Dual Mandate in British Tropical Africa.* 5th edn. London: Frank Cass, 1965.

Luke, Sir Harry, and Keith-Roach, Edward (eds.). *The Handbook of Palestine and Transjordan.* London: MacMillan and Co., 1934.

McDonnell, Michael, and Baker, Henry E. (eds.). *The Law Reports of Palestine . . . : [1920–1946].* 14 vols. London: Waterlow & Sons, 1933–47.

McLaren, John, Buck, A. R., and Wright, Nancy E. 'Property Rights in the Colonial Imagination and Experience.' In John McLaren, A. R. Buck, and Nancy E. Wright (eds.), *Despotic Dominion: Property Rights in British Settler Societies,* 1–21. Vancouver: UBC Press, 2004.

Macpherson, C. B. 'The Meaning of Property.' In C. B. Macpherson (ed.), *Property: Mainstream and Critical Positions.* Oxford: Blackwell, 1978.

Maine, Henry S. *Village Communities in the East and West.* London: John Murray, 1871.

Meek, Charles Kingsley. *Colonial Law: A Bibliography with Special Reference to Native African Systems of Law and Land Tenure.* London: Oxford University Press, 1948.

—— *Law and Authority in a Nigerian Tribe: A Study in Indirect Rule.* New York: Barnes and Noble, 1970.

Metcalf, Thomas. *Land, Landlords and the British Raj: Northern India in the Nineteenth Century.* Berkeley and Los Angeles: University of California Press, 1979.

—— *Ideologies of the Raj.* Cambridge: Cambridge University Press, 1997.

—— 'Laissez-Faire and Tenant Right in Mid-Nineteenth Century India.' In Thomas R. Metcalf (ed.), *Forging the Raj: Essays on British India in the Heyday of Empire,* 74–81. New Delhi: Oxford University Press, 2005.

Metzer, Jacob. *The Divided Economy of Mandatory Palestine.* Cambridge: Cambridge University Press, 1998.

Michaelis, Dolf. 'One Hundred Years of Banking and Currency in Palestine.' In *Research in Economic History*, 155–97. Greenwich: Jai Press Inc., 1986.

Migdal, Joel S. (ed.). *Palestinian Society and Politics.* Princeton: Princeton University Press, 1980.

Miller, Ylana N. *Government and Society in Rural Palestine, 1920–1948.* Austin: University of Texas Press, 1985.

Mitchell, Timothy. *Rule of Experts: Egypt, Techno-Politics, Modernity.* Berkeley and Los Angeles: University of California Press, 2002.

Mommsen, Wolfgang J., and Moor, Jaap de. *European Expansion and Law: The Encounter of European and Indigenous Law in 19th- and 20th-Century Africa and Asia.* Oxford: Berg Publishers, 1992.

Morris, Henry Francis, and Read, James S. *Indirect Rule and the Search for Justice: Essays in East African Legal History.* Oxford: Clarendon Press, 1972.

Mundy, Martha. 'Village Land and Individual Title: *Musha'* and Ottoman Land Registration in the 'Ajlun District.' In Eugene L. Rogan and Tariq Tell (eds.), *Village, Steppe and State: The Social Origins of Modern Jordan*, 58–79. London: British Academic Press, 1994.

—— 'The State of Property: Late Ottoman Southern Syria, the *Kaza* of Ajlun (1875–1918).' In Huri Islamoglu (ed.), *Constituting Modernity: Private Property in the East and West*, 214–47. London: I. B. Tauris, 2004.

Nadan, Amos. 'Colonial Misunderstanding of an Efficient Peasant Institution: Land Settlement and Musha' Tenure in Mandate Palestine, 1921–47.' *Journal of the Economic and Social History of the Orient*, 46/3 (2003), 320–54.

—— 'Competitive Advantage of Moneylenders over Banks in Rural Palestine.' *Journal of the Economic and Social History of the Orient*, 48/1 (2005), 1–39.

Ongley, F., and Miller, Horace Edward (eds.). *The Ottoman Land Code.* London: W. Clowes and Sons, 1892.

Osterhammel, Jurgen. *Colonialism: A Theoretical Overview.* Trans. S. L. Frisch. Princeton: Markus Wiener, 1997.

Ostrom, Elinor, and Schlager, Edella. 'The Formation of Property Rights.' In Susan S. Hanna, Carl Folke, and Karl-Goran Maler (eds.), *Rights to Nature: Ecological, Economic, Cultural, and Political Principles of Institutions for the Environment*, 127–56. Washington: Island Press, 1996.

Owen, Roger. *The Middle East in the World Economy, 1800–1914.* London: Methuen, 1981.

—— 'Introduction.' In Roger Owen (ed.), *Studies in the Economic and Social History of Palestine in the Nineteenth and Twentieth Centuries*, 1–9. Carbondale: Southern Illinois University Press, 1982.

—— 'Defining Traditional: Some Implications of the Use of Ottoman Law in Mandatory Palestine.' *Harvard Middle Eastern and Islamic Review*, 1/2 (1994), 115–31.

Owen, Roger. 'The Population Census of 1917 and its Relationship to Egypt's Three 19th Century Statistical Regimes.' *Journal of Historical Sociology*, 4/9 (1996), 457–72.

—— 'Introduction.' In Roger Owen (ed.), *New Perspectives on Property and Land in the Middle East*, pp. ix–xxiv. Cambridge, Mass.: Distributed for the Center for Middle Eastern Studies of Harvard University by Harvard University Press, 2000.

—— *State, Power and Politics in the Making of the Modern Middle East*. 3rd edn. London: Routledge, 2004.

Phillips, Anne. *The Enigma of Colonialism: British Policy in West Africa*. London: J. Currey and Indiana University Press, 1989.

Provence, Michael. 'Ottoman and French Mandate Land Registers for the Region of Damascus.' *Middle East Studies Association Bulletin*, 39/1 (2005), 32–43.

Quataert, Donald. 'Dilemma of Development: The Agricultural Bank and Agricultural Reform in Ottoman Turkey, 1888–1908.' *International Journal of Middle Eastern Studies*, 6 (1975), 210–27.

—— 'The Age of Reforms, 1812–1914.' In Halil Inalcik with Donald Quataert (eds.), *An Economic and Social History of the Ottoman Empire, 1300–1914*, 759–887. Cambridge: Cambridge University Press, 1994.

Razzaz, Omar M. 'Examining Property Rights and Investment in Informal Settlements: The Case of Jordan.' *Land Economics*, 69/4 (1993), 341–55.

Reiter, Yitzhak. *Islamic Endowments in Jerusalem under British Mandate*. London: Frank Cass, 1996.

Robb, Peter. *Ancient Rights and Future Comfort: Bihar, the Bengal Tenancy Act of 1885 and British Rule in India*. Richmond: Curzon Press, 1997.

—— 'Landed Property, Agrarian Categories, and the Agricultural Frontier: Some Reflections on Colonial India.' In Gregory Blue, Martin Bunton, and Ralph Croizier (eds.), *Colonialism and the Modern World: Selected Studies*, 71–99. Armonk, NY: M. E. Sharpe, 2002.

Roberts, Richard, and Mann, Kristin. 'Law in Colonial Africa.' In Kristin Mann and Richard Roberts (eds.), *Law in Colonial Africa*, 3–58. London: J. Currey and Heinemann, 1991.

Rogan, Eugene. 'Incorporating the Periphery: The Ottoman Extension of Direct Rule over Southeastern Syria (Transjordan), 1867–1914.' Ph.D., Harvard University, 1991.

—— *Frontiers of the State in the Late Ottoman Empire: Transjordan, 1850–1921*. Cambridge: Cambridge University Press, 1999.

—— and Tell, Tariq (eds.). *Village, Steppe and State: The Social Origins of Modern Jordan*. London: British Academic Press, 1994.

Rose, Carol M. *Property and Persuasion: Essays on the History, Theory, and Rhetoric of Ownership*, New Perspectives on Law, Culture, and Society. Boulder, Colo.: Westview Press, 1994.

Ruedy, John. *Land Policy in Colonial Algeria: The Origins of the Rural Public Domain.* Berkeley and Los Angeles: University of California Press, 1967.

Saumarez Smith, Richard. *Rule by Records: Land Registration and Village Custom in Early British Panjab.* Delhi: Oxford University Press, 1996.

Schaebler, Birgit. 'Practising *Musha*': Common Lands and the Common Good in Southern Syria under the Ottomans and the French.' In Roger Owen (ed.), *New Perspectives on Property and Land in the Middle East,* 241–311. Cambridge, Mass.: Distributed for the Center for Middle Eastern Studies of Harvard University by Harvard University Press, 2000.

Schölch, Alexander. 'European Penetration and the Economic Development of Palestine, 1856–82.' In Roger Owen (ed.), *Studies in the Economic and Social History of Palestine in the Nineteenth and Twentieth Centuries,* 10–87. London: Macmillan Press Ltd., 1982.

Scott, James. *Seeing Like a State: How Certain Schemes to Improve the Human Condition Have Failed.* New Haven: Yale University Press, 1998.

Shafir, Gershon. *Land, Labor, and the Origins of the Israeli–Palestinian Conflict, 1882–1914.* Cambridge: Cambridge University Press, 1989.

Shaw, Walter. *Report of the Commission on the Palestine Disturbances of August, 1929.* London: HMSO, 1930.

Shehadeh, Raja. 'The Land Law of Palestine: An Analysis of the Definition of State Lands.' *Journal of Palestine Studies,* 11/2 (1982), 82–99.

Shepherd, Naomi. *Ploughing Sand: British Rule in Palestine 1917–1948.* New Brunswick, NJ: Rutgers University Press, 2000.

Sluglett, Peter. *Britain in Iraq, 1914–1932.* Ithaca, NY: Cornell University Press, 1976.

Smith, Barbara J. *The Roots of Separatism in Palestine: British Economic Policy, 1920–1929.* Syracuse, NY: Syracuse University Press, 1993.

Southard, Addison E. *Palestine: Its Commercial Resources with Particular Reference to American Trade.* Washington: Government Printing Office, 1922.

Stein, Kenneth W. *The Land Question in Palestine, 1917–1939.* Chapel Hill: University of North Carolina Press, 1984.

Stewart Wallace, Sir J. S. 'Land Registration in England in Relation to Maps and Surveying.' In *Conference of Empire Survey Officers 1931: Report of Proceedings.* London: HMSO, 1931.

Storrs, Ronald. *Orientations.* London: I. Nicholson & Watson, 1937.

Strahorn, A. T. 'Agriculture and Soils of Palestine.' *Geographical Review* (1929), 581–601.

Strickland, C. F. *Report on the Possibility of Introducing a System of Agricultural Cooperation in Palestine.* Jerusalem: Government of Palestine, 1930.

A Survey of Palestine: Prepared in December 1945 and January 1946 for the Information of the Anglo-American Committee of Inquiry. 2 vols. Washington: Institute for Palestine Studies, 1990.

Swearingen, Will D. *Moroccan Mirages: Agrarian Dreams and Deceptions, 1912– 1986.* Princeton: Princeton University Press, 1987.

Sykes, Christopher. *Crossroads to Israel.* Cleveland: World Pub. Co., 1965.

Thomas, Nicholas. *Colonialism's Culture: Anthropology, Travel and Government.* Cambridge: Polity Press, 1994.

Tully, James. *An Approach to Political Philosophy: Locke in Contexts.* New York: Cambridge University Press, 1993.

Tute, R. C. *The Ottoman Land Laws [Microform]: With a Commentary on the Ottoman Land Code of 7th Ramadan 1274.* Jerusalem: Greek Convent Press, 1927.

—— 'The Law of State Lands in Palestine.' *Journal of Comparative Legislation and International Law,* 9 (1927), 165–82.

Tyler, Warwick P. N. *State Lands and Rural Development in Mandatory Palestine, 1920–1948.* Brighton: Sussex Academic Press, 2001.

Walker, R. 'English Property Legislation of 1922–1926.' *Journal of Comparative Legislation and International Law,* 10 (1928), 1–13.

Warriner, Doreen. *Land and Poverty in the Middle East.* London: Royal Institute of International Affairs, 1948.

Washbrook, David. 'Law, State and Agrarian Society in Colonial India.' *Modern Asian Studies,* 15/3 (1981), 649–721.

—— 'Orients and Occidents: Colonial Discourse Theory and the Historiography of the British Empire.' In R. Winks (ed.), *Oxford History of the British Empire,* v: *Historiography,* 596–611. Oxford: Oxford University Press, 1999.

—— 'Sovereignty, Property, Land and Labour in Colonial South India.' In Huri Islamoglu (ed.), *Constituting Modernity: Private Property in the East and West,* 69–99. London: I. B. Tauris, 2004.

Wasserstein, Bernard. *The British in Palestine: The Mandatory Government and the Arab–Jewish Conflict, 1917–1929.* 2nd edn. Cambridge, Mass.: Blackwell, 1991.

Weaver, John C. *The Great Land Rush and the Making of the Modern World, 1650–1900.* Montreal: McGill-Queen's University Press, 2003.

Whitcombe, Elizabeth. 'The Benevolent Proprietor and the Property Law: A British-Indian Dilemma.' *History and Anthropology,* 1/2 (1985), 373–79.

Willats, E. C. 'Some Geographical Factors in the Palestine Problem.' *Geographical Journal,* 108/4/6 (1946), 146–73.

Worsfold, W. Basil. *Palestine of the Mandate.* London: T. Fisher Unwin Ltd., 1925.

Yapp, Malcolm E. *The Near East since the First World War.* London: Longman, 1991.

Young, George. *Corps de droit ottoman; recueil des codes, lois, règlements, ordonnances et actes les plus importants du droit intérieur d'études sur le droit coutumier de l'empire ottoman.* 8 vols. Oxford: Clarendan Press, 1900–6.

Index